Enfleshed Counter-Memory

Enfleshed Counter-Memory

A Christian Social Ethic of Trauma

Stephanie C. Edwards

ORBIS BOOKS
Maryknoll, New York 10545

Founded in 1970, Orbis Books endeavors to publish works that enlighten the mind, nourish the spirit, and challenge the conscience. The publishing arm of the Maryknoll Fathers and Brothers, Orbis seeks to explore the global dimensions of the Christian faith and mission, to invite dialogue with diverse cultures and religious traditions, and to serve the cause of reconciliation and peace. The books published reflect the views of their authors and do not represent the official position of the Maryknoll Society. To learn more about Maryknoll and Orbis Books, please visit our website at www.orbisbooks.com.

Copyright © 2024 by Stephanie C. Edwards

Published by Orbis Books, Box 302, Maryknoll, NY 10545-0302.

All rights reserved.

Permissions listed on page 218 represent an extension of this copyright page.

No part of this publication may be reproduced or transmitted in any form or by any means, electronic or mechanical, including photocopying, recording, or any information storage or retrieval system, without prior permission in writing from the publisher.

Queries regarding rights and permissions should be addressed to: Orbis Books, P.O. Box 302, Maryknoll, NY 10545-0302.

Manufactured in the United States of America

Library of Congress Cataloging-in-Publication Data

Names: Edwards, Stephanie C., author.
Title: Enfleshed counter-memory : a Christian social ethic of trauma / Stephanie C. Edwards.
Description: Maryknoll, NY : Orbis Books, [2024] | Includes bibliographical references and index.
Identifiers: LCCN 2024022797 (print) | LCCN 2024022798 (ebook) | ISBN 9781626985827 | ISBN 9798888660379 (epub)
Subjects: LCSH: Psychic trauma—Religious aspects—Christianity.
Classification: LCC BF175.5.P75 E38 2024 (print) | LCC BF175.5.P75 (ebook) | DDC 155.9/3—dc23/eng/20240527
LC record available at https://lccn.loc.gov/2024022797
LC ebook record available at https://lccn.loc.gov/2024022798

*To Pete,
pesniki in bojevniki,
until the end.*

CONTENTS

Acknowledgments ix
Introduction xi
   The Ground We Stand On xv
   A Christian Social Ethic of Enfleshed Counter-Memory xxi
   The Structure of the Book. xxvi

1. **From Trauma Basics to a
Christian Social Ethic of Memory** 1
   Global Mental Health and the PTSD Diagnosis. 5
   Culture and the Hermeneutics of Trauma. 12
   Critics of Trauma 30
   Traumatic Memory: Moving from Self to Society 36
   Conclusion 44

2. **Womanist Ethics and Traumatic Memory** 46
   The Cultural Production of Health, Morality,
      and Embodiment. 53
   Connecting "Flesh" and Theology:
      A Womanist Theological Anthropology
      for Trauma Memory 67
   Womanist Practices of Healing:
      Lament, Self-Definition, and Storytelling. 77
   Conclusion 88

3. **The "Traumatic Imagination":
Trauma as Theological Hermeneutic** 91
   The Hermeneutical Basis for the Traumatic Imagination . . . 94
   Hermeneutics "for Life" 100
   Trauma Encountering Hermeneutics 102
   Trauma as Theological Hermeneutic 108
   Conclusion 124

4. **Reading Liberative Theologies with a Trauma Lens:
   Metz and Trauma's "Dangerous Memory"** 125
   Theology from Catastrophe 129
   Trauma as "Dangerous" Memory:
       Reading Metz with a Traumatic Imagination 143
   Traumatic Memory in a Mystical-Political Framework 150
   Bringing Metz to "Life" 160
   Conclusion 167

5. **Christian Enfleshed Counter-Memory** 169
   Disability Theology and
       the Fundamentals of Ethics in Healing 175
   Christian Liberation Psychology and
       Enfleshed Counter-Memory 180
   The Ethical Expansion of Christian Enfleshed
       Counter-Memory 184
   Enfleshed Counter-Memory as the Work of Justice 195
   Conclusion 212

Epilogue: et lux in tenebris lucet 215

Permissions 218

Index 219

ACKNOWLEDGMENTS

This book would not be in your hands without the immeasurable support of the people who have brought me into my being. Its words are the result of my thinking life to this point, and pieces of each place, face, and moment of the last forty years are scattered in its pages.

Specifically, this project is indebted to my dissertation director at Boston College, Lisa Sowle Cahill, and my readers Steve Pope and Kristin Heyer. Your wisdom, compassion, and belief in my scholarship are the bedrock of these pages. I also want to thank my early readers, teachers, and dialogue partners: M. Shawn Copeland, O. Ernesto Valiente, and Shelly Rambo.

To my editor, Tom Hermans-Webster, thank you for your astute eye, loving-kindness, and making this book the best it could be—I look forward to our next meeting at Wrigley.

To my students, those I get to share a classroom with, and those who come through the many doors of the Boston Theological Interreligious Consortium, I am continually humbled by your authenticity, your drive, and your commitment to creating a world of healing for all.

I believe, with Aristotle, that a friend is the greatest of all good things, and I am so lucky to be surrounded by a chorus that made this book possible: Debbie Brubaker and Timon Kaple, Amy Clearwater and Alexa Plotkin, Lynn Cooper, the Dirksen family, the Elements crew (specifically Katie Pinard and Michael Macomber), Thea Hollman, Blake Huggins and Lindsey Richard, Lauren Kimball and Chris Endersby, Mike, Sarah, Marah, and

Zoe Lafortune, Megan Raimondi-Musser, and Annie Selak (and so many more).

To my families—West and East—from Oregon to Maine, I am so grateful for your love, support, and continual confusion with my chosen career path. Thank you for sticking with me.

To my husband, Pete, for putting up with the long days, the emotional roller coaster that is the writing life, and somehow always having dinner ready—I love you. For our dog, EmmyLou, who made sure I took walk breaks, stopped to smell . . . everything, and generally reminded me of the important things throughout this process: naps, lots of snacks, and jaunts to the ocean.

Finally, to the people of Eden—friends for life who saw my truth earlier than I ever dared to imagine who I would become or what I would accomplish. You all were right in 2007: I wrote a book!

INTRODUCTION

November 2005

    I'm feeling my way forward more than seeing the path. The dark is only broken by the dim orbs of dying flashlights scattered among our group. Hot, dry wind tugs my hair from its tie, catching in my eyes. I have no idea where we're going. José's mom is dead, and I don't know what I'm doing here. A gringita in the Salvadoran countryside, watching a family mourn. I stare awkwardly at the packed dirt floor as sobs mingle with gentle guitar chords, played in a daze by a man sitting on a plastic stool in the corner. My mind wanders to last month. In two days, Ilamatapec erupted, raining ash around the city, dropping a blanket of gray that would be unceremoniously erased the next day by Tropical Storm Stan slamming into the country.[1] The catastrophe left in its wake the brown slick of mudslides and the sickening green of exposed rot, ravaging the poorest sections of El Salvador. The beating felt somehow timed. It brought to my front door what I had watched from afar a month before, my classmates helplessly gathered around a 12-inch TV screen at the hotel bar near campus: people in our home country buried in Katrina's water, in mud, in neglect and apathy.

---

    [1] On October 1, 2005, the explosion rocked El Salvador, see Teresa Scolamacchia et al., "The 2005 Eruption of Ilamatepec (Santa Ana) Volcano, El Salvador," *Journal of Volcanology and Geothermal Research* 189 (2010): 291–318. Then on October 3–5, 2005, Stan hit the country; see United Nations Office for the Coordination of Humanitarian Affairs (OCHA), "Analysis of Tropical Storm Stan in El Salvador" November 15, 2005.

August 2007

Sweat trickles down my back, pooling at my waistband. It's silent, eerily so, amid the packed-together railroad homes. I pick my way slowly down the narrow street, more pothole than even ground. As I turn a corner, my breath catches. The seemingly tidy house on my left reveals its back: shorn completely off. The first floor is a jumble of broken furniture and weeds; a kettle still balances precariously on the stove. The second floor is pristine—aside from the twisting vines reaching across the still-made queen bed with its pink bedspread, the exercise bike with a T-shirt tossed over the handlebars, the smiling family portrait in its heavy wooden frame hanging on the wall over the dresser. Looking down the street of my new home, huge "X" marks are spray-painted on every house's front, blaring out messages from each quadrant: 9.25 / GAS OFF / Food and Water / 1. That last number a ghostly stand-in for a person—sometimes dead, sometimes alive. All abandoned. Some house-checkers were more literal: "Dog dead," "Went to Bishop Francis," "1 Dead in Attic."[2]

April 2013

My hands are shaking as I call again. And again. Again. I get nothing but infuriating beeps and static. The trees outside my window are still covered in frost as I try desperately to figure out what's happening. We don't have internet at the house yet,

---

[2] I moved to New Orleans as a Jesuit volunteer and served there for a year. See Christopher Romaguera, "Spray-Painted FEMA X Still Marks the Storm in New Orleans," *Curbed,* August 19, 2015, and Chris Rose, *1 Dead in Attic: After Katrina* (New York: Simon & Schuster, 2015), for the stories of the X marks that became enduring public memorials after the storm and the man-made aftermath that ravaged the city August 23–31, 2005.

INTRODUCTION xiii

and my cell service is spotty at best. All I know is that we always go to the Marathon. Mike (and whoever he can convince over morning mimosas) always goes to the finish line. Of course, they'd be there today. Images of bloody shoes and smoky chaos seem superimposed onto my library's downtown branch, the church where my friend is interning, and the bar where I was clinking glasses just a week ago, celebrating my recent move to Maine.[3] "How many this time?" my brain keeps prompting—not "why" or even "how"—simply a plea: I know there will be some, there always are. Please, God, let it be none whom I call mine.

~

Pain, confusion, helplessness, fear—these emotions feel all too present as I recall myself in these moments. Rather than stay in nicely encapsulated boxes, most of my brushes—or collisions—with the death, destruction, and pain that we all carry seep into my everyday. Echoes of our distinct, yet shared losses reverberate each time I turn on the radio or get a news alert on my phone, reminding me of the thin boundary between "normal" and another world-shattering moment. Our shared stories of precarity are the "why" of this book: attempting to reckon with deeply personal tragedy *and* with the massive, global, and systemic trauma intertwined within. Communal, visceral pain ripples through our corporate body—wounded again and again and again—and cries out for healing. Each of our scabbed, scarred, and changed flesh charts its own, personal course, yet I find myself constantly seeking "more." I pull at the thread of connection that ties *me* to *us*, wanting to understand what binds us together in both our suffering and our rising.

---

[3] On April 15, 2013, two explosions near the finish line of the Boston Marathon killed three people and physically injured 281. The violence was followed by an unprecedented city lockdown and manhunt that lasted four-and-a-half days.

I don't start from such a dour footing to be pessimistic, determinist, or hyperfocused on pain. Rather, I start with Ruby Sales's first question: "'Where does it hurt?' because it's a question that drives to the heart of the matter—and a question we scarcely know how to ask in public life now."[4]

In this way, I hope that the snippets of my story brush up against something in your own life. I do not mean to shock or to trigger any certain response. I give these moments instead as an offering, an invitation to start with our hearts, in our bodies, probing our memories, asking ourselves to be honest about where it hurts. Such honesty is a prerequisite because exploring the contents of this book—trauma, faith, memory, and resistance—is deeply personal and embodied work, as well as a theological task.

Our feelings give us insight not only into our pain, but they also give insight into our hopes. The edges of our hurt tell us about our loves and reveal our knowledge that things as they are, are not how they should be.[5] Conversely, our joys, the times where we feel free and alive and unburdened, are a foretaste of the promise of liberation. In these pages, I hope to create a community of learning focused on these embodied knowings—connecting across time and space to tease apart the finely woven threads of our lives to understand ourselves, our challenges, and our faith more fully. In so doing, I ask that you join me in cultivating what bell hooks calls a "pedagogy of hope," a way of engaging that lives in our very bones and extends well beyond these words. This mode of learning—alive, forceful, grounded in gritty hope—is essential to

---

[4] Krista Tippett, "Ruby Sales: Where Does It Hurt?," *On Being*, NPR, September 15, 2016, https://onbeing.org/programs/ruby-sales-where-does-it-hurt/.

[5] I am not essentializing pain as necessary for knowledge, but rather here I am recalling Edward Schillebeeckx's "negative contrast experience," where one need not have the "answer" to suffering, but rather respond strongly with a feeling of "not this!" that spurs one to protest and social action toward creating healing and fullness of life (Schillebeeckx frames this in salvific terms).

Introduction xv

understanding and healing trauma, in all of its personal, social, and theological forms. In this book I offer a powerful Christian social ethic that provides the gut-level, formational, realistic hope that is the only gospel response to the multifaceted, collective experience of trauma that pervades our world and ourselves. The "enfleshed counter-memory" framework I develop is deeply theological and heartbreakingly realistic. This book is not an instruction manual for, a pastoral theology guide to, or a systematic theology of trauma. Rather, I aim to break open communities of shared lament, embodied compassion, and active resistance by presenting Christian enfleshed counter-memory as an engaged social ethic.

This is not a triumphalist project. It is deeply rooted in the liminal space in which so many of us find ourselves, struck down and unable to see through the dark. Here, rather than waiting for the heavens to break open and offer perfect clarity, we "stammer out redemption" in the face of systems that either demand our forgetting or create an obsession with our pain.[6] Here, in the dark, we practice emergent, creative forms of healing that reshape our hope, our vision, and even our world. A Christian enfleshed counter-memory offers a vocabulary and a framework that honors the truth of the circuitous path of healing widespread trauma and the particularities of how we each experience the "already but not yet."

The Ground We Stand On

To better understand what I will construct in the coming chapters, it is useful to briefly clarify where we enter this conversation. I am writing this book still relatively early in the discussion of theology

---

[6] Carlos Mendoza-Álvarez and Thierry-Marie Courau, eds., "Introduction," in *Concilium: Decolonial Theology: Violence, Resistance and Spiritualities* (London: SCM Press, 2019), 7, regarding the task of decolonial theology.

and trauma but simultaneously in a culture that is nearly obsessed with "trauma." From climate crises to global clergy sexual abuse to war to the coronavirus pandemic, it is easy to see why the word "trauma" gets tossed around daily, risking (and sometimes in fact losing) its content. Yet trauma's ubiquity and potency speak to our need to express the depth and impact of our experiences; that we are wounded[7] and seek recognition and healing. There is much debate around trauma, from its original development as a psychological diagnosis in the United States to its medical parameters, treatment modalities, theodicy, and philosophy. Here, it is helpful to note that (with a few nuances outlined in chapter 1) I assess trauma prima facie—I accept the overwhelming expression and use of this term to point toward a widespread lived human reality, one of deep harm and unfulfilled healing.[8]

Trauma, in its scope and power, exposes theological problems that demand both an indictment of interpersonal harms and the condemnation of and actions against systems of social sin that perpetuate such devastation. We need theological ethics that extend beyond the individual to meet the unsettling social nature of trauma, and then to sit within that complexity instead of repeating ready-made "answers." Here, I follow Karen O'Donnell and Katie Cross, who name how trauma theology is unique in its capacity "to create spaces for such difficult questions ... to feel God's presence and God's absence at the same time."[9] In this book, I sit

---

[7] The word "trauma" originates from the Greek word for "wound," "hurt," or "defeat." In the late 1600s, "trauma" was a Latin medical term for "physical wound," which remains in use today. By the late 1800s, mostly thanks to the work of Sigmund Freud, it came to represent "psychic wounds" as well.

[8] Since this is a work in social ethics, I find this approach valid. In other systems of thought, particularly in bioethics, the nuances of the medical diagnostical use of "trauma" and its other applications must be more intricately parsed.

[9] Karen O'Donnell and Katie Cross, *Bearing Witness: Intersectional Perspectives on Trauma Theology* (Norwich, UK: SCM Press, 2022), 2, 4. This

Introduction xvii

at such intersections. I revel in the paradoxes, the contradictions, and the unknown that trauma demands we investigate. I seek to shape a theological ethic that intertwines both lived experience and theological construction, moving beyond a purely clinical or purely philosophical discussion, always opening the door to further inquiry, rather than presenting a completed system.

In traditional accounts, trauma is variously interpreted as an individual deficiency, one that curative medical and spiritual models purport to solve. This individualization also leads to the "vulgar" usage of trauma—where everything from a stubbed toe to a disappointing or uncomfortable interaction is labeled as "trauma" in the cultural parlance. Yet there is no doubt that clinical cases of chronic traumatic disorders are increasing as well. In response, almost innumerable clinical interventions are being explored in the field of posttraumatic stress disorder (PTSD) alone—medical, spiritual, and otherwise—as the distinctions of specific cases and the staggering diversity of global human needs emerge.

Ethicists as well as medical practitioners are raising questions around these emerging treatments, including access (e.g., high cost limiting their use to elite groups), safety (as some drugs studied are not legal in the United States, or are being tested for uses beyond their original purpose), cross-cultural appropriateness, availability of representative test groups that can assess harm and benefit across diverse persons, and the dominant Western orientation of the concepts of trauma and medical healing themselves.[10] Yet it is

---

builds upon work by Gloria Anzaldúa (among others) to explicate theologies on the "borders" as sites of embodied wholeness rather than division.

[10] "Trauma" and "PTSD" have become terms commonly referenced in our shared cultural scripts in the United States. However, what such glib usage elides is the astronomical growth in PTSD diagnoses over the past thirty years, and the persistently insufficient responses to this trend in realms as varied as bioethics, theology, social work, and cultural studies. What to *do* for and with this growing number of people, as well as understanding what we are talking about when we talk about trauma, is a central concern of this project.

not unfettered access to medical treatments that can fully respond to trauma. As philosopher Michael Sandel points out,

> Worry about access ignores the moral status of [the treatment] itself. Is the scenario troubling because the unenhanced poor would be denied the benefits of bioengineering, or because the enhanced affluent would somehow be dehumanized? ... The fundamental question is not how to ensure equal access ... but whether we should aspire to it in the first place.[11]

If our aspirations for healing remain rooted in the perpetual narrative of consumerist "improvement," only limited by the most meager assurances of safety, then our humanity will forever be bound to the market, limiting our created, transcendent selves to whatever definitions the market wants to sell.

A vision of the environments, communities, religious structures, and social spaces in which persons live is often missing from clinical interventions, as well as ethical inquiries, into trauma treatment.[12] I belong to the millennial generation, a group that throws "trauma" around like a Pokémon card, counting how many

---

[11] Michael Sandel, "The Case against Perfection," *The Atlantic,* April 2004, https://www.theatlantic.com/magazine/archive/2004/04/the-case-against-perfection/302927/.

[12] Here I align myself methodologically and philosophically with Paul Farmer (see, e.g., *Pathologies of Power: Health, Human Rights, and the New War on the Poor* [Berkeley: University of California Press, 2004]) and Van Rensselaer Potter, *Bioethics: Bridge to the Future* (New York: Prentice-Hall, 1970), who both orient their scientific research and medical practice toward an interdisciplinary vision that bridges science and the humanities toward developing a normative global ethic that takes seriously the context around a specific illness or diagnosis (e.g., the role of the natural world / disasters, socioeconomic status, political affiliation, geographic location, and so on). These large-scale structural factors are essential for situating the experience of trauma, rather than the exclusive focus on medical case studies of the Georgetown bioethics model that has dominated the field.

"unprecedented" disasters we can collect before we hit forty. In this case, for example, even if an individual is treated successfully to alleviate suffering, there remains collective memory of the trauma, either directly through witnesses, secondhand through family members or friends, and the often social nature of the event(s). Despite the potential efficacy of certain interventions in one person's distinct body, the ripples of trauma throughout communities go un-, or at least under-, interrogated.

Further, the overwhelming emphasis on "curing" individual trauma occurs in a broader social context, one that urges "moving on" from the event, regardless of the health of those involved. The hyperindividualization of treatment, coupled with the US cultural demand for perfection, serves to negate ongoing communal and personal needs such as reconciliation, justice, or community healing. In response to this environment, victims may position their agency, selfhood, and even entire identity within the trauma itself, emphasizing all that has been suffered and lost, and the need for vindication within a triumphalist vision of survival.[13] This orientation positions their suffering as the center of their personhood. The traumatized are thus held in an impossible bind: the pressure to find a perfect cure at all costs, *and* to unceasingly repeat their suffering to attest to its truth in their life. Individuals and groups can both carry forward this suffering-as-identity, even repeating or exacerbating harmful actions in the name of their trauma. Not limited to the directly traumatized, the emerging field of epigenetics attempts to reckon with the biological reality of this identity-based trauma, and how the direct suffering of a person or group of people can be passed down to future generations.[14]

---

[13] Flora Keshgegian, *Redeeming Memories: A Theology of Healing and Transformation* (Nashville: Abingdon Press, 2000), 64.

[14] While this medical research is currently ambiguous, what we do know is that the person who suffered a trauma directly does change epigenetically, and their body is forever marked by that experience. The likelihood, therefore,

The field of trauma studies exists within this murky context. As an area of inquiry, trauma studies is interdisciplinary, intersectional, already large in scale—and growing. From psychology to medicine to philosophy to theology, a chorus of voices tries to encounter this nebulous experience and offer a path toward resolution from their specific vantage point. Yet too often these responses are either pointedly specific (addressing only one type of trauma, often solely on the individual level), overly systematic (placing a conceptual answer in place of real action), or unrealistic (advocating a type of systemic change that feels far out of reach, or relying on a model that is exclusively eschatological in hope). More specifically, a social ethics of trauma, particularly in its theological form, is largely undeveloped.

So where do we begin to build an embodied, realistic ethic that can meet the challenge of trauma in its multiple forms? I propose that *memory* is the feature of our human selves most useful for this task. Memory is the connective tissue between trauma and theology, conceptually as well as physically. While not simple by any means, our memories are often constitutive of our very selves, and often the site of our most realized connection to God.[15] Yet individually and socially, not to mention theologically, we are regularly unable to rightly hold memories of harm. Too often, we live

> with the unbearable by pressuring those who have been traumatized to forget and by rejecting the testimonies of those who are forced by fate to remember. As individuals and as cultures, we impose arbitrary term limits on memory and recovery from trauma: a century, say, for slavery, fifty years, perhaps, for the Holocaust, a decade

---

that something is passed down to future generations is quite strong (whether it is resilience, harm, or a mix of both is still outstanding; see more in chapter 1).

[15] While a simple reflection on the dignity and fullness of persons with dementia (John Swinton) or other disabilities disproves the "we are our memories" hypothesis, there is still something rich within the ongoing centrality of memory to our sense of self, both individual and corporate (more in chapter 1).

or two for Vietnam, several months for mass rape or serial murder.[16]

What is missing from this hegemonic process of forgetting is just what Christ demands, as Wendy Farley reminds us: that Jesus's lived ethic was an optics—it matters who we see, to whom we give our attention, who and what we remember—not just to our here-and-now, but to the kin-dom of God.[17] In fact, as Jesus mandates, we *must* see the persons and events society would like to forget, we *must* pay attention to the wounded, we *must* remember. But remember what exactly? Attend to what wounds? In the pages that follow, I offer my attempt to answer these questions: to hold myself, and my faith, accountable in the grounding life of Jesus, the original "enfleshed counter-memory." Through this social ethic, I hope to provide a framework that has the potential to hold a fundamentally different truth than what the world tries to tell us about our pain—an ethic that emboldens memory for life, rather than represses or sells it for profit. I offer an ethic that is dedicated to process rather than "success," an ethic that promises what theologian Flora Keshgegian calls "with-ness," rather than isolation.

A Christian Social Ethic of Enfleshed Counter-Memory

To this end, I work with womanist and feminist constructions of incarnational, embodied personhood, trauma as a theological hermeneutic, and Johann Baptist Metz's "dangerous memory."

---

[16] Susan Brison, *Aftermath: Violence and the Remaking of a Self* (Princeton, NJ: Princeton University Press, 2002), 57.

[17] "Jesus's presence among the poor is not a social program. It is in a sense more radical than that. For Jesus, the poor were persons who mattered.... His ethics is an optics.... He sees in society's throwaways beings to cherish, enjoy, befriend." *Gathering Those Driven Away: A Theology of Incarnation* (Louisville, KY: Westminster John Knox Press, 2011), 194. I draw "kin-dom" from Ada María Isasi-Díaz and her work to remove patriarchal language from theological terminology.

Using these theological building blocks, enfleshed counter-memory provides conceptual grounding for concrete social action that engages our shared yet particular traumas. The wording is purposeful: "enfleshed," in relation to complex and incarnational embodiment; "counter," as traumatic memory often runs up against structures of power; and "memory," as the essential category that unites trauma studies with Christian theology. Resisting socially encouraged "forgetting" through this model does not deny individual agency and the right to seek treatment to alleviate suffering. Rather, it illuminates the political, religious, and historical context of harm *and* healing. With a vision of the person beyond a presenting disorder, and trauma beyond its individual confines, our definition of healing must encompass incarnate persons and communities. These are "whole selves in struggle," already fighting for recognition in situations of extreme harm.[18]

Within the construction of enfleshed counter-memory, larger questions regarding moral agency, the role suffering often plays in an individual's development, and individual and social responsibility will emerge. These three areas explicitly resurface in a variety of ways in the following chapters, and I do not claim to resolve them. I think trauma, however, can *trouble* our assumptions about agency, development, and responsibility in generative ways. Our growing knowledge of trauma disrupts the traditional Western view of the individual: that one's own intellect, will, and intention create a fully capable, responsible individual, and, by extension, one who can deal with their problems alone.[19] Just as

---

[18] Emilie Townes, *Womanist Ethics and the Cultural Production of Evil* (New York: Palgrave Macmillan, 2006), 48.

[19] From a scientific perspective, such biological plasticity within neurology is explored in the work of Bruce McEwen, who was a highly influential neuroscientist who died in 2020, and is remembered specifically for the translational nature of science from the perspective of the individual to society across the lifespan. See Matthew Hill, Richard Hunter, and Lawrence Reagan, eds., *Neurobiological Stress: Special Issue Dedicated to Dr. Bruce S. McEwen* 25

the nature of traumatic experience itself is shared (by occurring in a society, if nothing else), our existential selves are similarly intertwined. Instead of an isolated, internally cohesive individual, trauma studies brings to the fore (at least) three related factors that influence one's agency: (1) individual consciousness and intention, qualified by biological factors including neurological patterns and genetics; (2) the formational role and impact of families, social and religious groups, and societal norms; and (3) epigenetic modification posttrauma, which changes how our genes express themselves, and in so doing very concretely re-creates and changes our bodies and our minds.

While bioethics is not the focus of this book, theology (and the theological anthropology that is the basis of my ethic in particular) must engage honestly with scientific trauma research that helps expose these aspects of agency, as we increasingly understand the connections between individual psychological experiences of trauma, the social context in which trauma is experienced, and trauma's physiological effects on the brain.[20] To ignore the very real neuroscience and psychological research into trauma is to build a disingenuous ethic. Unfortunately, this is a tendency seen all too often in theology: the impulse to paper over anything difficult, contradictory, or nuanced with, "Well, you just need a little more Jesus."[21]

This supposedly theological response works hand-in-hand with the emphasis of medical models on autonomous, isolated trauma treatment. Our penchant to isolate and burden the trauma

---

(July 2023). *Note:* Throughout I use the gender-neutral "their" as singular.

[20] J. D. Bremner, "Traumatic Stress: Effects on the Brain," *Dialogues in Clinical Neuroscience* 8, no. 4 (2006): 445–461; T. Y. Kim, S. J. Kim, H. G. Chung, J. H. Choi, S. H. Kim, and J. I. Kang, "Epigenetic Alterations of the *BDNF* Gene in Combat-Related Post-traumatic Stress Disorder," *Acta Psychiatrica Scandinavica* 135 (2017): 170–179.

[21] As theologian Monica Coleman was told when sharing her struggles with trauma with a pastor, *Bipolar Faith: A Black Woman's Journey with Depression and Faith* (Minneapolis: Fortress Press, 2016).

victim/survivor[22] with their own healing is further supported by the culturally pervasive "blame the victim" mentality as well as interpersonal interactions with the trauma experience that often serve to highlight our own fragility.[23] Countering such attitudes is a tremendous task. As theologian Willie James Jennings outlines, however, Christianity has at its core a claim of deeper intimacy, a foundational reality grounded in incarnational relatedness that bonds humanity with God and persons to each other as *imago Dei*.[24] For Jennings, whose central work explores the embedded racism within Christianity, the intimacy of the Incarnation requires honest wrestling with suffering within communities who refuse to settle for *talking about* reconciliation, seeking to implement it concretely instead. Failing to face history and suffering means that, despite claims of a higher sense of relatedness based in God's creation and the Incarnation, Christianity's call to "brother and sisterhood" actually reinforces various oppressive frameworks. Without doing the real work, hollow calls for reconciliation or healing only negotiate social power or perform "exhausted idealist claims masquerading as serious theological accounts."[25]

---

[22] There is a long-standing debate around the words to use to describe a person who has been through trauma. Best clinical practice lets individual self-identification be the guide (personal preference). In this book, as the emphasis is on systems of victimization and power, rather than individuals, I follow the common practice of dual "victim/survivor" identification.

[23] Think of how most rape victims are spoken about, or the burden of proof laid upon them to attest that they did not somehow deserve to be violated or were responsible in some way for another's actions.

[24] Willie James Jennings, *The Christian Imagination: Theology and the Origins of Race* (New Haven, CT: Yale University Press, 2011), 8–9.

[25] Jennings, *The Christian Imagination*, 10. While this short summary paints "Christianity" with a very broad brush, Jennings provides a much more nuanced and intricate exploration of how Western Christianity became and continues to be a racialized project that has too often served social power rather than the gospel, especially in the United States. The particularity of race and racialization in the Catholic context, which upholds its own particular

Introduction

xxv

My aim is to develop a theological method for taking seriously Jennings's call to incarnational intimacy in the context of trauma, rather than cooperate with social and theological scripts that tell us to forget or reason away complex and difficult past experiences. The core of a Christian social ethic of enfleshed counter-memory moves past empty idealism. It instead demands mores and practices of building incarnational intimacy bound up with justice. For, as M. Shawn Copeland reminds us, our faith asks us to remember suffering *rightly*; the "Christian exercise of memory purports to be radically different: We pledge to remember, we are obliged to do so."[26] Approaching ethics in this way asks us to undertake the demanding work of reimagining ourselves and our communities, walking the circuitous, often painful path toward long-term healing of all.

Creating a framework for action via enfleshed counter-memory does not mean the task is "finished" at the end of this book. If, as *Gaudium et Spes* states, we are to read the "signs of the times," our work will remain necessarily open-ended. We are *status viatoris*—beings on the way—both knowing we are unfulfilled yet oriented toward fulfillment; making the way by walking.[27] This is a particular asset of trauma theology: that our becoming-ness is central, that our seeking is in itself a good, our unfinished nature a gift. As the oft-cited Rilke, I do not seek to provide answers in this book, but to live the right questions[28]—without which our theology dies in thrall to power—rather than living into the transformational, liberatory promises of the gospel.

---

commitments to such paltry responses, is explored by Bryan Massingale in *Racial Justice and the Catholic Church* (Maryknoll, NY: Orbis Books, 2010).

[26] M. Shawn Copeland, "Memory, #BlackLivesMatter, and Theologians," *Political Theology* 17, no. 1 (2016): 1.

[27] Josef Pieper, *On Hope* (San Francisco: Ignatius Press, 1986), 13. Also drawing on Roberto Goizueta, *Caminemos con Jesus: Toward a Hispanic/Latino Theology of Accompaniment* (Maryknoll, NY: Orbis Books, 1995).

[28] Rainer Maria Rilke, *Letters to a Young Poet* (1934; New York: W. W. Norton, 1993), 35.

The Structure of the Book

Chapter 1—From Trauma Basics to a Christian Social Ethic of Memory

Necessarily, this book cannot be a comprehensive treatment of clinical trauma or memory studies, but it will review current, relevant literature to determine the major components of the interdisciplinary conversation. I outline the multivalent connections between "trauma" and Christian ethics, helping the reader establish a baseline for understanding what we talk about when we talk about trauma, and how theology might interact with this experience. In the understanding of trauma that is presented here, the problem is framed not only as recurring, individual chronic suffering, but also as one of endemic and hegemonic social forgetting. From individual to social, trauma in its multitude of forms is clearly a "sign of the times" that calls for a social ethic, particularly rooted in the Christian tradition. The first chapter also briefly addresses critiques of the trauma diagnosis and trauma discourse, concluding with how a focus on memory within trauma resolves much of this tension and provides a fruitful way forward toward a Christian social ethic.[29]

Chapter 2—Womanist Ethics and Traumatic Memory

The second chapter focuses on womanist theology, in particular the work of Monica Coleman, Phillis Sheppard, M. Shawn Copeland, and Emilie Townes. It elicits from their work the theological concepts of embodiment and social flesh that emphasize the

---

[29] While it is useful to debate terms for many reasons, I am focused here on finding frameworks for ethical action, over and against any preoccupation with definitional debate.

INTRODUCTION

incarnational reality of creation. This reality enlivens the "flesh" of the world, and the traumatized person in particular, that resists dualism and seeks the salvation and integrity of whole persons.[30] Theological anthropology is the essential basis of enfleshed counter-memory, as who and why we *are* is at stake within any consideration of trauma. Trauma does not happen "out there"—it is always within bodies, breaking and forming integrated persons. To consider any proposal that reaches toward healing, we must first understand where we are to begin. Here, the body is inextricable. Positioning womanist enfleshment as the cornerstone of a Christian social ethic in response to trauma also centers voices too often ignored in trauma literature. This chapter posits womanists as founders of trauma theory, although they are rarely recognized as such.[31]

Chapter 3—The "Traumatic Imagination":
Trauma as Theological Hermeneutic

With a theological anthropology of enfleshment central, how do we engage trauma? Chapter 3 outlines trauma's function as a hermeneutic, a way of reading and interpretation that can lead to new ways of seeing and acting. I propose three central aspects of the "traumatic imagination"—time, position, and praxis. While obviously blunt tools for such a delicate task, I introduce these broad categories as a starting point for our thinking on the hermeneutical implications of trauma and the ways it might

---

[30] Further, their work illuminates the larger historical, social, political, and religious context of the individual who experiences extreme trauma, and the ways in which traditional Western bioethics often ignores the wisdom and practices that emerge from a community's negotiations for survival and adaptation. See Emilie Townes, *Breaking the Fine Rain of Death: African American Health Issues and a Womanist Ethic of Care* (Eugene, OR: Wipf and Stock, 1998).

[31] Trauma studies has been rightly critiqued for its whiteness, of which I am a part and will discuss in this chapter.

challenge us to read theology anew, particularly liberative theology. When we "read with a trauma lens," we change how we interpret ourselves and our theology. Practicing the traumatic imagination from within a womanist theological anthropology begins to hint at the depth of the work necessary to live out a social ethic that has the power to respond to trauma.

Chapter 4—Reading Liberative Theologies with a Trauma Lens: Metz and Trauma's "Dangerous Memory"

The fourth chapter explores the work of twentieth-century German Catholic theologian Johann Baptist Metz, engaging his concepts of memory, narrative, and solidarity to contextualize the experience of trauma within a Christian mystical-political framework.[32] Metz offers a particular way of interpreting suffering theologically that connects individual memory to the stories of communities. This insight suggests ethical practices of rendering trauma as "dangerous memory" that require a community of resistance, never resigning the individual to isolated struggle. This reading of Metz is itself a demonstration of the traumatic imagination as theological hermeneutic. Reading Metz with a trauma lens (through the work of Flora Keshgegian) provides an interesting interlocutor for my proposed social ethic, rereading "classic" liberative theological writing in a new context. The chapter concludes by demonstrating how Metz helps concretize the roles we—even "observers" or "witnesses" to trauma—all play in liberation and healing, as together we are enmeshed in

---

[32] While Metz was broadly focused on society's victims and hegemonic power post-Shoah, his work is directly applicable to the ethics of trauma, and to this project in particular, as he demonstrates how communal memory can interfere with the renegotiation of memory of an individual, as well as providing a communal, ethical response to mass suffering, which speaks to the need for communal re/integration of the traumatized person and their memories.

suffering alongside direct victims. Moving from enfleshment, to imagination, to community, the theological foundation of each aspect of enfleshed counter-memory is made clear.

Chapter 5—Christian Enfleshed Counter-Memory:
A Practical Social Ethic

Finally, the fifth chapter outlines the content of a Christian social ethic of enfleshed counter-memory. Enfleshed counter-memory is inherently practical, made real through the practice of seeking justice within three distinct yet interrelated spheres: individual agency, intimate community, and the global preferential option for the poor.[33] It is a necessarily "thin" social ethic, meant to be adaptable to particular circumstances, continually emerging in specific contexts. I explore how embracing *enfleshment* is one necessary theological move, and that, while *accompaniment* in light of our incarnational reality is ethically necessary, an enfleshed counter-memory is meant to be *revolutionary*. Enfleshed counter-memory is dangerous. It is disruptive. It asks us all to reach beyond our comfort and into the struggle for justice. It is the call of the gospel. As in chapter 2, I tease out

---

[33] The poor and marginalized are much more likely to experience preventable death and disease, including trauma. See J. S. Seng, W. D. Lopez, M. Sperlich, L. Hamama, and C. D. Reed Meldrum, "Marginalized Identities, Discrimination Burden, and Mental Health: Empirical Exploration of an Interpersonal-Level Approach to Modeling Intersectionality," *Social Science and Medicine* 75, no. 12 (2012): 2437–2445. Inspiration for this idea comes from Paul Farmer, "Health, Healing, and Social Justice: Insights from Liberation Theology," in *On Moral Medicine: Theological Perspectives in Medical Ethics*, 3rd ed., ed. T. Lysaught, J. Kotva, S. Lammers, and A. Verhey (Grand Rapids: William B. Eerdmans, 2012), 140. Farmer frequently laments the lack of a larger social justice framework for addressing bioethical issues worldwide. He finds that it is in fact liberation theology that offers particular as well as universal ways of approaching global health that balance subsidiarity with social justice, which I take up in this chapter with regard to trauma.

initial insights into the ways certain communities/individuals are living out an enfleshed counter-memory and how a Christian social ethic can inform believers' participation in action for justice and healing.

Though enfleshed counter-memory may appear to propose mere academic jargon, I hope to provide a theoretical grounding and a concrete evaluative mechanism for Christians to build communities that truly sit with pain and work toward transformation. Importantly, this project does not urge what Shelly Rambo calls a "rush to redemption." I follow her approach of the much more difficult work of Holy Saturday: embodying a community of faith within the aftermath of traumatic loss.[34] In this space we build the physical, spiritual, and relational conditions to remember rightly. Positioning the healing of trauma in this way is a unique contribution of theological ethics, which creates and holds space for relationship, fruitful tension, and "unknowing" that medicalized, profit-driven models do not and cannot offer.

---

[34] Shelly Rambo, *Spirit and Trauma: A Theology of Remaining* (Louisville, KY: Westminster John Knox Press, 2010), 35. A community that does not move "to" a prescribed goal but authentically moves "through" pain together.

1

FROM TRAUMA BASICS TO A CHRISTIAN SOCIAL ETHIC OF MEMORY

> At the site of the former concentration camp Belzec, in South-eastern Poland, when the Memorial Mausoleum was being built, planners decided to remove the younger trees that had been planted by the SS during the camp's heinous years of operation. The only trees to be retained were the old oaks, which had witnessed the atrocities.... How does atrocity defy memory and simultaneously demand to be remembered? How do we collectively mark it and honor it—while addressing its inevitably complicated aftermath? As we examine the inheritance of trauma within the mosaic of human history, is it ever possible to move beyond it?
>
> —Elizabeth Rosner[1]

Very rightly, most of trauma studies, theological or otherwise, is victim-centered, uncovering what is happening in the experience of the (so-called) victim. While what is happening "in them" is

---

[1] Elizabeth Rosner, *Survivor Café: The Legacy of Trauma and the Labyrinth of Memory* (Berkeley, CA: Counterpoint, 2017), 56, 9.

deeply important and necessary work, this tendency to emphasize the victim experience is often translated by those on the outside of trauma as a phenomenon that happens "over there." This creates a culture of what theologian Laurie Cassidy calls "the up close but far away."[2] Cassidy argues that our modern world allows us intimate access into a slice of people's experiences (namely through media), creating a sense of ethics that ends in an outsider's "knowledge" of suffering. Simply think of scrolling your news app or social media feed every morning, reposting about the war of the day with a link to an NGO, and feeling you've done your daily duty. For Cassidy, and her reading of Christ, this is simply not enough. While those of us outside of the day's direct trauma may feel an intimacy in our witnessing through a screen, the same is assuredly *not* felt by those in pain.

Here, I want to trouble our default sense of solidarity and compassion as people of goodwill. How are those of us who most often sit "outside" of direct traumatic experiences *implicated* by trauma? How do we feel, or not feel, *bound up with* the suffering of the world?

I am interested in action in the model of Jesus as our ethical end, not in mere awareness. Christian theology is tasked with cultivating "right" attitudes, actions, and beliefs as it responds to what Christ himself asks of the faithful. To believe, act, and feel "rightly"—orthodoxy, orthopraxy, and orthopathy, respectively rendered from the Greek—such that we cultivate "right memory" is the theological backdrop of this book, and a response to the questions Rosner asks of us, uncovering our profound obligations as well as our profound gifts within our faith.[3]

---

[2] Laurie Cassidy, "Grotesque Un/Knowing of Suffering: A White Christian Response," in *Christology and Whiteness: What Would Jesus Do?*, ed. George Yancy (New York: Routledge, 2012), 36–58.

[3] Nancy Ramsey inspired the obligations language. "Psychology, Culture, and Religion: Session 1," *American Academy of Religion*, Annual Meeting, San Antonio, TX, November 17, 2023.

Encountering trauma and memory is a challenging task in multiple ways. The first and foremost challenge is resisting the desire to own, control, or mandate memory or a particular shape of remembering—despite, or even because of, our best intentions. Yet, we are challenged as Christians to create the conditions for "remembering rightly in a violent world," as Croatian theologian and political abuse survivor Miroslav Volf puts it.[4] We are part of a "community of memory" as Christians, he argues, framing our existential claim in the midst of trauma, always together— never alone. As such, we must understand what we mean when we ask people to remember their pain or engage their trauma. We must recognize how Christian conceptions of memory of suffering shapes how we ask people to hold their pain toward healing and how prior approaches to memory have caused great harm.

To take this task seriously, this chapter first outlines the scope and definition of trauma, posttraumatic stress disorder (PTSD), and current treatment models.[5] Rather than assume a blithe interpretation that meets our theological aims, an honest engagement with the best scientific and biological understandings of trauma is necessary so we can examine the issue in its fullness. I then outline the culture and hermeneutics of trauma, including a brief history of the term and diagnosis, as well as the still-emerging field of trauma and theology. From this multifaceted understanding of trauma, I address some critics of trauma discourse and trauma studies, who help illuminate the complexity

---

[4] Miroslav Volf, *The End of Memory: Remembering Rightly in a Violent World* (Grand Rapids: William B. Eerdmans, 2006).

[5] Note that this chapter is meant to be illustrative, not exhaustive. Also, the definition of mental health and wellbeing/illness itself is contested and debated. The development of psychology as a field and in particular the definitions in the American Psychiatric Association *Diagnostic and Statistical Manual* are the subject of much conflict and disagreement. While I do not wade into the extreme particulars of this debate, I orient myself from a position that seeks to heal, or at least address, aspects of mental functioning that inhibit a person's quality of life and potential flourishing.

of this work. The foundation laid in the first three sections is necessary to ground the final, fourth section, which focuses on memory itself and the particular role of Christian memory as a social ethic in the face of trauma.

Throughout this chapter, I aim to move our understanding of trauma and healing from clinical to cultural, from individual to social, from disease diagnosis to shared experience. While there is much good work to be done to theologically address traumatized persons directly in the fields of bioethics, clinical preparedness, and clergy training (to name just a few arenas), here I remain focused on the broader ethical implications of widespread trauma and trauma discourse. Trauma, and all disabling experiences, must be understood as a universal aspect of human life, defined by socially constructed impediments as well as the physical and/or mental limitations in themselves. Trauma is, truly and frustratingly, always a "both/and."

Rather than seek a precise, rigid, single definition of trauma, I explore complex information to ask good questions that trouble our embedded assumptions about trauma and suffering. How does our theological ethics change when we confront trauma as part of our shared being, rather than as isolated cases of "bad luck"? How do we move from sole clinical focus on the victim/survivor to social responsibility for harm—or rather, how do we ask both of these questions in tandem? How can I understand my role in the multitude of traumatic experiences and see Christ amid the ruin?[6] Can an understanding of Christian memory help suggest what justice or healing might look like in our broken world? Does this impact our conceptions of "right" belief, feeling, and action?

---

[6] Robert A. Orsi explores similar questions in relation to the climate crisis in "Religion(s) in the Ruins of the Temples," in *Theology and Media(tion): Rendering the Absent Present*, ed. Stephen Okey and Katherine G. Schmidt, College Theology Society Annual 69 (Maryknoll, NY: Orbis Books, 2024), 227–243.

Global Mental Health and the PTSD Diagnosis

To begin to define trauma in its multiple forms, it is helpful to start with how it acts in bodies and impacts individual mental health. For context, the World Health Organization (WHO) considers neuropsychiatric conditions the most common, long-term health problem on earth. Yet even the WHO itself may be underestimating the issue, as some research finds that, although the WHO ranks the "disease burden"[7] of mental illness in the top six leading causes of ill health globally, with more precise measurement mental illness is in fact "a distant first in the global burden of disease."[8] Despite such staggering data, the gap between the need for treatment and its provision is cavernous. "In low- and middle-income countries, between 76% and 85% of people with mental disorders receive no treatment.... In high-income countries, between 35% and 50% of people with mental disorders are in the same situation."[9] Generally speaking, most people who

---

[7] Disease burden is a data analysis term used by global public health researchers to demonstrate the impact of health on an individual life. It is calculated using "years lived with disability" (YLDs) and disability-adjusted life-years (DALYs), where the DALYs also reflect mortality related to disease. As the WHO states, "Mental health is an integral and essential component of health. The WHO constitution states: 'Health is a state of complete physical, mental and social well-being and not merely the absence of disease or infirmity.' An important implication of this definition is that mental health is more than just the absence of mental disorders or disabilities. Mental health is a state of well-being in which an individual realizes his or her own abilities, can cope with the normal stresses of life, can work productively and is able to make a contribution to his or her community." World Health Organization, "Mental Health: Strengthening Our Response," March 30, 2018, http://www.who.int/mediacentre/factsheets/fs220/en/. This will be used as an orientating definition of health/healing for the purposes of this project, and is complicated by disability scholars in later chapters.

[8] D. Vigo, G. Thornicroft, and R. Atun, "Estimating the True Global Burden of Mental Illness," *The Lancet* 3, no. 2 (2016): 171–178.

[9] World Health Organization, "Mental Disorders," April 9, 2018, http://

suffer from any type of mental illness (roughly one in eight people globally) will likely never receive proper treatment, and many will never even be properly assessed.[10] This treatment gap widened during the COVID-19 pandemic, which, during just the first year, saw an estimated 25 percent rise in both anxiety and depressive disorders globally while service locations closed and providers left mental health professions in droves.[11]

The burden of mental illness (episodic or chronic) is exacerbated by individual contexts: your positionality—geography, economic status, race, gender, and so on—will directly impact your experience of illness and recovery. For example, those most vulnerable globally during the COVID-19 pandemic suffered more severe illness and died at higher rates than those with more privilege as defined in their local context. COVID-19 also acted as what epidemiologists call a "syndemic" or synergistic epidemic, where two or more sequential events act in aggregate to worsen multiple burdens of disease. In this case, COVID-19 itself combined with the psychological impacts of isolation, fear, and general upheaval at every social level, micro to macro. The combined harm is again heightened for persons with preexisting vulnerabilities.[12] While those with access increased

---

www.who.int/mediacentre/factsheets/fs396/en/. For a discussion of the nuances of "access" to health care, which is a complicating factor of mental health treatment, see Martin Gulliford, José Figueroa-Munoz, Myfanwy Morgan, David Hughes, Barry Gibson, Roger Beech, and Meryl Hudson, "What Does 'Access to Health Care' Mean?" *Journal of Health Services Research & Policy* 7, no. 3 (2002): 186–188.

[10] World Health Organization, "Mental Disorders," June 8, 2022, https://www.who.int/en/news-room/fact-sheets/detail/mental-disorders.

[11] World Health Organization, "World Mental Health Report: Transforming Mental Health for All," June 16, 2022, https://www.who.int/publications/i/item/9789240049338, xiv.

[12] "The COVID-19 pandemic can be recognized as a syndemic due to: synergistic interactions among different diseases and other health conditions, increasing overall illness burden, emergence, spread, and interactions between

usage of pharmaceuticals and medical interventions to deal with the psychological impacts of the pandemic, the WHO stressed the particularly social nature of the pandemic, resulting in what philosopher Matthew Bretton Oakes calls "ontological instability."[13] Very plainly, many of us do not know who we are anymore. The ways that many of us assumed the world "worked" were shaken or broken by the pandemic, not just individually but as social, national, and global beings.[14]

The important stress on the psychosocial nature of the pandemic emphasizes what many mental health practitioners, particularly those who identify as "trauma-informed," have long used as part of their assessments: the biopsychosocial model. This model highlights the fact that many illnesses, particularly mental illnesses, hold direct ties to one's environment as well as to one's biology. Viewing mental health in this way is essential to understand what mental health, as well as trauma, is and how it works, both in particular bodies and within our shared humanity.[15]

---

infectious zoonotic diseases leading to new infectious zoonotic diseases; this is together with social and health interactions leading to increased risks in vulnerable populations and exacerbating clustering of multiple diseases." See Kiran Saqib, Afaf Saqib Qureshi, and Zahid Ahmad Butt, "COVID-19, Mental Health, and Chronic Illnesses: A Syndemic Perspective," *International Journal of Environmental Research and Public Health* 20, no. 4 (2023): 3262.

[13] Matthew Bretton Oakes explores this in more detail: "Ontological Insecurity in the Post-COVID-19 Fallout: Using Existentialism as a Method to Develop a Psychosocial Understanding to a Mental Health Crisis," *Medicine, Health Care and Philosophy* 26 (April 24, 2023): 425–432.

[14] It is essential not to isolate a public crisis into only its individual forms; there is a unique "shared" nature to the trauma of the pandemic. Beijing-based neurologists Fei-Fei Ren and Rong-Juan Guo compare COVID-19 with the SARS outbreak to better understand the public nature of mental health in "Public Mental Health in Post-COVID-19 Era," *Psychiatria Danubina* 32, no. 2 (2020): 251–255.

[15] This is one of the genesis points for the field of public health, and figures such as Paul Farmer. Because of the world-shaking impacts of trauma, and other painful events, many social workers add "-spiritual" to the BPS assessment,

Within measures of all global mental health disorders, before and after the pandemic, a significant portion of illnesses are labeled as "trauma."[16] Trauma occurs when an event, a series of events, or a corrosive overall environment overwhelms one's capacities. Statistically, most of us will experience a traumatic event in our lifetimes; car accidents, complicated childbirth, tragic deaths, and violence name a mere few. However, only a relatively small number of individuals who experience trauma develop a disordered response.[17] The human brain and body are quite resilient, and an initial traumatic response is one of the ways our bodies cope with overwhelming suffering. In fact, the negative traits that define PTSD—initial fight, flight, freeze, and fawn, followed by a variety of distresses—constitute a completely *normal* reaction to an abnormal experience. A disease occurs when those reactions persist over time and develop into maladaptive traits. Once developed, such traits are extremely difficult to eliminate and, often, become chronic.

---

as understanding a patient's metaphysical claims as well as their negative and positive experiences of religious/spiritual life has shown direct correlations to healing in situations where "meaning" has been impacted.

[16] A 2017 global study, still the top-cited statistic in 2023, showed that "The cross-national lifetime prevalence of Post-Traumatic Stress Disorder (PTSD) was 3.9% in the total sample [71,083] and 5.6% among the trauma exposed." See K. C. Koenen, A. Ratanatharathorn, et al., "Posttraumatic Stress Disorder in the World Mental Health Surveys," *Psychological Medicine* 47, no. 13 (October 2017): 2260–2274.

[17] "Unbiased estimates suggesting a conditional risk of 9% following trauma." J. W. B. Elsey and M. Kindt, "Breaking Boundaries: Optimizing Reconsolidation-Based Interventions for Strong and Old Memories," *Learning & Memory* 24 (2017): 473. However, further case studies are showing an increase in diagnosable symptoms, such as the finding that one-fifth of a study group of cancer patients were living with PTSD (with the inciting incident being their diagnosis). See Wiley, "Many Cancer Survivors Are Living with PTSD," *ScienceDaily,* November 20, 2017, www.sciencedaily.com/releases/2017/11/171120085442.htm.

Here I use PTSD to help sharpen our exploration of trauma and memory and to give us an example of how those concepts "work" in a person's body. PTSD is the clinically accepted indicator of the most common severe mental illness related to the traumatic event(s) that occur within the lifespan of most people. PTSD can result from a variety of experiences, including direct involvement in a traumatic event, being a witness to a trauma, learning of the trauma of a close family member or friend, or firsthand repetitive and intense exposure to details of trauma (e.g., military drone operation bases in Nevada where troops never witness in-person violence but participate in it through technology).[18] Four main clusters of experience define PTSD: reexperiencing (often called "flashbacks"); avoidance (of distressing memories or reminders of the event); negative cognitions and mood (such as a persistent sense of blame, estrangement, or disinterest, all commonly associated with the "flight" response); and arousal (aggression, recklessness, or hypervigilance, associated with the fight response).[19] Trauma also acts across the lifespan, with impacts

---

[18] Sarah McCammon, "The Warfare May Be Remote but the Trauma Is Real," National Public Radio, April 24, 2017, https://www.npr.org/2017/04/24/525413427/for-drone-pilots-warfare-may-be-remote-but-the-trauma-is-real. It is as-yet unstudied, but the real-time nature of video platforms such as TikTok offering near-immediate, unfiltered exposure to war, terrorism, and death (seen recently in Ukraine and Gaza) may also have wider implications for how we engage with trauma.

[19] In the most recent, fifth edition of the American Psychiatric Association's diagnostic manual, commonly referred to as the *DSM-V*, the PTSD diagnosis was greatly expanded. Yet it is important to note that the development of these parameters was not without conflict; for a brief survey of the development of PTSD as a diagnosis in the 1980s, see N. C. Andreason, "Editorial: Acute and Delayed Posttraumatic Stress Disorders: A History and Some Issues," *American Journal of Psychiatry* 161, no. 8 (2004): 1321–1323; this is discussed later in the chapter. For the current diagnostic parameters, updated in 2022, see American Psychiatric Association, *Diagnostic Manual 5 Revised (DSM-5-TR)* (Washington, DC: American Psychiatric Association, 2022).

that are cumulative (where any future traumas show increase in impact/force), additive (where a combination of trauma with other life occurrences changes the shape/experience), and summative (shown to have "sticky" outcomes across years).

Yet for a constellation of reasons, not all, or even most, individuals who suffer from PTSD receive a clinical diagnosis.[20] Many will live, diagnosed or not, with the chronic nature of PTSD for most or all of their lives. Some will experience only episodic suffering, whereas others cannot access necessary long-term care to ever break out of its cycles, often resulting in further loss of quality of life, including lack of employment, substance abuse, housing instability, or all three.[21]

A further implication of the chronic nature of PTSD is how it potentially impacts the person's offspring. This emerging aspect of biological trauma research and of the PTSD diagnosis is explored in the field of epigenetics. Epigenetics is the study of potentially heritable changes in gene expression—active versus

---

[20] The US Department of Veterans Affairs estimates that anywhere from 6 to 8 percent of people will have PTSD at some point in their life. About five of every one hundred adults (5 percent) in the United States had PTSD in 2020, with women twice as likely to develop PTSD than men, mostly due to the type of trauma (women are more likely to experience sexual harm, which is correlated to higher rates of PTSD). USVA, "How Common Is PTSD in Adults?," National Center for PTSD, December 6, 2023, https://www.ptsd.va.gov/understand/common/common_adults.asp.

[21] Julie Williams, "'I Have No One': Understanding Homelessness and Trauma," *Psychiatric Times,* September 1, 2022, https://www.psychiatrictimes.com/view/i-have-no-one-understanding-homelessness-and-trauma. A related aspect of trauma is the media inundation of traumatic stories, from everyone from combat veterans to football players, where traumatic life events are now often accepted as functional, or even expected. This occurs especially in cases where trauma is linked to weakness or blame that is then associated with shame, such as trauma suffered by veterans or sexual assault survivors; or in the case of athletes, that they more or less signed up for such physical abuse. This is dealt with in the field of moral injury. As it is a distinct subfield of ethics and trauma studies, I gesture to it in this project, but it is not my central focus.

inactive genes—that do not involve changes to the underlying DNA sequence: a change in phenotype without a change in genotype. Epigenetic changes affect how cells read our genes, and these changes can impact the expression of human appearance and behavior. Such changes come about in our lives through our environment and, most notably, through events that have large impacts, such as a severe lack of nutrition or the stress of living in a war zone. Epigenetic fluctuations can be thought of as a change in our "software" versus our "hardware": the software (epigenetic) change exists in us and is heritable, but it is also highly malleable and subject to variation across one's lifetime. While research in this vein is in its early stages, epigenetics is yet another data point in our understanding of the shared nature of trauma, even in its strictest biological form.[22]

With emerging scientific research, however, it is imperative not to leap too quickly to deterministic conclusions. A deterministic reading of epigenetic research comes very close to the fallacy that phenotypic changes give rise to genotypic modifications; for example, a blacksmith's children do not necessarily inherit strong forearms, and a person with a severely traumatized parent does not necessarily develop PTSD. To date, no consistently proven direct causal link between parental trauma—an environmental factor that changes their gene behavior and is potentially inheritable—and

---

[22] See R. Yehuda, N.P. Daskalakis, et al., "Influences of Maternal and Paternal PTSD on Epigenetic Regulation of the Glucocorticoid Receptor Gene in Holocaust Survivor Offspring," *American Journal of Psychiatry* 171, no. 8 (2014): 872–880; and Jana Švorcová, "Transgenerational Epigenetic Inheritance of Traumatic Experience in Mammals," *Genes* 14, no. 1 (2023): 120. There is also ongoing, and very promising, research identifying the exact genes involved in PTSD, and therefore, as the researchers conclude, these genes can be recommended as targets for gene therapy/intervention. See Ghazi I. Al Jowf et al., "The Molecular Biology of Susceptibility to Post-traumatic Stress Disorder: Highlights of Epigenetics and Epigenomics," *International Journal of Molecular Sciences* 22 (2021): 10743.

a child's predisposition to the development of PTSD in the wake of trauma has been established. What we do know is that the individual who suffered trauma *did change epigenetically* and that there is a strong likelihood that *something* related to a parent's trauma is inherited, with the current research goal being to disentangle positive, adaptive changes from negative, maladaptive ones.[23]

Rachel Yehuda, one of the leading researchers in epigenetics, observes, "People say, when something cataclysmic happens to them, 'I'm not the same person. I've been changed. I am not the same person that I was.' ... Epigenetics gives us the language and the science to be able to start unpacking that."[24] It is crucial to lift up this emerging biological reality when considering how theology might engage with trauma. How families, groups, and entire communities experience and interpret trauma is important, and yet it may not be the full picture. Our behaviors may be impacted by, and family members potentially physically linked through, biological trauma. Trauma, then, in this first definition, is a biological, material reality, with distinct, embodied impacts as an experience, a disability, a diagnosis, and even an inheritance.

Culture and the Hermeneutics of Trauma

Another component of trauma's definition is constructivist, where the meaning of a term is co-created by the people learning about it. While clinical studies and statistics are powerful and all too real, the experience of trauma and its related disorders exceed

---

[23] A. S. Zannas, N. Provençal, and E. B. Binder, "Epigenetics of Posttraumatic Stress Disorder: Current Evidence, Challenges and Future Directions," *Biological Psychiatry* 78 (2015): 327–335. See also Meenu Ghai and Farzeen Kader, "A Review on Epigenetic Inheritance of Experiences in Humans," *Biochemical Genetics* 60 (2022): 1107–1140.

[24] Krista Tippett, "Rachel Yehuda: How Trauma and Resilience Cross Generations," *On Being*, NPR, July 30, 2015, https://onbeing.org/programs/rachel-yehuda-how-trauma-and-resilience-cross-generations/.

their confines. Trauma is a communal phenomenon that, while linked to interpersonal violence, is intimately tied to shared experiences such as war, disaster ("natural"[25] or man-made), and social unrest. In this public sense, "trauma" has become a buzzword of academics and pop culturistas alike. It saturates common conversation via debates on topics as wide-ranging as "trigger warnings," campus sexual assault, and generational social issues such as racism and income inequality.[26] However, few of these uses of "trauma" take seriously the history of the term's development and use (both clinically and culturally), its diagnostic content (as discussed earlier), or trauma's psychobiological functions (both individual and communal). It is necessary to address these complex factors in tandem with the strict medical understanding of trauma to move toward a grounded theological ethic.

In this section, therefore, I explore three components of the concept and culture of trauma, followed by a brief introduction to the current theological conversation about trauma. I conclude by addressing a few of the major critiques of the interdisciplinary field of trauma studies. While each of these topics could be (and in some cases

---

[25] I have previously written at length about the "unnatural" results of "natural" disasters such as Hurricane Katrina (2005) and the Haiti earthquake (2011), in work funded partially by the Boston University Pardee Center for the Study of the Longer-Range Future. While the cause of suffering may be natural (although with human-caused climate change even that is in question), the impacts of disasters are disproportionately shouldered by the poor and vulnerable, including psychological ramifications.

[26] "When a person lives in poverty, a growing body of research suggests the limbic system is constantly sending fear and stress messages to the prefrontal cortex, which overloads its ability to solve problems, set goals, and complete tasks in the most efficient ways.... They are constantly struggling to make ends meet and often bracing themselves against class bias that adds extra strain or even trauma to their daily lives." Tara García Mathewson, "How Poverty Changes the Brain," *The Atlantic,* April 19, 2017, https://www.theatlantic.com/education/archive/2017/04/can-brain-science-pull-families-out-of-poverty/523479/?utm_source=twb.

already are) books in and of themselves, it is crucial to review these topics to locate ourselves in relation to previous work and understand the multivalent functions of trauma in our corporate body.

Trauma beyond Individual Clinical Diagnosis

"Trauma" is the Greek word for "wound," more precisely, physical wounds. While it has retained this use in medical practice, it has also become a catchall term in colloquial usage, most likely referring to psychological impacts of difficult events. Popularized by Sigmund Freud in the late nineteenth and early twentieth centuries,[27] trauma is now broadly understood within American culture to be the destructive result of painful experiences such as surviving disasters, serving in a war zone, rape, near-death experience, adverse childhood experiences, witnessing a violent act, or living within an ongoing corrosive environment.

While the individuated clinical symptoms are largely agreed upon as outlined above, the rapid growth of the diagnosis has

---

[27] This project does not linger in Freudian psychoanalysis, where the study of Freud's concepts of memory, repression, and trauma are still pervasive. The most useful and illustrative of Freud's work to understand the roots of the modern trauma diagnosis is found in *Beyond the Pleasure Principle* (1920; New York: W. W. Norton & Company, 1990). For a wider view of the modern inheritance of Freud on the field of trauma, see Bessel A. van der Kolk, "The History of Trauma in Psychiatry," in *Handbook of PTSD*, First Edition: *Science and Practice*, ed. Matthew J. Freidman, Terence M. Keane, and Patricia A. Resick (New York: Guilford Press, 2007), 19–36. For a concise history of clinical trauma, see chapter 1 in Judith Herman, *Trauma and Recovery: The Aftermath of Political Violence—from Domestic Abuse to Political Terror* (New York: Basic Books, 1992); and Paul Verhaeghe, "Trauma and Hysteria within Freud and Lacan," *The Letter (Dublin)* 14 (1998): 87–106. The construction of mental health and wellness is also rooted in the Western embrace of "reason," wherein equilibrium and balance are prized and any disruption is to be eliminated. For a classic discussion of the social construction of mental illness and "madness," see Michel Foucault, *Madness and Civilization: A History of Insanity in the Age of Reason* (New York: Mentor, 1967).

caused concern. *The Body Keeps the Score* by Bessel van der Kolk, trauma specialist and founder of the Trauma Center at the Justice Resource Institute in Brookline, Massachusetts, spent 141 weeks on the *New York Times* best-seller list, and as of October 2023 had spent three years on Amazon's best-seller list.[28] Van der Kolk suggests that mainline psychology often seeks to numb the patient—out of an honest effort to treat debilitating symptoms—and focus on available cognitive processing. Psychology in this mode overlooks the power of and need for more affective, embodied treatments such as yoga, dance, or simple movement therapy to target the often unspoken/unspeakable ramifications of trauma stored in the body. While van der Kolk is a licensed psychiatrist, this turn toward self-help marketing of trauma treatment, paired with lack of access to mental health care in the United States, has led to a wave of "self-diagnosis" and cultural overidentification with trauma as disease.

But what are people saying when they identify as "traumatized"? Cultural variation in beliefs around mental health and related treatments are deeply and particularly embedded, even if some in the Western psychiatric world treat diseases as if they are inalienable, universal concepts. While PTSD may be used as a marker by, for example, an aid agency in a war zone, the disaster and its effects must be understood through the views of those harmed, without presupposing a diagnosis that can alter, mask, or repress the actual experience. In Sri Lanka, victims of the 2004 tsunami reported understanding disaster impacts as operating outside of their minds, in the social realm. Any personal

---

[28] Bessel van der Kolk, *The Body Keeps the Score: Brain, Mind, and Body in the Healing of Trauma* (New York: Viking, 2014). See also Babette Rothschild, *The Body Remembers: The Psychophysiology of Trauma and Trauma Treatment* (New York: W. W. Norton & Company, 2000). In 2018 van der Kolk was fired from the Trauma Center after allegations of conducting a hostile workplace, and the center eventually closed. Liz Kowalczyk, "Allegations of Employee Mistreatment Roil Renowned Brookline Trauma Center," *Boston Globe,* April 7, 2018.

"symptom" was not within themselves, but a direct result of communal life. Therefore, the "solution" to their symptoms was not to be found within their minds, but in altering/restoring the social life of the group. Ignoring this culturally specific understanding of trauma and its healing, outsiders diagnosed the victims with a condition that did not resonate with their interpretation. Broadly, Sri Lankans did not wish to be treated by psychologists, but rather to have their relational, physical spaces restored. By recognizing trauma only within limited parameters, outsiders simply reinforced the dominant Western medical worldview at the cost of the self-determining humanity of those suffering.[29]

Frankly, we often don't know what people are talking about when they talk about trauma, as the limited exploration of practices of healing memory used by groups and societies as well as individuals in the wake of great suffering is subsumed under the overwhelming focus on framing trauma through "psychiatric nosology."[30] Even if a person uses trauma language to describe their experiences, it is likely that their definition is unique and not easily generalized. There is also evidence that the professional "appraisal" of a symptom—such as intrusions of memory after trauma—affects the frequency of reported symptoms. For example, subjects who were told that intrusions indicate negative psychological functioning reported higher rates of intrusions as opposed to those who were told nothing or told that intrusions had no particular

---

[29] Eric Watters, "Opinion, the Big Idea: Invasion of the Mind-Snatchers," *New Scientist* 205, no. 2744 (2010): 26–27.

[30] Nosology is a classification system in medicine for defining diseases. Penny Summerfield, *Reconstructing Women's Wartime Lives: Discourse and Subjectivity in Oral Histories of the Second World War* (UK: Manchester University Press, 1998) as cited by Ruth Kevers, Peter Rober, Ilse Derluyn, and Lucia De Haene, "Remembering Collective Violence: Broadening the Notion of Traumatic Memory in Post-conflict Rehabilitation," *Culture Medicine, and Psychiatry* 40, no. 4 (2016): 620–640.

significance.[31] This "helping" can easily become its own end, emphasizing the importance or necessity of a particular medical framing and intervention. The therapist defines what constitutes problems as well as solutions, rather than the presenting person: the tail wagging the dog.[32] There is no one-size-fits-all approach to trauma treatment, and "therapists who claim that treatment of trauma victims is easily accomplished with standard protocols run the danger of minimizing the profound personal, social, and biological disruption caused by trauma."[33]

Further, and particularly salient in large-scale traumas like the pandemic, therapists themselves are caught up in the harmful environment with the patient. Demonstrated in one way by the ongoing workforce loss within the "helping professions" post-pandemic, mental health professionals are subject to high rates of compassion fatigue even in healthy societal contexts. Compassion fatigue is "a state experienced by those helping people or animals in distress; it is an extreme state of tension and preoccupation with the suffering of those being helped to the degree that it can create secondary traumatic stress for the helper."[34] Compassion

---

[31] Jessica Cheung and Richard A. Bryant, "The Impact of Appraisals on Intrusive Memories," *Journal of Behavioral Therapy and Experimental Psychiatry* 54 (2017): 108–111.

[32] Jo Ann Allen "The Constructivist Paradigm: Values and Ethics," *Journal of Teaching in Social Work* 8, no. 1-2 (1994): 31–54. as cited by Hussein H. Soliman and Mary E. Rogge, "Ethical Considerations in Disaster Services: A Social Work Perspective," *Electronic Journal of Social Work* 1, no. 1 (2002): 9.

[33] A. C. McFarlane and Bessel A. van der Kolk, "Trauma and Its Challenge to Society," in *Traumatic Stress: The Effects of Overwhelming Experience on Mind, Body, and Society*, edited by Bessel A. van der Kolk, Alexander C. McFarlane, and Lars Weisaeth (New York: Guilford Press, 2006), 44.

[34] Compassion Fatigue Awareness Project, "What Is Compassion Fatigue?," 2017, http://www.compassionfatigue.org/pages/compassionfatigue.html. See also Charles R. Figley, *Compassion Fatigue: Coping with Secondary Traumatic Stress Disorder in Those Who Treat the Traumatized* (London: Brunner-Routledge, 1995).

fatigue can lead to apathy/detachment or substance abuse, and the caregiver can even develop similar symptoms to their patients. K. S. Coddington applied this observation to her study of Aboriginal community organizing in Australia, noting that trauma is not so much "vicarious" in nature, but rather "contagious":

> Advocates experience contagious trauma as the effects of witnessing trauma combin[ing] toxically with their own life traumas. Contagious trauma expands the destructive effects of traumatic public policy [in her case study Aboriginal policies that mirror the treatment of Native Americans by European colonists], and simultaneously shrinks the capacity of advocacy that contests these policies. Capacity shrinks as advocates construct barriers to keep trauma at bay.[35]

Not only does the contagious trauma harm the caregiver and their helping capacities, it also potentially limits any ability to advocate for broader systemic change and social justice on behalf of the community. The psychological repercussions of trauma build beyond the initial event, becoming a chronic disaster within the community as all its members struggle with long-term recovery. The event becomes a condition.[36]

---

[35] K. S. Coddington, "Contagious Trauma: Reframing the Spatial Mobility of Trauma within Advocacy Work," *Emotion, Space and Society* 24 (2017): 66.

[36] K. T. Erikson, *Everything in Its Path: Destruction of Community in the Buffalo Creek Flood* (New York: Simon & Schuster, 1976), 230. This brief assessment of developments within the trauma diagnosis is not meant to indicate that all of psychology functions in one way, monolithically, and that the field is not already deeply involved in this discussion. Rather, an entire subset of psychology and psychiatry attempts to tackle these interconnected and complex issues, including feminist psychology (see M. B. Lykes and G. Moane, "Editor's Introduction: Whither Feminist Liberation Psychology? Critical Explorations of Feminist and Liberation Psychologies for a Globalizing World," *Feminism Psychology* 19, no. 3 [2009]: 283–297); liberation psychology (Ignacio Martín-Baró, *Writings for a Liberation Psychology*, ed. Adrianne Aron

I raise the nuances of trauma's popularity, "objectivity," and enmeshment here to problematize from the start any ease with which the concept "trauma" is applied, particularly in interdisciplinary research. While the medical/psychological diagnosis is still being refined and treatments advanced, both the definition of trauma and its healing exist within social and political contexts that determine trauma's shape, emphases, interpretation, and attempts at healing. These brief observations demonstrate how the Western psychological model initially presented often focuses on certain aspects of individual treatment rather than a wider, more comprehensive assessment of the traumatic experience and its attendant ongoing social challenges. If we are to take trauma seriously, then we must also take seriously the remaining ambiguity in its definition and our understanding of its use, including and beyond the individual.

Emergence of the Hermeneutics of Trauma

Some of these wider ripples of trauma discourse became immediately apparent to early researchers, namely Judith Herman in her now-seminal 1992 work, *Trauma and Recovery: The Aftermath of Violence from Domestic Abuse to Political Terror*. Herman, a clinical psychiatrist holding an MD degree, defines trauma through a distinctly feminist lens, where the personal is also understood as political. Therefore, any trauma is rooted in larger social patterns, and its healing is only achieved through the inclusion of public

---

and Shawn Corne [Cambridge, MA: Harvard University Press, 1996]); and critical psychology (T. Teo, "Critical Psychology: A Geography of Intellectual Engagement and Resistance," *American Psychologist* 70, no. 3 [April 2015]: 243–54), among others. It is with these dialogue partners, who are pushing the boundaries of "Western" psychotherapy, that this project finds resonance. The discussion in this section is meant to thicken our understanding of the PTSD diagnosis and treatment, always including the particularity of the individual experience, but also necessarily situated beyond an individual experience, defined and shaped by the sociocultural realm.

truth-telling. She argues that "denial, repression, and dissociation operate on a social as well as an individual level," and that the narrative of secrecy and silence around inflicted harms must be broken for any sort of healing to occur.[37] The cycle of secrecy is visible, yet difficult to counter: "After every atrocity one can expect to hear the same predictable apologies: it never happened; the victim lies; the victim exaggerates; the victim brought it upon herself; and in any case it is time to forget the past and move on."[38] Those who inflict violence are often propped up by warped social standards (e.g., judgments on the lives and habits of Black men and boys killed by police) and powerful social norms (e.g., racism, misogyny, inequality, etc.). Herman insists that the role of the therapist is not only to attempt to support victims in their healing spaces but to also become activists on their behalf. In fact, this social recognition can complete the integration of severe harm into a victim's life. Bystanders—the category of "the rest of us" for Herman, which includes therapists—must stand publicly with the expressed truth of the victim: "moral neutrality in the conflict between victim and perpetrator is not an option ... [and] those who stand with the victim will inevitably have to face the perpetrator's unmasked fury."[39] This allyship will cost and potentially be painful, but such is the mandate for all in response to trauma.

Herman's book sparked a renaissance in trauma studies in clinical research and within interdisciplinary application and cultural parlance. In expanding the definition of trauma beyond its individual clinical diagnosis, she uncovered a broader cultural understanding of the perpetuation of trauma and why certain populations are at greater risk of experiencing harm. She applied the observations of psychologists regarding patterns of harmful repetition from intrasubjective experience and mapped them

---

[37] Judith Herman, *Trauma and Recovery: The Aftermath of Violence from Domestic Abuse to Political Terror* (New York: Basic Books: 1997), 2 and 8.

[38] Herman, *Trauma and Recovery*, 8.

[39] Herman, *Trauma and Recovery*, 247 (afterword in 2007 edition).

onto larger societal trends. In so doing, Herman created a new framework to understand repetitions of suffering where trauma is based on the behavior of individual, interpersonal perpetrators, *as well as* on the characteristics of whole groups and societies, and even the entire modern world.

Also in 1992, literary scholar Shoshana Felman and clinical psychologist Dori Laub published *Testimony: Crises of Witnessing in Literature, Psychoanalysis and History*.[40] Focused on the communication and reception of traumatic stories, specifically from the Yale Holocaust Archives, Felman and Laub explore how memory is transmitted through speech and art, including literature, and how trauma is relayed. Despite multiple and abundant communication methods posttrauma, particularly in the case of the Shoah, they argue that the reality of trauma remains incommunicable.[41] Their work shares many themes with Herman's, including an attempt to parse the cycles of silence and repression posttrauma that exist for individuals as well as entire societies.

Picking up on the conversation of witness and testimony to trauma, literary scholar Cathy Caruth published *Unclaimed Experience: Trauma, Narrative, and History* in 1996.[42] Since this

---

[40] Shoshana Felman and Dori Laub, *Testimony: Crises of Witnessing in Literature, Psychoanalysis, and History* (New York: Taylor & Francis, 1992).

[41] This echoes the work of Elaine Scarry, *The Body in Pain: The Making and Unmaking of the World* (New York: Oxford University Press, 1985). I tend to use the Hebrew word "Shoah," as it is terminology preferred by Jewish trauma scholars; although "Holocaust" is the more common term, it also holds the historical/religious meaning of "burnt offering" on an altar. Metz also hated the word "Holocaust," as it flattened out the particular experiences of the Shoah into supposedly comparable events, such as the concerns of "nuclear holocaust." See J. B. Metz, "Communicating a Dangerous Memory," in *Communicating a Dangerous Memory: Soundings in Political Theology*, ed. Fred Lawrence (Atlanta: Scholars Press, 1987), 43.

[42] Cathy Caruth, *Unclaimed Experience: Trauma, Narrative, and History* (Baltimore, MD: Johns Hopkins University Press, 1996). See also Caruth, ed., *Trauma: Explorations in Memory* (Baltimore, MD: Johns Hopkins University Press, 1995); Caruth, *Literature in the Ashes of History* (Baltimore: Johns

work, Caruth has continued to publish on the topic and has become one of the most referenced thinkers in interdisciplinary trauma studies, chiefly because of her contribution to the field of trauma as a "way of reading." Caruth's work is rooted in the Freudian and psychological assessment that the full extent of trauma is so overwhelming that it is in some ways "missed," but also repeated, by the implicated individual as well as any witnesses. Here, she echoes the 1985 work of Elaine Scarry, who attests that pain is unspeakable, an "invisible geography" that

> for the person whose pain it is, it is "effortlessly" grasped (that is, even with the most heroic effort it cannot *not* be grasped); while for the person outside the sufferer's body, what is "effortless" is *not* grasping it (it is easy to remain wholly unaware of its existence; even with effort, one may remain in doubt about its existence or may retain the astonishing freedom of denying its existence; and finally, if with the best effort of sustained attention one successfully apprehends it, the aversiveness of the "it" one apprehends will only be a shadowy fraction of the actual "it").[43]

Caruth argues that this "missing" should be attended to and identified within texts and testimonies of trauma. She even goes a step further than Scarry, who is focused primarily on physical pain.

Hopkins University Press, 2013); Caruth, *Listening to Trauma: Conversations with Leaders in the Theory and Treatment of Catastrophic Experience* (Baltimore, MD: Johns Hopkins University Press, 2014). However, it is important to note that Caruth is not an uncontroversial figure. Her reading of trauma has been questioned by many in the practical professions and notably by philosopher Susan Brison in her own philosophical work dealing with her near-death rape and assault: *Aftermath: Violence and the Remaking of a Self* (Princeton, NJ: Princeton University Press, 2002). However, as Caruth is arguably the "founder" of modern trauma studies, it is important to attend to the impact her work has had on shaping the field.

[43] Scarry, *The Body in Pain*, 4.

She asserts that the distinct inaccessibility of the "event" of psychic trauma, even to the individual who experienced it, as well as the fundamental incommunicability of the traumatic story, contribute to the community's inability to receive and understand it.

Caruth's works of postmodern literary criticism indicate again and again that the "gap" of the unknown is such that an objective "truth" of a traumatic experience is not possible.[44] It thus becomes clear that perhaps *truth* is not what will be asserted in the communication of trauma, but rather a fundamental *departure* into the creation of a new story. The complexity of departure as Caruth presents it—and indeed the central premise of a "gap" within communication—continues to inspire the rethinking of history itself within trauma studies as not strictly referential.[45] Thus, rather than sit neatly within preexisting categories, Caruth insists on a fundamental challenge to the mores of traditional philosophy and theology in response to the harm of trauma.

From such an understanding of history, Caruth also offers an explicit challenge to ethics. For "the shock of traumatic sight reveals at the heart of human subjectivity not so much an epistemological, but rather ... an *ethical* relation to the real."[46] Here, Caruth points toward the potential healing of history beyond individual experiences of trauma—beyond those localized in population, geography, time, and so forth. She argues that a method or pedagogy defined by trauma must explore new ways of holding history and rereading the political. She goes so far as to propose that we in fact make history by erasing it.[47] Such erasure is

---

[44] "Truth is not referential for Caruth and therefore not 'true knowledge' in the philosophical sense" (Shelly Rambo, email message to author, November 18, 2015).

[45] Caruth, *Unclaimed Experience*, 11.

[46] Caruth, *Unclaimed Experience*, 92.

[47] Caruth, *Literature in the Ashes*, 79. See also D. LaCapra, *Writing History, Writing Trauma* (Baltimore, MD: Johns Hopkins University Press, 2001); M.

posited on the departure—the listener/witness is one who merely glimpses the real and, in response, opens up new avenues for how to tell the story.[48] It is, then, "a matter not only of what we see and know but also of what is ethical to tell."[49] Such a movement is complex, questioning *what* we can put into words within the recognition of the Derridian "ever-submerging shore," as well as *how* such trauma is told and retold.[50] As such, "stories of trauma cannot be limited to the catastrophes they name, and the theory of catastrophic history may ultimately be written in a language that already lingers, in these texts, after the end, in a time that comes to us from the other shore, from the other side of the disaster."[51]

Rothberg, *Multi-Directional Memory: Remembering the Holocaust in the Age of Decolonization* (Stanford, CA: Stanford University Press, 2009).

[48] Caruth, *Unclaimed Experience*, 112. Or, for Dirk G. Lange, the "force of the return": *Trauma Recalled: Liturgy, Disruption, and Theology* (Minneapolis: Fortress Press, 2010), 98.

[49] Caruth, *Unclaimed Experience*, 26. A question Caruth asks of the work she is examining, the 1959 film *Hiroshima mon amour*.

[50] Distinctly positioned in a postmodern milieu, she is uncovering through a trauma lens what Jacques Derrida called the "regular *submerging* of the shore," meaning that one attempts to glimpse the truth of the other as it slips beyond our sight, again and again, in reference to an encounter with written works, as well as with other people. Jacques Derrida, "Living on Border Lines," in *Deconstruction and Criticism,* trans. James Hulbert (London: Routledge, 1979), 81. The site of this submersion is where, for Caruth, we must train our eyes—to recognize that such hiddenness can in fact reveal the *real*. Here the absence urges the *departure* into new words, metaphors, and stories to assert the experience of the self. Uniquely, in trauma it is also this hidden site that repeats itself unwittingly, a continual return as well as departure (as in the Freudian *fort/da* of the child [*Beyond the Pleasure Principle,* 11]). Thus the submersion, or gap, at once reveals the unknown self and/or the event, as well as demanding concrete attention despite its absence of solid "fact" or essence. In the tradition of Derrida, Gadamer, and Lacan (among others), Caruth uses this seeming paradox to point toward the necessity of relationship or encounter for self-definition. For Caruth, there is a latent component within history that (via trauma) binds together in a common story the world and the selves within it. *Unclaimed Experience,* 18.

[51] Caruth, *Literature in the Ashes*, 92.

While Caruth's ethical construction depends largely on the unintelligibility of trauma, it simultaneously offers some hope from the other shore, namely the hope of ethical relationality, the willingness and ability to hold "discourse at the site of catastrophe."[52] Her concept of departure asks the witness to turn away from the event and toward the "other" (as concept and as a self). The "other" may be a concrete individual with whom one can form a relationship, or a concept, as in the suffering we witness through the lens of media or history. In this way, witnesses "listen to departure" to give primacy to the *person* speaking through their trauma, rather than seeking a factual re-accounting of traumatic events. Such a factual re-accounting, while important for other tasks of justice in the wake of trauma, is peripheral to Caruth's concerns. Although much of Caruth's work is deeply theoretical, she concludes with a call toward practical ethics, wherein the burden of work is given to those of us who witness trauma, either directly or indirectly. She argues that the distinct role of witnesses is to continue to listen, empower, and build new futures (as well as histories) with the most deeply wounded persons in our world. The vision of trauma, history, and ethics from Herman, Felman and Laub, and Caruth ignited a new way of understanding human suffering, applying trauma and trauma language to larger cultural modes that far exceed individual clinical cases.

Theology and Trauma

In the late 2000s, the field of Christian theology saw a burst of publications explicitly dealing with the field of trauma studies, both developing theological reflections on trauma itself and theological engagement with trauma studies produced by social scientists and literary scholars. Notably, theologians Shelly Rambo, Jennifer Beste, Dirk G. Lange, and Serene Jones, among others,

---

[52] Caruth, *Unclaimed Experience*, 34.

all published books explicitly addressing trauma.[53] While each is oriented toward different topics—Holy Saturday for Rambo, survivors of childhood sexual assault for Beste, Lutheran liturgy for Lange, and pastoral theology for Jones—these authors took seriously the challenge of trauma studies and the new answers it demanded of Christian theology. Standing in the tradition of works of theodicy, these theologians sought ways forward that could authentically address the call to public witness and communal healing from trauma studies, as well as the clear cases from clinical research that unfortunately proved that complete healing may indeed never come. Writ large, these authors sought literal and theoretical spaces within Christian theology to hold the uncertainty of trauma experience and trauma healing.

All resist, in their own ways, what Rambo terms the "rush to redemption" that too often befalls Christian practices and community building: a hurry toward the promise of resurrection while ignoring the totality of the Holy Week story. Rambo critiques modern American Christian communities, namely in her Protestant context, as unable to reflect the true depth of trauma and doubt that was experienced by those who witnessed the events of Christ's crucifixion, preferring to rush toward the promised resurrection of Easter. By too quickly becoming an "Easter people," she argues, Christianity loses the unique, liminal space that can

---

[53] Shelly Rambo, *Spirit and Trauma: A Theology of Remaining* (Louisville, KY: Westminster John Knox Press, 2010); Jennifer Beste, *God and the Victim: Traumatic Intrusions on Grace and Freedom* (Oxford: Oxford University Press, 2007); Dirk G. Lange, *Trauma Recalled: Liturgy, Disruption, and Theology* (Minneapolis: Fortress Press, 2010); Serene Jones, *Trauma and Grace: Theology in a Ruptured World* (Louisville, KY: Westminster John Knox Press, 2009). This brief summary is by no means comprehensive, but should at least establish that this project is part of a robust discussion within theology. It is also essential to note the contributions of these authors on the formation of my thinking on trauma and theology, before turning toward the specific focus of this project. It should also be noted that Rambo and Lange studied directly with Caruth, and her interpretation of trauma studies is evident in their work.

honor experiences of trauma. Instead, she encourages a theological and practical approach focused on the much more difficult work of Holy Saturday, of embodying a community of faith in the aftermath of great loss.[54] In this way, Christian communities do not move "to" a prescribed goal but move "through" pain together.

Lange argues that Christian liturgy has the unique ability to hold the "unknowing" asserted by trauma studies. He outlines how our liturgy is built to interrupt the remembering of the Christ event as the violence of the cross, centering instead the eucharistic bread and wine. Liturgy, for Lange, is "the disorientation and reorientation of a radical commensality" that, when illuminated through trauma theory, enables us "to understand ritual not as passing on violence [the crucifixion] but as pointing toward, as repeating, something inaccessible, something that breaks the cycle of violence [the Christ event]."[55]

Serene Jones identifies this "something" as grace. In her work, she holds together the "excruciatingly particular" forms of trauma with the experience of grace itself as "always vibrantly particular in its shape."[56] She reads trauma theory within the Christian tradition, using Herman's three steps to trauma recovery with Calvin's work on the Psalms, and the silence and fractured speech of trauma theory with the original ending of the Gospel of Mark. She concludes that "perhaps habits of heart and imagination, rather than grand doctrinal stories, must carry the weight of our hopes for healing."[57] Centering these daily or weekly practices, both Lange and Jones are writing practical theology, carving pathways for pastors and ministers to follow to better serve their congregations.

---

[54] Rambo, *Spirit and Trauma*, 35.
[55] Lange, *Trauma Recalled*, 10. See also David Farina Turnbloom, Megan Breen, Noah Lamberger and Kate Seddon, "Liturgy in the Shadow of Trauma," *Religions* 13 (2022): 583.
[56] Jones, *Trauma and Grace*, ix.
[57] Jones, *Trauma and Grace*, xiv.

Finally, and important for its resonances with this project, Beste focuses on Christian theology in conversation with survivors of childhood sexual abuse, particularly incest. Using German Jesuit Karl Rahner's "fundamental option" as the foundation of the Christian person's salvation as well as ethical life, Beste uncovers how one's capacities may be deeply harmed by such abuse, but how potential for healing and moral growth remain.[58] She concludes that, while trauma problematizes a simplistic reading of Rahner's fundamental option, his theology can nonetheless be interpreted through the devastating harm that shapes one's capacity for free choice. Beste argues that theology cannot rest only in "mystery" as the response to trauma, as apophaticism is a thoroughly problematic response to incest, clergy-perpetrated sexual abuse, and other trauma as it can be, and indeed has been, used as an excuse for inaction or even for the continuation of injustice.[59] Instead, we must foster a more complex vision of the virtue of relationality and community. This is both a call to a truthful reckoning with the behavioral and neurobiological damage that trauma causes, as well as a call to a fuller understanding of how God's grace is mediated through supportive relationships.[60]

Rahner's concept of freedom that Beste embraces is anti-fatalistic. It maintains that the choice for grace is open to all, no matter the circumstance. She presents a hopeful vision that reaches

---

[58] Rahner's work is widely considered to be some of the most influential theological writing in the twentieth century. He explores the permeation of grace throughout creation and the dynamic, dialogic mode of God's communication of God's grace. As grace is a free gift, humans are then free to respond to the gift: Beste, *God and the Victim*, 22–24. See also Karl Rahner, *Grace in Freedom* (New York: Herder and Herder, 1969); and Rahner, "Reflections on the Experience of Grace," in *Theological Investigations*, vol. 3 (London: Darton, Longman and Todd, 1967), 86–90.

[59] Beste, *God and the Victim*, 93.

[60] Beste argues that Rahner does not develop either of these aspects sufficiently in his work.

beyond determinism of experience and neurobiological harm, and toward the "awesome responsibility" we have for ourselves.[61] This responsibility should not be read as a burden but as the ever-existing, enduring option to continue in a path toward an actualizing "yes" within one's context, not a one-off, perfect act in an ideal world.[62] Beste's theological engagement of trauma demonstrates how deterministic accounts of the acting person can further damage and debilitate, a conclusion I follow here. Her interpretation maintains the freedom to change within a developmental vision of the will. The self and its actions are not one monolithic decision but emerge over time and with care, as has been shown through successful therapies.[63] It is essential to think of selves as continua, not as static categories, and, as such, maintain a nuanced vision of the always-developing human person.[64] Rather than condemn anyone to predetermined results based on situation or

---

[61] Beste, *God and the Victim*, 98. Julia Feder released a new book on this population/trauma in 2023: *Incarnating Grace: A Theology of Healing from Sexual Trauma* (New York: Fordham University Press, 2023).

[62] Especially in Rahner's later works on suicide and death as well as his consideration of free response even after death, as with babies and those with limits on functional reason. Beste, *God and the Victim*, 106. Further, "there is always hope for each and every living person to forge supportive relationships, actualize her freedom to accept God's grace, and continually deepen her 'yes's to God's self offer" (109).

[63] J. M. Pierre, "The Neuroscience of Free Will: Implications for Psychiatry," *Psychological Medicine* 44 (2014): 2465. Rahner's epistemic humility is also key to reading traumatic experience, neuroscience, and the pursuit of virtue: "The actual situation of a person's freedom ... is not completely accessible to reflection ... as we cannot with certainty know our fundamental option from categorical moral acts." Beste, *God and the Victim*, 29.

[64] R. M. Sapolsky, "The Frontal Cortex and the Criminal Justice System," *Philosophical Transactions of the Royal Society* 359 (2004): 1789. For recent collected works of trauma theology, see Karen O'Donnell and Katie Cross, eds., *Feminist Trauma Theologies: Body, Scripture & Church in Critical Perspective* (London: SCM Press, 2020); *Bearing Witness: Intersectional Perspectives on Trauma Theology* (London: SCM Press, 2022).

experience, Beste's interpretation of Rahner's theology encourages a complex understanding of the potential for virtue and healing in traumatized populations, the communal responsibility to work for an end to suffering, and the pursuit of human flourishing for those who have been subjected to great suffering.[65]

While this brief summary of major works in theology and trauma is far from comprehensive, it demonstrates the foundations of the conversation into which this project enters. The interchange between theology and trauma builds upon the emergence and ongoing definition of clinical trauma, uses the hermeneutics of trauma as a "way of reading," and dialogically engages trauma to interpret not only traumatic experience but also the Christian story itself.

Critics of Trauma

Before proceeding further, it is important to note that there is ongoing, robust critique of the pervasiveness of trauma / trauma language / trauma studies. One of the major criticisms is that trauma theory is not holistic in nature. It separates the prevailing medical/psychological paradigm of trauma from its broader moral and historical dimensions. As should be clear by the complex definitions of trauma offered in this chapter, a central aim of my work is to avoid such a dualistic or isolated reading of trauma. I instead center the connections that individual-level trauma has with mezzo-level institutions and macro-level systems (cultural, religious, and

---

[65] Beste, *God and the Victim*, 101–103. Especially tied to neuroscientific findings around the ties of empathy and action. See E. Gleichgerrcht and L. Young, "Low Levels of Empathic Concern Predict Utilitarian Moral Judgment," *PLOS One* 8, no. 4 (April 2013): e60418. Beste ends with a meditation on pastoral changes and expanded visions of Rahner's "neighbor-love" but with the caution that communal response is not easy—the choice for this type of accompaniment requires patience, living with tension, and the pain of the lack of resolution for many survivors. Beste, *God and the Victim*, 125. I revisit these themes in chapter 5.

social). To support this integrated view of trauma, I address three general areas of trauma critique: the social construction of trauma; the Western, colonial structure of diagnosis and treatment; and the political manipulation of trauma and memory. While by no means a complete survey of the critiques of trauma, I engage these three directly to enliven all future work of trauma and theology, and to hold it authentically accountable to its interdisciplinary interlocutors.

First, in *Empire of Trauma*, anthropologist Didier Fassin and psychiatrist Richard Rechtman argue that modern trauma discourse elides the true nature of particular suffering. They consequently "denaturalize" the experience of trauma and "repoliticize" its victims.[66] Using the work of Derek Summerfield, Fassin and Rechtman even question the legitimacy of "trauma" itself, arguing that, rather than objectively discovering something already in existence (which occurs with diseases), society and politics conspired to create a useful category, the result of which was trauma.[67] They argue that the pervasiveness of trauma emerged from victim advocacy, seeking a social utility.[68] As such, trauma is a social rather than psychological or clinical category.

Fassin and Rechtman conclude that the truth of trauma actually exists outside the psyche or the physical brain, and that its true location is within "the moral economy of contemporary societies."[69] In other words, while some people do develop mental health disorders, the category of "trauma" is wholly located in the social realm. Its power and content have little to do with the individual's brain; rather, society defines trauma by marking

---

[66] Didier Fassin and Richard Rechtman, *The Empire of Trauma: An Inquiry into the Condition of Victimhood*, trans. Rachel Gomme (Princeton, NJ: Princeton University Press, 2009), xi.

[67] Derek Summerfield, "The Invention of Post-traumatic Stress Disorder and the Social Usefulness of a Psychiatric Category," *BMJ* 322, no. 7278 (2001): 95–98.

[68] Fassin and Rechtman, *The Empire of Trauma*, 126.

[69] Fassin and Rechtman, *The Empire of Trauma*, 276.

certain groups to suffer (or making their suffering acceptable), and then using a label to manipulate resources, spaces, and attitudes. Fassin and Rechtman emphasize that the "moral economy" is what we use to define the good as well as the bad, and concrete resources follow such determinations. While I still hold to the biological and psychological realities of trauma as a diagnosis, Fassin and Rechtman's critique illuminates an essential aspect of this project: trauma is a moral category, named and created by society, and it must be seen in a social perspective rather than reduced to a solely individual experience.

Second, psychologist, ethicist, and theologian Maryanne Loughry also resists the current emphasis on trauma/PTSD in global contexts. Her work, predominantly in international refugee camps, focuses on some of the most traumatized populations in the world. Yet, in her estimation, the popularity of trauma discourse distracts from the real needs present in such extreme cases (e.g., funding for psychologists, rather than rebuilding housing). Further, the definition of trauma is based on Western treatment models that are neither culturally competent nor dedicated to the long-term accompaniment needed for successful psychological treatment.[70] Instead, "minimum responses ... should be implemented as soon as possible in an emergency" and are most critical to those in need.[71] After safe and secure shelter and food, these "minimum" efforts include mental health assessment via participatory systems, recruiting local staff, organization and training of aid

---

[70] Drawn from conversations with Loughry, and Maryanne Loughry, "The Representation of Refugee Women in Our Research and Practice," in *Not Born a Refugee Woman: Contesting Identities, Rethinking Practices,* ed. M. Hajdukowski-Ahmed, N. Khanlou, and H. Moussa (New York: Berghahn Books, 2009): 166–172. Other selections from this volume also support Loughry's critique.

[71] Inter-Agency Standing Committee, *IASC Guidelines on Mental Health and Psychosocial Support in Emergency Settings* (Geneva: IASC, 2007), 5. This is also supported by training in FEMA- and WHO-endorsed "Psychological First Aid."

workers, identification/monitoring/prevention of threats through social and legal mechanisms, and facilitating community mobilization. All such efforts seek to maximize the utility of international aid and disaster response, while supporting the community itself to address mental health and suffering as it sees fit.

This approach does not focus on trauma but on factors shown to bolster mental health in crisis situations: the establishment of safety, practical assistance, and social support. Loughry's resistance to the pervasive use and labeling of trauma emerges from its current myopic focus on clinical, Western treatment models (and the resulting redirection of funding within the contexts in which she works) rather than as a critique of trauma as a diagnosis/disease and authentic cultural phenomenon. Given this practical critique, it is essential that this project take seriously the global context of trauma, and the ways in which the discourse has been and continues to be manipulated, most often by those with socioeconomic and political power.[72]

Finally, as trauma so often occurs in communal space, the memory of trauma is recalled socially as well as individually. Such collective memory[73] is an aspect of trauma and memory studies that often challenges individual experiences and is of supreme importance in situations of memorialization (or lack thereof).

---

[72] This critique is most easily applied in postdisaster contexts, and gains another layer of complexity when approaching inter- or intragroup conflict. Here, the reintegration/processing strategies emerging from the field of restorative justice and postconflict studies is essential. While this is clearly another aspect of trauma, I do not address these particular ramifications in this project. Rather, I maintain focus on the larger concept of trauma and its relation to the moral/theological concept of memory.

[73] Collective memory is another branch of memory studies and generally deals with manipulation of group memory—either for healing or the machinations of social/political/economic power. The field locates its roots in the work of Maurice Halbwachs, *On Collective Memory*, trans. Lewis A. Coser (1925; Chicago: University of Chicago Press, 1992).

Political scientist Jenny Edkins maintains a critical view toward trauma memory's usurpation by political powers in communal trauma cases such as the Shoah, genocide, and chattel slavery. She resists the ease with which trauma is discussed publicly, and instead highlights the production of a "trauma narrative" as an aspect of a complicit body politic.[74] The attempt to force trauma into language and the public sphere is arguably impossible, as our language and expressions are so thoroughly mediated by the status quo of a given power structure. Thus, any account of suffering is immediately translated into digestible language for consumption, rather than service to the real experience of pain.[75]

In constructing ethical communal traumatic memory, therefore, a linear, exacting narrative must not be the main goal, yet translation remains necessary and sought by communities dealing with trauma. Edkins recognizes this tension and points toward a new way of communicating trauma, one that presents "an alternative, that of *encircling the trauma*. We cannot try to address the trauma directly without risking its gentrification. We cannot remember it as something that took place in time, because that would neutralise it."[76] Her proposal instead focuses on local practices of "truth testimony," allowing for broader expressions of trauma and its lived experience, rather than an emphasis on "explaining away" the event by forcing it into a preestablished

---

[74] Jenny Edkins, *Trauma and the Memory of Politics* (Cambridge: Cambridge University Press, 2003), 7.

[75] This view is also supported by J. B. Metz drawing on Karl Marx, explored further in chapter 4.

[76] Edkins, *Trauma and the Memory of Politics,* 15, drawing on Slavoj Žižek's construction of an open social order with an "acceptance of lack" at its center. Used in this way, "gentrification" is meant to indicate the refining or "improving" of a narrative to fit the parameters of social acceptability and politeness, usually defined by the powerful, or even the perpetrator. Like Caruth, Edkins instead emphasizes the permeable nature of trauma, and the need to bow to its "ongoingness" in people's lives.

social category or series of legal facts. In this way, Edkins supports much of the above critiques, adding a keen, suspicious, unwavering attention to the damaging political, social, and cultural structures of power that are all too often responsible for trauma and all too willing to coopt and reinscribe traumatic memory for oppressive purposes.

While brief, these three critiques name important points of accountability for this book. First, Fassin and Rechtman clarify the social construction of trauma that emphasizes contextualization of traumatic events and seeks the active empowerment of the person through recognition of trauma as a moral category. Second, Loughry illuminates the Western bias in diagnosis, treatment, and resource allocation, and calls for a more localized, robust, and nuanced approach to suffering in global contexts. Finally, with Edkins, collective memory studies recognizes the frequent production of trauma narratives as an aspect of broader social complicity in suffering.[77] Rather than weaken the case for the study of trauma within Christian social ethics, these critiques bolster my aim of a holistic view of trauma as psychological experience as well as communal phenomenon. In response, this project explores how trauma itself has become embedded in our bodies and minds, as well as in our culture, history, and theology. This is by no means a clean definition of trauma. I hope that, by raising the term to the light and turning it about like a prism, we can now hold together a complex and multifaceted conceptual engagement that inspires further inquiry.

---

[77] This is evident in cases such as the conflict in the former Yugoslavia, where narratives of suffering were manipulated by multiple political and military factions to incite further violence and still today support ongoing divisions in the region. See Stephanie C. Edwards, "Creating a Multidirectional Memory for Healing in the Former Yugoslavia," in *Healing and Peacebuilding after War: Transforming Trauma in Bosnia and Herzegovina*, ed. Marie Berry, Nancy Good, and Julianne Funk, Routledge Studies in Peace and Conflict Resolution, ed. Tom Woodhouse and Hugh Miall (New York: Routledge, 2020), 89–105.

Traumatic Memory:
Moving from Self to Society

The need for a social ethic is evident considering this exploration of trauma's manifold operation in our world. *Memory* is the aspect of both our embodied selves and our communal practices that is most useful for the task. The human mind, especially when viewed from our Cartesian inheritance, is often considered to hold our essential being, over and sometimes against our physicality.[78] As such, our memories are central to our understanding of the human person and, for Christian theology, potentially sacred as part of our createdness as *imago Dei*. In this final section, we shift from peeling back the layers of trauma as psychological experience, potential disorder, cultural reality, and social/theological hermeneutic and turn toward a focus on the role of memory in trauma, specifically as the ground of an enfleshed social ethic.

After first briefly explaining the biological functions of traumatic memory, I offer a succinct exploration of the bioethical debate regarding memory. Examining the secular debate regarding traumatic memory grounds theological ethics in emerging research. Christian social ethics do not arise in a vacuum, nor does the church's life in Christ happen in a separatist and exclusionary antagonism to the world. Theological and ethical reflection on Christian memory, particularly as it provides vital ground for a social ethic that can address trauma, renders itself inadequate for Christian life if it ignores the debates and contexts that shape the world in which such reflection happens. The ethical considerations regarding the role of human memory, therefore, contextualize my proposal of Christian enfleshed counter-memory and play an important role in demonstrating the centrality of womanist theological anthropology presented in the next chapter. Focusing

---

[78] I reject this dualism, but it indicates the importance of our minds in the Christian tradition.

on trauma memory rather than trauma experience reinforces that, regardless of the particularity of individual cases, trauma permeates our shared existence in the form of overwhelming harm and unfulfilled healing of our corporate body. Trauma in this usage indicates a remainder, something that lingers after the pain itself, something that is remembered, not just by one but by all. Trauma, at its core, is a disease of the memory. Therefore, the central category of ethical concern within this book is memory, as memory is at once embodied, individual, corporate, and active.

Traumatic Memory and Memory in Patients with PTSD

Starting, then, with the material reality of trauma, a basic understanding of biological memory is required: how memories are formed, how trauma impacts our memories, and how any intervention in memory recollection, integration, or healing acts in our bodies and brains. The body stores physical and psychological markers of our memories, particularly those extreme in nature, like trauma, or those that occur in an important developmental stage, like childhood. Even if memories are not immediately apparent, or strictly "accessible" in a factual sense, a formative aspect is stored. This "storage" leads to our development, both for evolutionary need (safety vs. danger) and preferences (the reason you no longer eat salsa with corn in it).[79] Yet even if we feel we can "recall it like it was yesterday," we now know that our memories are delicate, malleable entities. Far from being static once "stored," memories are actually modified each time they are remembered.[80]

---

[79] Rothschild, *The Body Remembers*.

[80] The understanding of memory as dynamic, rather than static, is first found in historic studies dating to the 1930s. Yet as we see in ongoing neurobiological research, our memories and how they function are still relatively shrouded in mystery. However, while reconsolidation theory continues to be tested, it is the functioning paradigm for all ongoing research. More broadly, and accessibly, a reference for the development of neuroscience in general is Sam

When we remember, we re/create[81] cellular protein linkages, and initiate cascades of chemical responses throughout the brain and physical body. We do not "re-member" (put back together) or replicate those protein linkages perfectly—*we actually change the event recalled in our memory through the act of remembering it.* This phenomenon represents a neural "plasticity" that filters out important memories to be consolidated from the commonplace, often discarded, data in the memory formation process.[82]

In a brain with PTSD, the trauma memory is encoded differently to the extent that an individual can either remember every detail of the event (a burden of detail that the brain eliminates in normal experience), to nothing at all (at least consciously, the extreme neural example of the "flight" response). This "misfiring" of chemicals is the brain's attempt to protect itself from extreme trauma. If this neural pattern continues, however, it has corrosive impacts on the life and memory of the individual, specifically seen in the breakage from normal, chronological time exhibited through PTSD "flashbacks."[83] Memories associated with PTSD have also shown themselves to be difficult to forget or modify,

---

Kean, *The Tale of the Dueling Neurosurgeons: The History of the Human Brain as Revealed by True Stories of Trauma, Madness, and Recovery* (New York: Back Bay Books, 2014).

[81] Used on purpose, as sometimes we are re-creating pathways, other times we are creating completely new ones.

[82] "The brain acts as a computer both to store information and to process that information. In a computer, separate devices perform these roles; while a hard disk stores information, the central processing unit (CPU) does the processing. But the brain is thought to perform both these functions in the same cells—neurons—leading researchers to ask if distinct molecules within the brain cells serve these different functions." SUNY Downstate Medical Center, "Spotless Mind? Unwanted Memories Might Be Erasable without Harming Other Brain Functions," *Science Daily,* December 24, 2008, https://www.sciencedaily.com/releases/2008/12/081223121137.htm.

[83] Rachel Yehuda, Marian Joëls, and Richard G. M. Morris, "The Memory Paradox," *Neuroscience* 11 (2010): 837.

even over time, as there is potentially a "limited role for memory updating consistent with evolutionary accounts of associative learning for threat and reward."[84] In other words, we remember traumatic events deeply, as their extreme impact potentially benefits our survival (what to avoid, what to seek) in the broader evolutionary context of human life. While our memories are dynamic, they can get stuck in repeated grooves and patterns that can be difficult to change.

Memory Healing, Elimination, and Enhancement:
The Debate about Human Memory

With this basic understanding of memory and trauma in hand, it is helpful to introduce the current debate about memory healing to determine the broad strokes of ethical action based in memory. Most medical memory experiments look at both elimination and enhancement to find the best potential clinical applications for everything from PTSD (memory elimination) to Alzheimer's (memory enhancement). The debate around any sort of human enhancement (e.g., genetic, cybernetic, pharmaceutical) has been long established, and its cautions well-known.[85] With the ever-increasing number of available, relatively low-impact pharmaceuticals, however, "cosmetic neurology" or "cosmetic psychopharmocology"[86] is

---

[84] M. Treanor, L. A. Brown, J. Rissman, and M. G. Craske, "Can Memories of Traumatic Experiences or Addiction Be Erased or Modified? A Critical Review of Research on the Disruption of Memory Reconsolidation and Its Applications," *Perspectives on Psychological Science* 12, no. 2 (2017): 291. Yet boundary conditions are by no means permanent, and some scholars are more hopeful about their abilities to break through the blockade. See Elsey and Kindt, "Breaking Boundaries."

[85] For example, see Michael J. Sandel, *Case against Perfection: Ethics in the Age of Genetic Engineering* (Cambridge, MA: Belknap Press of Harvard University Press, 2007).

[86] C. Elliott, "The Tyranny of Happiness: Ethics and Cosmetic

becoming a growing concern in scientific and lay conversations about memory elimination.[87] Today, you can order everything from psilocybin in a clinic to ketamine to your door, with the oft-sought goal of eliminating harmful memories or breaking free from trauma symptoms. This level of unprecedented access to drugs specifically targeting traumatic memory raises immediate practical questions (e.g., appropriateness, supervision) and indicates a dubious regard for the value of such memories.[88]

For example, political scientist Łukasz Kamieński argues that preventively using the beta-blocker propranolol in combat troops instrumentalizes their humanity, eliminating the existential element of war by blunting their memories. What is at stake is truly life and death both for the medicated soldier and those with whom they interact. Yet if we can protect "our own" from harmful memories, shouldn't we be mandated to do so, especially considering astronomical PTSD rates in US combat troops? Kamieński says no. In such cases, it is not only morally right that soldiers should be able to maintain their own pharmaceutically unaltered moral compass within war zones, but also that society has a "right to know" about the full truth of actions taken on its behalf and even has "an obligation to remember."[89] Kamieński

---

Psychopharmacology," in *Enhancing Human Traits: Ethical and Social Implications,* ed. E. Parens (Washington, DC: Georgetown University Press, 1998): 177–188.

[87] A. Chatterjee, "The Promise and Predicament of Cosmetic Neurology," *Neuroethics* 32 (2006): 110.

[88] Oregon decriminalized "mushrooms" along with other formerly illegal drugs in 2020 for clinical use only (not recreational), and now the company Joyous will send you ketamine doses in the mail nationwide for $129/month (as of December 2023).

[89] Łukasz Kamieński, "Helping the Postmodern Ajax: Is Managing Combat Trauma through Pharmacology a Faustian Bargain?," *Armed Forces & Society* 39, no. 3 (2012): 405. Kamieński's argument is based on the view that soldiers do have a moral compass, which is contradicted by "situationist"

argues we are "all Aristotelian *zoon politikons*, gaining our identity and humanity only within and through the society in which we live."[90] As such, pharmaceutical prophylaxis of combat troops also abrogates legal responsibility, further medicalizes society as well as individuals, and strips individual soldiers of their agency, as "our agency is built on what we have experienced and how we remember."[91] Despite the devastating impacts of war and its memories, Kamieński concludes that our human weakness, our vulnerability, should never be lost, especially in contexts that are created exclusively to do just that. Bioethicist Elisa A. Hurley agrees, proposing that sensitive and spontaneous reactions of emotion can actually assist individuals in determining the "evaluative significance" of traumatic events.[92] For example, if the horror is removed from a trauma such as rape, it may become impossible for the victim to recognize the full extent of the harm done, or even to hold "the perpetrator accountable for the *full extent* of the injury."[93]

Despite such concerns, Jessica R. Cadwallader argues that, by centering the figure of "hysterical rape victim" in memory discourse, we only reify a problematic narrative. The significance of a painful event is not universal, and all too often judgment is cast by communities, society, and justice systems based on emotive response or lack thereof. Drawing on Sara Ahmed's work on race, Cadwallader contends that discussions around

---

ethicists (known for rejecting virtue ethics) who argue that individual conscience flows with group membership.

[90] Kamieński, "Helping the Postmodern Ajax," 405.
[91] Kamieński, "Helping the Postmodern Ajax," 407.
[92] Elisa A. Hurley, "The Moral Costs of Prophylactic Propranolol," *The American Journal of Bioethics* 7, no. 9 (2007): 35. A further complication is cases of moral injury, most often spoken about in contexts of war, where the perpetrator may be the self (as soldier) carrying out actions that are morally repugnant to the self (as individual in society).
[93] Hurley, "The Moral Costs," 35.

therapeutic forgetting must be restructured, that survivors should have the real choice

> to maintain the affect of pain, to refuse to forget that which contemporary institutions and political structures would much rather we did.... The responsibility that we have is not to maximise access to [drugs].... It is, rather, to bring into being worlds in which we do not catch ourselves on the horns of the choice between treating individual suffering and redressing systematic injustice.[94]

This balance requires much more attention to the nuances of remembering as well as forgetting, the intense pain and suffering caused by traumatic experience, and the transformation of individual and social scripts regarding trauma and its memory.

All of this ethical debate hinges upon the moral valence we have attached to the "production and recollection of past experiences," that these cognitive functions are central to humanity, and that memories "should be maintained even in opposition to the wishes of the memory holders."[95] Many scholars from disability studies and beyond struggle with the desire for an end to suffering while not mandating a type of healing or diminishing one's personhood based on "perfect" functioning.[96] Palliative care physician Leah B. Rosenberg resists the assumption that memories form the basis of our moral judgments, instead focusing on how

---

[94] Jessica R. Cadwallader, "Figuring (Wounded) Detachment: Rape, Embodiment and Therapeutic Forgetting," *Somatechnics* 3, no. 2 (2013): 265–266.

[95] Leah B. Rosenberg, "Necessary Forgetting: On the Use of Propranolol in Post-traumatic Stress Disorder Management," *The American Journal of Bioethics* 7, no. 9 (2007): 27.

[96] Disability theology is discussed further in chapter 5. For an interesting framework based on Amartya Sen and Martha Nussbaum's "capabilities approach," see Christopher A. Riddle, *Disability and Justice: The Capabilities Approach in Practice* (Lanham, MD: Lexington Books, 2014).

intrusive, painful memories actually inhibit life development. She argues that we should focus on what traumatic memories *actually do* (i.e., harm), and that, "as such, the ethical value of memories must be formulated solely by the only stakeholder that matters— the patient."[97] This is echoed by legal and healthcare ethics scholar Adam Kolber, who argues that "excessive hand-wringing now over the ethics of tampering with memory could stall research into preventing post-traumatic stress in millions of people [as well as those already suffering]."[98]

If we are made from our memories in some form, then our experiences and our memories of them shape us into coherent selves, families, and communities no matter how painful the content. Yet it is also true that the severe disorders that can result from traumatic events are "*not* a critical part" of a person's humanity, instead breaking a person's sense of self.[99] Traumatic memory should then be eliminated to restore a person's "real" self, as memories of trauma are an external assault on the person. In either perspective, embodied individual memories, especially those that reflect shared traumas, map onto our corporate body, passing through families and cultural groups, often defining identity, beliefs, and social ethics. Whether the memory is repressed or rehearsed regularly, it remains. Sitting within this complex tension, trauma memory is a contested site. Within this struggle, however, is an essential moment for Christian ethics, a way of being and believing centered on a complex, painful memory.

---

[97] Rosenberg, "Necessary Forgetting," 28.

[98] Adam Kolber, "Give Memory-Altering Drugs a Chance," *Nature* 476 (August 18, 2011): 275.

[99] Adam Piore, "Totaling Recall: Scientists Can Put Memories in a Precarious State—And Manipulate, or Even Erase, Them," *Scientific American*, January/February 2012, 45.

Conclusion

While understanding the biological realities of trauma and memory, trauma's diagnostic content and cultural construction, and the ethical nuances of memory healing are necessary to ensure that we tread carefully in our expansion of trauma into the theological realm, we leave our analysis of trauma itself here.[100] From this footing, I propose that individualized solutions are not the easy, sole, or complete solution to the most challenging aspects of our cognition. It should be clear from the above analysis that social, political, religious, economic, and cultural contexts are foundational concerns when encountering trauma and traumatic memory. Understanding traumatic memory in this way, the problem is framed not only as recurring, individual chronic suffering. It is a problem of endemic and widespread social enablement of pain and willed ignorance of responsibility. As such, our questions going forward are in line with theologian Miroslav Volf:

> So from the start, the central question for me was not *whether* to remember. I most assuredly would remember and most incontestably should remember. Instead, the central question was *how to remember rightly*. And given my Christian sensibilities, my question from the start was, How should I remember abuse as a person committed to loving the wrongdoer and overcoming evil with good? What does "remembering rightly" actually involve?[101]

I propose that memory is a site of opportunity for a constructive, enfleshed Christian social ethic in response to trauma, not just the locus of individual discernment. Christian ethics is

---

[100] To reiterate—this does not make what I have outlined exhaustive, but merely sufficient for our discussion moving forward. In this shift to social ethics I stand solidly in the tradition of Latin American liberation theology, with such authors as Ignacio Martín-Baró (liberation psychology), discussed in chapter 5.

[101] Volf, *Remembering Rightly in a Violent World*, 9, 11.

particularly equipped to hold the tension of transcendent persons and communities seeking to break out of self-fulfillment for self-fulfillment's sake, reaching beyond the evolutionary or social concerns of secular/medical ethicists outlined above.[102] Instead, the approach to Christian memory that I build in the remaining chapters addresses the existential contours of trauma, beyond but also encompassing specific cases of trauma.

We are asked to remember, tasked with doing so by Jesus not only for our own sake but for the entirety of creation. As such, Christian enfleshed counter-memory takes trauma seriously, attempting to discern its shape within our shared body, and providing practices of justice that can hold and attempt to heal harmful memories. In the next chapter, I attend to the first theological intricacy necessary for this task, engaging womanist notions of incarnational, embodied, and relational personhood to root this social ethic within our created selves.

---

[102] Drawing here from Charles Taylor, *The Ethics of Authenticity* (Cambridge, MA: Harvard University Press, 1992). Yehuda and her colleagues also recognize that there is a fundamental existential component to trauma that must be addressed, see Rachel Yehuda, D. Spiegel, S. Southwick, L. L. Davis, T. C. Neylan, and J. H. Krystal, "What I Have Changed My Mind about and Why," *European Journal of Psychotraumatology* 7, no. 1 (2016): 33768.

2

WOMANIST ETHICS AND TRAUMATIC MEMORY

The social surd that *is* our nation is the product of *structural historical amnesia*. The massacre of indigenous peoples, expropriation of their lands, trampling on treaty after treaty, and centuries of black enslavement, segregation, and discrimination compose the "tough stuff of American memory." We conspire to not remember; we choose to forget. We repress and erase; we edit and delete. The result is a peculiar and unsettling, even puerile, ignorance that seeks to pass as political innocence. Christian exercise of memory purports to be radically different: We pledge to remember, we are obliged to do so. We are marked with a sign that neither can be erased nor easily forgotten. The cross of the Crucified Jew traced on our bodies at Baptism initiates us into a promise of new life and reminds us of our intimate and irrevocable relatedness to all creatures in the here-and-now through His name.

—M. Shawn Copeland[1]

---

[1] M. Shawn Copeland, "Memory, #BlackLivesMatter, and Theologians," *Political Theology* 17, no. 1 (2016): 1.

While secular bioethics can discern some of the pertinent issues around traumatic memory, there remain untreated existential contours to which Christian theological ethics is particularly suited to respond. As Copeland points out, Christian memory purports to be radically different. We must be abundantly clear, however, that the aims of theological inquiry are distinct from the medical or psychological fields. Individual biomedical and psychological healing are the aim of the healthcare industry, making patient autonomy and resource allocation their central ethical concerns. Theology, at its best, contends with the larger meaning-making structures and metaphysical claims within which we live, often shifting focus beyond the individual alone, while simultaneously upholding the uniqueness and value of each person.

From this distinctive position, theology can offer a powerful reframing of trauma and suffering. Yet much harm, it must be said, has been done by pastors, lay ministers, and theologians who speak to the traumatized with an authority that excludes or denigrates the medical and therapeutic fields (e.g., "God never gives you more than you can handle"). I do not aim to replace or contradict scientific best practices through a focus on theology. In fact, I resist the "spiritual bypassing"[2] that is too often the response of faith structures in their encounter with suffering. Rather, I want to trace how theology speaks alongside emerging medicine, best therapeutic practices, and the larger context of structural injustice in which both operate. While it may not be apparent at first blush, this orientation actively resists a type of traumatic memory manipulation that already exists both in medicine and the Christian faith: the ease with which some medical treatments

---

[2] Generally, spiritual bypassing is when a person or institution uses spirituality-based explanations to dismiss or avoid hard situations, emotions, questions, or psychological issues. Overdependence on "God's plan," silver-lining rhetoric, and karmic justice (as used in US cultural parlance) are roots of the term's development in the 1980s by Buddhist psychotherapist John Welwood.

are considered "answers" to suffering from the medical community and, on the other hand, a type of acceptance of suffering that can become pathological within Christian theology. Neither of these responses are adequate to the challenge posed by trauma, nor are they the compassionate, healing, and holistic response sought by both camps.

With this critique at the forefront, womanist theological anthropology is foundational for a robust Christian ethic of traumatic memory, one that takes seriously the nuances of subjugated, enfleshed, and empowered personhood. The work of Emilie Townes on the cultural production of health in conversation with Monica Coleman and Phillis I. Sheppard on the experiences of Black women and mental health in the United States clarifies the lived reality of trauma and the intimate ties between morality and disease. Together, these theologians center what Copeland calls the "new theological subject": Black women, who are too often considered peripherally, if at all, in mainstream Western theology. Orienting enfleshed counter-memory within womanist theological anthropology, I draw connections between issues of "flesh" and broader Christian theology with M. Shawn Copeland and Eboni Marshall Turman. I introduce the nuances of incarnate embodiment in conversation with trauma, advancing the position that an intersectional, womanist theological anthropology is essential to Christian enfleshed counter-memory. Persons and their identities are formed by and with their communities: what womanists identify as a distinctly relational existence, tied directly to God's sharing in humanity through the person of Christ. By centering a deeply incarnational vision, traumatic memory is seen through a distinctly Christian lens, highlighting the responsibility to do theology—in academic circles and beyond—that engages ethical action to encounter and interpret traumatic memory.

Finally, the chapter follows the practical nature of much womanist theology, explicitly identifying three broadly construed practice realms involved in a Christian ethical response to trauma: (1) lament as public prophecy, (2) personal narrative and the power of self-definition, and (3) intergenerational storytelling. These practices of memory in response to trauma form initial insight into the lived expressions of the social ethic of enfleshed counter-memory. Specifically, they suggest the ways trauma response is not limited to individual healing work and consequently propose that integrated memory-holding must include acts beyond the isolated person. While necessarily broad, I introduce these practices here, early in our consideration of trauma and Christian ethics, to lift up the necessary application of our thinking in actions that cultivate communal memory. Rooting enfleshed counter-memory in the relational theological anthropology of womanist thought is the inextricable backing on which I will weave all that follows: a framework deeply committed to the sacrality of the person, our enmeshment with others, and actions toward liberation.

A Note on My Embodiment

It is important to note that I, a white woman speaking from a location of social and economic privilege, am choosing to focus on womanist thought with intention and purpose. Womanism, in some forms, adamantly opposes the appropriation of its thought by outsiders, as repetitive reinscription of colonial and tokenizing abuse of the work of people of color is often the result.[3] Works of people of color, particularly women, tend to be shunted

---

[3] On figuring out how one can "*do* womanism even if they cannot *be* womanists," see Stacey M. Floyd-Thomas, *Mining the Motherlode: Methods in Womanist Ethics* (Cleveland: Pilgrim Press, 2006), 4. I do find that, as Monica Coleman states as her purpose, "The theology that emerges from my experiences is meaningful to those with whom I share similar embodiment and those with whom I largely do not." See Coleman, "Speak Like Christ, Adorn Like Plaskow: Embodied Theologies," *Journal of Feminist Studies in Religion* 33, no. 2 (2017): 105–109.

aside as "just stories" or "cultural" works that add some flavor to the "norm," rather than foundational and central to shaping the issue at hand—trauma studies or otherwise.[4] While the roots of womanist discourse—the lived experiences of Black women—are distinctly outside my access, I center the voices of womanists as methodologically essential: womanists are some of the most complex and insightful thinkers on trauma and theology, although they are rarely acknowledged as such. My intention is not to speak "for" these authors but rather "with" their scholarship.[5] Further, womanists themselves are also more likely to have experienced trauma directly, or to attend actively to familial, communal, and historical traumas. In this way they are the very people with whom a Christian ethic of trauma must ground itself.

Importantly, being linked to trauma is *not only* what Black communities are; they are also "proud, rich, and supportive cultural heritages."[6] I am in no way attempting to reify the story of despair that is often the only story told of Black communities in the United States. Yet because my work centers on the experience of trauma, this volume necessarily casts its gaze there. Throughout this project, I read harmed communities and individuals through

---

[4] While virtue is not my focus here, M. Therese Lysaught and Cory D. Mitchell similarly explore how the embodied trauma of racism has resulted in malformed virtue ethics: "Vicious Trauma: Race, Bodies, and the Confounding of Virtue Ethics," *Journal of the Society of Christian Ethics* 42, no. 1 (2022): 77–100. Donna Maeda also explores speaking across difference in "The Other Woman: Irreducible Alterity in Feminist Theologies," *Religion* 27, no. 2 (1997): 123–128; as does Patricia Hill Collins in *Black Feminist Thought: Knowledge, Consciousness, and the Politics of Empowerment* (London: Routledge, 1990).

[5] See Monica Coleman, "Introduction: Ain't I a Womanist Too?," in *Ain't I A Womanist Too?: Third-Wave Womanist Religious Thought*, ed. Monica Coleman (Minneapolis: Fortress Press, 2013), 1–34.

[6] Wynetta Scott-Simmons, "The Other Side of Silence: The Look of Separation," *Journal of Curriculum Theorizing* 28, no. 3 (2012): 22–39, for a more extensive discussion of speaking and relationship building across racial/cultural difference.

the social work theory of "strengths-based" analysis, where a person or community's struggles are read first for strength rather than need.[7] Womanism is particularly attuned to reading these "matrices of oppression" that reveal the ways intersecting and overlapping systems, experiences, social locations, and so on, influence our harms as well as our empowerment, which is of particular importance in the consideration of trauma.[8]

Finally, I believe it to be of the upmost importance to foreground womanist thought and method in Christian theology writ large because endemic knowledge has long been marginalized in the fields of theology and bioethics.[9] Mainstream white-dominant theology's near obsession with pain, and people as objects (not subjects) of that pain, has created a vacuous Christian ethics, foreclosing from the outset deep exploration of and listening to the resilience, strengths, and joys of persons and groups forced to the "margins."[10] As a white woman listening to and applying womanist theological modes, I align myself with Emilie Townes: where "other" stories do not embrace the "Other" as

> a social problem or an object of too many Derridas, Foucaults, or Spivaks; but the folk who are really just round the corner—but we act as if we do not know them because this is what we have been trained to do as "natural." Frankly, this use of "the Other" is neither liberatory nor transformative. In postmodern America, discourse on

---

[7] In a strengths-based analysis, that child who always eats at the neighbor's house evidences strong kinship bonds in the community. In a needs-based analysis, the same situation would be interpreted as a lack of food in the home that must be remedied by external forces.

[8] Patricia Hill Collins, *Black Feminist Thought: Knowledge, Consciousness, and the Politics of Empowerment* (New York: Routledge, 2000), 227.

[9] See Emilie Townes, *Breaking the Fine Rain of Death: African American Health Issues and a Womanist Ethic of Care* (New York: Continuum, 1998).

[10] Gloria Anzaldúa is a great example of resisting this tendency, offering the construction of theologizing on and within the frontera/boundary.

"the Other" often becomes an excuse to remain ignorant and arrogant about our illiteracy of other peoples—their thoughts, their religions, their politics, their values, their social structures, their moral landscapes—their isness/ontology—both mundane and radical.[11]

Or, as Townes cites Toni Morrison more poetically, I meet womanism in its model/method of a "dancing mind."[12] This is where the writer's "real life is about creating and producing and distributing knowledge; about making it possible for the entitled as well as the dispossessed to experience one's own mind dancing with another's."[13] My contention, with fellow white theologian Laurie Cassidy, is that, within womanist anthropology, "there is an intersection between the work of love and our ability to critically understand what it means 'to live in the master's house,'" where we can recognize *resonances with radical difference*, and determine different responsibilities as well as common goods.[14] As such, I

---

[11] Emilie Townes, *Womanist Ethics and the Cultural Production of Evil* (New York: Palgrave Macmillan, 2006), 31.

[12] Townes, *Womanist Ethics*, 2. This is also in keeping with the work of Karen Baker Fletcher, *Dancing with God: The Trinity from a Womanist Perspective* (St. Louis: Chalice Press, 2006).

[13] Toni Morrison, "The Dancing Mind," Acceptance of the Medal for Distinguished Contribution to American Letters, November 6, 1996, https://www.nationalbook.org/tag/the-dancing-mind/. This is not meant to be a flippant or overly trite summary of my role as a white scholar. I make mistakes and I always need additional learning and evolution. For a process of just engagement, I look to adrienne maree brown, a Black queer femme community organizer, who outlines the tough work of growing together as a diverse community seeking justice in *We Will Not Cancel Us: And Other Dreams of Transformative Justice* (Chico, CA: AK Press, 2020).

[14] Laurie Cassidy, "Learning to Enflesh Freedom: Returning to the Clearing," in *Enfleshing Theology: Embodiment, Discipleship, and Politics in the Work of M. Shawn Copeland*, ed. Robert J. Rivera and Michele Saracino (Lanham, MD: Lexington Books / Fortress Academic, 2018), 50–51, 54.

attempt to resist colonial appropriation of womanist thought, as well as the drive to convenient social forgetting of suffering that Copeland outlines at the beginning of this chapter. Instead, I aim to explore how womanists might define the task of memory in light of trauma, and to describe the contours of the "Christian exercise of memory [that] purports to be radically different."[15]

The Cultural Production of Health, Morality, and Embodiment

Theological anthropology, who we are in light of our understanding of God, is tightly linked with our socio-cultural-historical and embodied location. If, as Scripture claims, we are created *imago Dei* (in the image of God), then who and why we are is intimately bound with the divine. Thus, our bodies have been a near-constant site of theologizing throughout the history of Christianity, in particular because of Jesus's Incarnation (God become flesh).

Here, as gestured to by Copeland, we must consider our memory as an inextricable part of who we are within our physical selves. Inextricable does not mean flawless and essential, however. Arguments that equate our memories to our purest, true selves quickly deteriorate when we recognize the good humanity of persons with developmental delays or elders with Alzheimer's. Even the mundane experience of failing to remember anything that I have not written down raises concerns about hastily accepted claims defining our true selves as a perfect mind or memory. Too often, we accept overly simplistic renderings of ourselves and force

---

Copeland also mines this vein in "Racism and the Vocation of the Theologian," *Spiritus: A Journal of Christian Spirituality* 2, no. 1 (2002): 15–29.

[15] Copeland, "Memory, #BlackLivesMatter, and Theologians," 1. For a classic treatment of the white/Black divide in systematic theology, see Jacquelyn Grant, *White Women's Christ and Black Women's Jesus: Feminist Christology and Womanist Response* (Atlanta: Scholars Press, 1989).

such renderings upon others. These simplistic approaches harm our own complexity and, through a Christian lens, do a disservice to God's gifts of creativity in our very selves. Yet we essentialize our most basic embodiment (race, gender, etc.), and, with seemingly even more readiness, our minds.[16] The rush to find a solution to our "unruly," finite, death-bound bodies often ends with a perfunctory supremacy of the mind, even if given the guise of "spirit" or "soul."[17] The theological anthropology presented here resists such dualism, following instead the womanist construction of situated, incarnate selves, who hold the experience of trauma in body, mind, and spirit.

To understand such a theological anthropology, however, it is first important to clarify how health and disease operate within and around our embodied selves. While it may appear on the surface that health and illness are two simple categories interpreted via our physical state, both are tightly tied to cultural conceptions, those directly referencing bodily wellness (e.g., "health") and those that at first seem unrelated (e.g., race and gender).[18] Our definitions, experiences, and interpretations of our bodies are not limited to how one views one's condition or lack thereof. They are tied to existing social categories.

---

[16] Essentializing is the process wherein we make something true of the essence of a person, a critique often raised by feminists who resist the biological essentialism created by certain readings of Scripture or biology: that we are destined to do only that to which our physical bodies are shaped.

[17] Here I'm gesturing toward the body of disability theory, discussed in chapter 5, and particularly the work of Susannah B. Mintz, *Unruly Bodies: Life Writing by Women with Disabilities* (Chapel Hill: University of North Carolina Press, 2007). Coleman can be read as a disability theologian as well, centering her work on her own mental health.

[18] See, for example, the work on the value of epilepsy for the Hmong people explored in Anne Fadiman's book *The Spirit Catches You and You Fall Down: A Hmong Child, Her American Doctors, and the Collision of Two Cultures* (New York: Farrar, Straus and Giroux, 1997). Also of particular interest is Michel Foucault's social construction of mental health in *Madness and Civilization* (1961; New York: Vintage, 1988).

Further, our understanding of bodily experience also influences how a person is treated when they seek healing, and whether they choose to pursue assistance. A result of this complexity—the value-laden beliefs about health and disease, as well as speaking across differences in those definitions—is to "render invisible" many of the relevant presenting factors of one's needs.[19] This is particularly salient within mental health treatment, where some of the only methods to assess treatment needs are in discussions between provider and patient. As this tangled web surrounding our biological well-being suggests, it is important to begin with a brief parsing of the meanings and "morality" often intertwined with health.

The "Morality" of Health and Illness

Michael Pestana's theoretical philosophical work deconstructs the oft-conflated topics of virtue and mental health and is a relevant exploration of this topic for our focus on trauma and memory.[20] Virtue is a crucial category in considerations of trauma, as victims are very often blamed for their suffering, and persons who perpetrate crime are often reduced to single incidents of action.[21] In a departure from the project at hand, Pestana takes

---

[19] As a result of social inequality and gaps in health access, many individuals who do seek treatment in the United States will encounter a service provider with a distinctly different background from their own. Phillis I. Sheppard, "Culture, Ethnicity, and Race: A Womanist Self Psychological Perspective," in *Transforming Wisdom: Pastoral Psychotherapy in Theological Perspective,* ed. Felicity B. Kelcourse and K. Brynolf Lyon (Eugene, OR: Cascade Books, 2015), 46.

[20] Michael Pestana, *Moral Virtue or Mental Health?* SFSU Series in Philosophy 10 (New York: Peter Lang, 1998).

[21] For example, rape victims are asked why they were walking late at night or wearing a certain outfit, and moral blame is placed on them for their experience of harm. Adding nuance to our assessment, perpetrators of crime can be acting through maladaptive traits brought on by untreated trauma. This does

great pains to avoid neuroscientific research, psychiatry, or indeed medical fields in general, and instead focuses on the need to deconstruct and divide the ways in which philosophy and studies of personhood (and resulting social systems) do or do not treat moral virtue and mental health.[22] Pestana defines moral virtue and mental health as, respectively, an act of the will and a capacity for enacting the will. Importantly, the former (virtue) requires the latter (mental health), not vice versa (mental health *does not* require virtue). Without such a strict divide in the definition of the two aspects of human functioning (virtue and mental health), he argues, inappropriate judgments of the person are made throughout society. Such judgments have direct impacts, which are particularly salient for Pestana in the treatment and understanding of persons involved in the criminal justice system. Persons in the US penal system are often judged and assigned value based on their mental health, demonstrating a loss of a dynamic and comprehensive social understanding of the person, as well as of virtue and vice.[23] The problem, for Pestana, is not the categories themselves, but the loss of a proper understanding of virtue and vice, and how they are influenced by social power.

Additionally helpful for our theological consideration of the person, Pestana identifies himself as "anti-Platonic" in that he resists

---

not excuse harmful action but refuses to reduce the person to that single action. This is in keeping with conversations around transformative and restorative justice, which while not the focus of this book do influence the ways I think about harm, right action, and repair.

[22] While I don't follow his methodology (as I believe addressing emerging science is crucial to proper theology in response to trauma), I include it here as much theorizing, particularly in the theological and philosophical realms, divorces itself from science. It is important to recognize how these arguments are constructed and to weigh for yourself the validity of such methodology, in particular whether you think theology and philosophy can and should stand on their own merits, and to what extent they can (or must) engage with interdisciplinary conversations that have very different metaphysical claims.

[23] Pestana, *Moral Virtue*, 3, 104–116. Arguably lost, if it was ever present.

the conflation of acts of virtue with the health of the soul.[24] Instead, he finds that mental health is unrelated to human good and that "specification of the human good is not necessary for adequately characterizing mental health and perfection in mental health."[25] Still, he examines the "perfection of mental health" that is so often sought, concluding that there is no clear connection between *health* as such and a healthy personality/psyche.[26] Throughout, Pestana stresses that just because a capacity is there, and is even considered "perfect," it does not mean that the individual will practice virtuous habits, or indeed be involved in any type of activity. However, practices of virtue and vice can indicate for Pestana a more or less "perfect" mental health.[27] Overall, Pestana seeks to recognize and perhaps begin a rejuvenation of philosophy within the mental health and medical fields—a conversation within which this book and theological bioethics are right at home. He believes that recognition of the conflation of virtue and mental health can address the social conflation of wickedness with negative mental health and help foster a true understanding of both radical evil and supreme good.[28]

---

[24] Pestana, *Moral Virtue*, 4. Theologians, particularly those rooted in disability studies, adamantly hold to *everyone's* createdness in the image of God—not just some, or those who we may view as "normal"—a decidedly anti-Platonic stance based in Scripture rather than our philosophical inheritance that often influences what we know to be "true."

[25] Pestana, *Moral Virtue*, 7. Here Pestana is attempting to account for the "good" of those with permanent limited mental functioning: in that their goodness is not reliant on having "perfect" mental health. He is also attempting to avoid wading into the related debate about what makes up the human good in general. Instead, he focuses quite narrowly on mental health.

[26] Pestana, *Moral Virtue*, 93.

[27] Pestana, *Moral Virtue*, 99. He does follow the Aristotelian line of development of habits—that such mental "perfection" must be exercised to be realized (cannot be simply given or inborn).

[28] Pestana, *Moral Virtue*, 107. While I am only dealing with one slim academic volume for the purposes of streamlining my argument, the discussion

While I agree with his assessment of virtue, specifically that it is not inherently tied to a conception of health or perfect mental functioning, Pestana has a tendency to isolate mental health as something that can be evaluated "in itself," which must be corrected to properly address trauma. Despite his reference to social power and the impact of constructions of health, trauma is a personal and social phenomenon that requires precise attention to its embeddedness. To attempt to separate mental health as an isolated and isolatable phenomenon does not provide the robust assessment of its nature that is required for a complete vision of how our bodies and brains are formed.

Nonetheless, Pestana's ability to disentangle virtue from health and illuminate the direct impacts our conceptions of personhood have on our construction of social systems (both of punishment and service) are central to the consideration of trauma and memory. We are not "good" because we are labeled healthy, neither are we "wicked" when we are ill. Too often, the sense of moral shame that goes hand in hand with assessments of mental health disorders prevents individuals from seeking treatment and can encourage the use of intense pharmaceutical or surgical modification to return to what society has deemed "normal," despite the true desire of the person. Understanding the basic morality discourse within our approach to our health and our fundamental personhood is the first step toward a more robust understanding of the experience of trauma and its theological contours.

The Cultural Production of Health

As explored in chapter 1, the experience of trauma is complex, and the resulting interpretations of the harm caused are equally fraught. With Pestana, we see that our assumptions about those

---

of definitions of health (and related considerations of definitions of illness, disease, dis/ability, etc.) constitute entire fields of academic, practical, and medical inquiry.

who suffer from less-than-perfect mental functioning (including ourselves) are not isolated to an assessment of individual well-being. Instead, categories of health carry within them social, cultural, moral, philosophical, and theological burdens. This way of reading the labels relevant to trauma (PTSD, abnormal, ill, etc.) are part of what womanist theologian Emilie Townes calls the "cultural production" of health.[29] While intrapsychic processes are very real and form mental health disorders, they are informed by cultural experience.[30] To put it simply, trauma and its diagnosis do not exist in a vacuum. Here, Townes's work better orients the experience of trauma and treatment within a social understanding of suffering, which is critical to the development of a theologically based enfleshed counter-memory.

Townes's project is concerned with uncovering and naming the structural operations—structural sins in theological terminology—that create suffering in the world. She sees clear ties between stereotypes created to support power structures (e.g., Mammy, Aunt Jemima) and the poor health and social outcomes present in Black Americans today. Such deeply embedded cultural images ignore the intersectional nature of identity and, instead, render "the marvelously complex interlocking character of our humanity" into one-dimensional, simplistic representations that serve the powerful for monetary gain and social control.[31] Townes argues

---

[29] Townes, *Breaking the Fine Rain,* 49; and Townes, *Womanist Ethics,* passim. Her larger project in both works is an ethic based in theodicy and the explication of "evil" itself as a cultural production, with ramifications for our social and individual lives, such as our experience, or lack, of healthcare.

[30] Jessica Henderson Daniel, *The Courage to Hear: African American Women's Memories of Racial Trauma* (New York: Guilford Press, 2000), as cited by Phillis I. Sheppard, "Mourning the Loss of Cultural Selfobjects: Black Embodiment and Religious Experience after Trauma," *Practical Theology* 1, no. 2 (2008): 236. See also Townes, *Womanist Ethics,* 112.

[31] Townes, *Womanist Ethics,* 164. M. Shawn Copeland also addresses this in *Enfleshing Freedom: Body, Race, and Being,* 2nd ed. (Minneapolis: Fortress Press, 2023), 97, and elsewhere.

that social and political power conspire to keep certain persons (in her work, Black people) sick and subjugated, *and* aims for those persons to internalize the blame for any struggle they encounter. This is an aspect of what Townes calls the "fantastic hegemonic imagination," or how our imaginaries emerge from conceptual life into reality, specifically our structures of domination and subordination.[32] In approaching trauma, we must recognize that the context of suffering is always social and, as such, is defined by racism, sexism, and other oppressive structures. These "isms" are so internalized that "getting into the interior worlds of those who endure structural evil" as well as personal evil is an essential part of the healing, and theological, task.[33]

Just as our imaginaries emerge into reality when considering someone's apparent race or gender, they also deeply inform how we witness, or ignore, mental health and trauma. Beyond the default US "bootstraps" mentality, wherein one should deal with any problems resolutely alone through individual fortitude, mental health/illness presents in and among a person's complex life situation. As reflected by trauma and disease burden statistics in the United States, traumatized persons are also likely to be poor, racially minoritized, and embody other marginalized positions.[34] When receiving these "difficult" cases, as one physician puts it, persons will present with "'sociomas'—social problems that range from not having a ride to the doctor's office, to drug addiction, to homelessness, to despair.... [This] sets up a deadly dynamic that makes it difficult to sort through the massive issues."[35] Rather than wade through such complexity, the dominant Western healthcare model is set up such that, when presented, "Ill health is seen as

---

[32] Townes draws on the work of Michel Foucault and Antonio Gramsci in her explication of this term.
[33] Townes, *Womanist Ethics*, 12.
[34] Townes, *Breaking the Fine Rain*, 59.
[35] Townes, *Breaking the Fine Rain*, 125.

the mechanical failure of some part ... [and] the task of medicine, then, is to repair the damage."[36]

While treatments, when accessible, may attend to some of the "broken" systems in an individual's body, brain, or both, Townes reminds us that what is still missing "is the realization that health is a cultural production and that an extreme concentration on a curative model that 'explains' the causes of diseases and explores the different ways in which we experience illness is too limited."[37] She instead encourages a shift of attention that "pushes us not only to focus on the biomedical model, but to consider the ways in which *how* we are influences, if not forms, our healthiness or lack of it."[38] The cultural production at play within considerations of trauma forms both how we view the suffering *and* what constitutes healing. Here, a theologically rooted approach to trauma and memory situates the individual person within constellations of relationships that influence and are influenced by the person's well-being. As such, we must expand beyond an individual right to treatment and consider communal responsibilities for harm and healing, specifically by determining the shape of traumatic memory grounded in Christianity's claims about the human person and God's promise of liberation.

---

[36] Townes, *Breaking the Fine Rain*, 111.

[37] Townes, *Breaking the Fine Rain*, 112. In this volume, Townes also explores the lack of research, particularly clinical trials, that include racial/ethnic minorities. This is an increasing area of concern in medical research generally, as clinical trials seek captive audiences, many of whom are undergraduates on college campuses and therefore majority-white, middle- to upper-class, and relatively young. While all responsible research names their target population, size, and its limits within the published study, news reporting of "breakthroughs" rarely do the same. This is of particular importance when certain therapies are marketed to populations upon which they have never been thoroughly tested.

[38] Townes, *Breaking the Fine Rain*, 112.

Black Women and Mental Health

A womanist theological anthropology is necessary to get to such an enfleshed counter-memory. I start with the multivalent experiences of Black women and mental health in the United States to build our understanding of this way of thinking about the human person. While brief, this practical reflection illuminates how some womanist authors have expressed and interpreted mental health issues, including trauma, and how they have constructively responded. I draw specifically on authors who interact directly with womanist thought and Christian theology, with the goal that this sampling will offer further nuance and context to the following theological and practical responses to trauma and Christian memory. Offering such particular reflections at this stage also enlivens the above considerations of the morality and cultural production of health, grounding our exploration of a womanist theological anthropology with real people. This approach takes one of the central methods of womanism seriously: a direct and purposeful attention to the real lives of Black women as the central subject that must inform our theological reflection.[39]

Monica Coleman's autobiography, *Bipolar Faith*, outlines her struggles with traumatic experience and bipolar disorder while simultaneously pursuing a career in theology and ministry. She powerfully recounts the ways in which the various churches, faith leaders, and seminary professors responded to her, often falling very short of a compassionate response to her experiences. While Coleman does not advocate for a "church-only" response

---

[39] This is in keeping with the ethical method of doing theology "from the margins," as now-classic liberation theology suggests—without primary attention to historically marginalized groups as central to thinking about God, the task of gospel action in the mode of Jesus goes unfulfilled. I reiterate: This is *not* to function as objectification, but engagement with the complex subjectivity and theological engagement of a robust vein of thought and experience central to trauma theology that often goes unrecognized in those conversations.

to trauma survivors, she does desire to hold religious institutions accountable for the construction of larger frameworks of meaning. Within these constructions of meaning, theology potentially holds and can help heal great harms, rather than rest in common platitudes ("You just need more Jesus"—the theological conclusion one pastor offered) or even perpetuate outright harm (e.g., the promotion of known domestic violence perpetrators in her church leadership).[40] Coleman agrees with Townes that contextualization of experience is key and that our health outcomes, particularly those tied to trauma, are bigger than our individual lives. For Coleman, "Understanding rape better didn't keep me from hurting . . . [but] in many ways the knowledge gave me strength to heal."[41] This contextualization is academic and deeply personal. At first, she "didn't understand that rape unravels everyone's life. It ripped holes in the fabric of my being, but it also frayed the material of which Mama and Daddy were made. Rape leaves many victims in its path."[42] The traumatic experience of one person is social; embedded in larger systems in its genesis and can be the undoing of families and communities in its aftermath.

Coleman's life also attests to the complexities of the lives of many trauma survivors. She is at once a person with depression (later determined to be bipolar disorder), a survivor of childhood domestic violence, a rape victim, and the latest heir to a familial lineage of suicide, social oppression, and economic struggle. This suffering demands a response that includes and addresses the particularity of a person as well as the exposure and healing, to

---

[40] Monica Coleman, *Bipolar Faith: A Black Woman's Journey with Depression and Faith* (Minneapolis: Fortress Press, 2016). She offers this example in her book, to which I would add harboring and hiding sexual predators in the Catholic Church. See *Theology in a Post-traumatic Church*, ed. John N. Sheveland (Maryknoll, NY: Orbis Books, 2023).

[41] Coleman, *Bipolar Faith,* 167.

[42] Coleman, *Bipolar Faith,* 174.

whatever extent possible, of the historical, and even universal, oppressions that surround one life.

To address such complexity, womanist theologian and psychologist Phillis I. Sheppard offers the response of community: there exists "the need to enter the fire together, as did Daniel *and his companions,* and not be burned ... [to] both recognize the reality of the outer world and the ways in which the inner world can become distorted, and help individuals and groups to come to recognize which domain (outer or inner) is active in relation to others."[43] Such distortions are not only the result of individual mental health or personality. They are deeply informed by our cultural imaginaries and resulting social structures. Wading through this process is not limited to persons in posttrauma settings. Sheppard argues that such intentional, communal psychological work is crucial to the healthy self-development and self-understanding of all persons, particularly Black women. We are not isolated brains, but deeply embedded, fully embodied persons who seek connection and security. A full response to this reality includes the practical and formational work of communities and groups that, while holding particularity, reach beyond individual experience.

Sheppard recognizes that this re/building of self, particularly after trauma, is doubly (if not further) bound for people of color and acutely so for Black women. Black women who seek treatment after a traumatic experience must overcome not only the traumatic experience but also such suffering within the context of social oppression. The concept of "mirroring" is used in psychology to explain how humans learn behaviors and cultural expectations: what we see is what we repeat, and what we see in the "gazer's" eye is what we internalize. For Black women in the United States, what is reflected back from society writ large is the identity of distinct "Other," a sexualized and distorted version of self. When

---

[43] Sheppard, "Mourning the Loss of Cultural Selfobjects," 242.

understood in tandem with racialized social structures, this othered self is, at times, an inescapable identity.[44] Sheppard argues that it is necessary to disentangle these issues in Black women's development and, if needed, mental health treatment. Yet she also recognizes that the image reflected to Black women via society is not solely an image, but that "abuse of Black women's bodies . . . reaches far beyond representation" into lived experience of ongoing exploitation.[45] Again, our imaginaries become all too concrete.

Just because this example of mirroring is negative does not inevitably mean that we ought to discount its ongoing utility overall, as "cultural selfobjects [i.e., examples of 'ourselves' in broader culture] can serve the mirroring, idealization, and kinship needs of groups, providing a sense of self continuity—or they can fail to serve them."[46] For Sheppard, this tension leads to a theological response that is inherently communal, and is imbued with a power that may have the potential to overcome negative societal mirroring. In this sense, "Theologically, we are speaking of (1) being *in* and recognized by a community that affirms our relationship to the *imago dei;* and (2) being in relationship to a community that is deeply related to the Idealized One."[47] The relational and practical center of a womanist theological anthropology is revealed within these communities, cultivating the context where God's promise of flourishing, not mere survival, can be realized. This anthropology does not require perfect foreknowledge or a perfect goal. Instead, it expects a commitment to relationship and process.

---

[44] Sheppard, "Mourning the Loss of Cultural Selfobjects," 247, drawing on Patricia Hill Collins.

[45] Sheppard, "Mourning the Loss of Cultural Selfobjects," 248. For Sheppard, "the loss of culture as a site for the gratification of selfobject needs is central to making a link between the individual and the social." See also the work of Elisabeth Schüssler Fiorenza.

[46] Sheppard, "Mourning the Loss of Cultural Selfobjects," 251.

[47] Sheppard, "Mourning the Loss of Cultural Selfobjects," 251.

Both Sheppard and Coleman explore how the cycles of death and rebirth that constitute traumatic experience can only be held *with*, not apart from, community. Coleman's recovery is ongoing and depends upon those to whom she holds herself accountable—if for nothing else but showing up. Her community gave her a new sense of movement in such accountability, though she describes at times feeling like the Israelites in the desert who asked Moses to return to what they knew, even though it was the condition of slavery. Black people fleeing southern slavery said the same thing to Harriet Tubman, but she "cocked a rifle on her shoulder and turned to those slaves with a new threat—we're moving forward no matter what.... Like a running slave, I know that with freedom there is no going back. I must keep moving."[48] As is commonly said in El Salvador among Christian base communities: *Hacemos camino,* "We make the way by walking."

This brief exploration into the formation and experience of health, mental health, and potential healing by Black women is foundational to any discussion of trauma and theology. Firstly, Townes, Sheppard, and Coleman demonstrate that our health is value-laden, social, historical, inextricably embodied, and essentially related to Jesus Christ. Second, they illuminate how the person is at once defined by and exceeds social determinants, exposing a fundamental theo-ethical orientation. Finally, womanist theology, speaking with health provision, emphasizes the incarnational nature of reality, and how the healing of personal and social trauma must be tied to an embodied vision of the divine. As Eboni Marshall Turman outlines,

> Black women are not consubstantial with Christ only because of suffering. It is rather the entirety of the logic of incarnation, that is, the logic of enfleshment that identifies a before (*en sarki*) and an after (*Parousia*) to suffering

---

[48] Coleman, *Bipolar Faith*, 339.

(*kata sarka*) that, taken together, tell the whole story of God's freedom and justice that is continuous with black women's lives—her loves, her joys, and her troubles.[49]

If the person, understood in this way, suffers trauma, what is an appropriate theological, as well as ethical, response?

Connecting "Flesh" and Theology: A Womanist Theological Anthropology for Trauma Memory

A womanist theological anthropology is crucial to answering this question because it considers the person in a way that does not gloss over suffering but looks directly at it. First, womanist theological anthropology sits within the traumatic past, both of direct experience and inherited cultural harm, and calls for a healing *without* forgetting. Forgetting, for these scholars, does a disservice to the trauma experience itself and the necessary call for justice that suffering elicits.[50] This call for memory is not rooted in a self- or other-punishing vision, but rather is meant to inspire a communal accounting for and concrete response to harm. Second, womanist theological anthropology takes seriously the preferential option for the poor, calling all to solidarity in a vision of God that supports those pushed to the many margins

---

[49] Eboni Marshall Turman, "'Today a Black [Wo]Man Was Lynched': A Womanist Christology of Sandra Bland," in *Enfleshing Theology: Embodiment, Discipleship, and Politics in the Work of M. Shawn Copeland*, ed. Robert J. Rivera and Michele Saracino (Lanham, MD: Lexington Books / Fortress Academic, 2018), 29.

[50] This orientation presents a direct connection to J. B. Metz's concept of the salvation of the dead in his theology, which is delineated in chapter 4. This is essential when discussing direct perpetrators of trauma as well as the somewhat nebulous but powerful social mores, such as white supremacy, that help enact suffering, and the role of those outside the direct trauma as responsible and response-able actors.

of our world. Third, it holds as central the person and life of Jesus Christ, whose "good news" is that we are much more than what human structures may tell us. Finally, womanist scholars give primacy to the interplay of theology and history, society and God, transcendence and materiality, which is an inextricable dynamic in any Christian ethic attempting to deal with trauma and memory. A womanist anthropology reveals a more holistic understanding of incarnate personhood, and what such createdness means for our responsibility in the face of suffering.

The primary component of a womanist theological anthropology asserts that *Black* embodiment must be a central theological and ethical category.[51] As Copeland points out,

> Our search for the humanum is oriented by the radical demands of the incarnation of God … [and] taking poor women of color as the subject" of theological anthropology is a crucial way forward to resist former theological constructions that ignored or explicitly harmed non-white, non-European, non-male persons.[52]

---

[51] Sheppard, "Mourning the Loss of Cultural Selfobjects," 255. See also M. Shawn Copeland, "The New Anthropological Subject at the Heart of the Mystical Body of Christ," *CTSA Proceedings* 53 (1998): 25–47; and M. Shawn Copeland, *Enfleshing Freedom: Body, Race, and Being* (Minneapolis: Fortress Press, 2010), 22. In this chapter I use Copeland's work as my central interlocutor, as a fellow Catholic. I would be remiss if I did not identify that much of my thinking is also influenced by Katie Geneva Cannon, *Katie's Canon: Womanism and the Soul of the Black Community*, 25th ann. ed. (Minneapolis: Fortress Press, 2021).

[52] And in so doing harmed the totality of humanity, circumscribing what is considered good, or even possible, for all existence. Copeland, "The New Anthropological Subject," 34. For example, philosopher Slavoj Žižek framed the media coverage of post-Katrina New Orleans as the subject (poor African Americans) that is supposed to loot and rape. He argues, "More and more, they [poor African Americans] live in another world, in a blank zone that offers itself as a screen for the projection of our fears, anxieties and secret desires." See Slavoj Žižek, "The Subject Supposed to Loot and Rape: Reality and Fantasy in New

What we take for granted as our norm for judgment, particularly what form we consider as the baseline for "full" humanity, determines not only how we speak but also social and governmental institutions, foreign aid, public policy, family units, healthcare provision, psychological support, and on and on. Further, if the norm for theological anthropology is a white, autonomous male (in the tradition of the Enlightenment), the potential for a full understanding of the pluralistic ways of being, healing, and flourishing in the world is, at best, circumscribed.

Not only are "other" lived ways of being limited, they are actually made invisible and even inhuman: "We build borders around our anthropology so that our functional theological anthropology reflexively denotes some people as human, but not others."[53] Sheppard argues that such personal and group "invisibility" must be countered via theological anthropology.[54] Centrally, this is not a reobjectifying or tokenizing task. It is not simply adding on another body to the list of considerations. Womanist anthropology is rooted in *the subject being seen*—an intimate as well as harrowing undertaking. As Marshall Turman outlines the task via Copeland, the construction of womanist anthropology

> reveals an important distinction between the act of *looking at* and the task of *looking for*. In short, [Copeland's] theological anthropology turns from the prevailing posture of *looking at* that is driven by racist-patriarchal imagination,

---

Orleans," *In These Times,* last modified October 20, 2005, https://inthesetimes.com/article/the-subject-supposed-to-loot-and-rape.

[53] Copeland quoting Michele Saracino, "An Interview with M. Shawn Copeland," in *Enfleshing Theology: Embodiment, Discipleship, and Politics in the Work of M. Shawn Copeland,* ed. Robert J. Rivera and Michele Saracino (Lanham, MD: Lexington Books / Fortress Academic, 2018), xxxvii.

[54] "Whether acknowledged or not, theological anthropology undergirds pastoral psychology's theories of health, healing, and transformation; being fully visible and fully seen are indispensable aspects of pastoral psychotherapy." Sheppard, "Culture, Ethnicity, and Race," 46.

to a counter-*attitude ferme* [standing on one leg without wavering in the face of injustice, from ballet] of *looking for* that is compelled by the realities of black women's bodies and blood.... This is linked in an agential looking for oneself that resonates with Copeland's "inscape"; that is, her argument for the nourishing and salvific interiority of enslaved people's lives that defiantly links their bodies with Jesus amid suffering and oppression.[55]

In this position of "counter-*attitude ferme*," womanist anthropology orients itself and encourages a *looking for* suffering persons that is aimed toward justice as well as an internal healing that is essential for any ethic dealing with trauma.

In the twentieth century, womanists emphasized *looking for* the lived experience of the first African (forced) converts to Christianity and demonstrated their strength and lived faith under the control of white power. Within the means of expression available, enslaved women found ways to express their faith in song and sass, as Copeland puts it, even while their lives remained in real bodily danger. Copeland takes seriously the physical body at the center of the Christian faith and what the expressions of Black Americans can reveal about the truth of its tenets. In considering the marked body of Jesus—a wounded, tortured, and death-bound subject who is fully human as well as fully divine—Copeland experiences echoes of enslavement and wonders how freedom can be found. Freedom, for Copeland, arises from an "incarnate spirit refusing to be bound."[56] Jesus, in suffering and rising, embodies the spirit of African Americans: particularly "subjugated in empire" and yet simultaneously beautiful, loved,

---

[55] Turman, "'Today a Black [Wo]Man Was Lynched'," 20, 23. This is in the spirit of Howard Thurman, *Jesus and the Disinherited* (1949; Boston: Beacon Press, 1996).

[56] Copeland, *Enfleshing Freedom*, 46.

and fully created in God's image.[57] Thus, theology is called to take seriously the markings of the world. Indeed, "The flesh of the church is the flesh of Christ in every age ... marked (as was his flesh) by race, sex, gender, sexuality and culture," as well as by harmful experiences such as trauma.[58]

The extreme "marking" of slavery did not condemn these persons to exclusion from the people of God. Rather, these persons expressed knowledge of the embrace of the God of Israel, who asserts the liberation of all things. While womanists caution against saying that suffering is redemptive, that the pain *itself* is liberative, Copeland argues that suffering and pain are not without meaning, nor is it right that the experience of suffering is forgotten, particularly in situations where larger social structures are to blame for individual or group suffering.

Marshall Turman takes this attention to suffering within womanist anthropology directly into the body of Christ. Where some position their inquiry in the social realm and its influences on the religion of Christianity, Turman is concerned with Black women's *bodies* and their interplay with the literal body of Jesus

---

[57] Copeland, *Enfleshing Freedom*, 57. This is a reality most perfectly expressed for Copeland in African American enslaved women's lives who were doubly or triply bound by their gender, race, and slave status.

[58] Copeland, *Enfleshing Freedom*, 81. Further, for Copeland, it is imperative that theology recognize its own markings of the same sociopolitical structures, as well as its power to create yet further wounds. Such theological wounds are created when theology remains ignorant of the bodies that constitute its churches, and how such bodies, as well as theology itself, are given over to modern "empires." Rather than resist the domination of the unjust, as Jesus did, modern theology too often ignores the very real physical and psychic wounds caused by its usurpation into narratives of domination and subjugation. For further discussion of empire and its interpretation in Jesus Christ, see Copeland, *Enfleshing Freedom*, 55–84. Further efforts toward embodied theology are present in feminist discourses such as E. Schüssler Fiorenza, "Struggle Is a Name for Hope: A Critical Feminist Interpretation for Liberation," *Pacifica* 10 (1997): 224–248.

Christ. She argues that the complex interplay between identity, institutions, and "I(i)ncarnation bodies" outlined above shapes our moral values, moral responses, and moral agency.[59] As a dancer, Turman uses embodied metaphor and relies on practical choreographic engagement to explore concrete bodies not as sites upon which we theologize but rather as sites that create and express theology directly. Here, a tie to trauma studies is clear, where she "formulates a theory of I(i)ncarnation that posits black women's *bodies* as the primary source for constructive womanist ethics … the criterion that necessitates consideration of black women's embodiedness as a significant method for not only articulating and understanding, but most importantly, for *doing* womanist ethics."[60] Again, this is not some light engagement of one population with a spirituality of Christianity, an "other" to add to the list of globally diverse Christians, but rather a deep and required reckoning with Christ:

> In other words, in accordance with Chalcedon's copulation of divergent perspectives concerning the "who" of God, the doctrine of the incarnation as womanist mediating ethic employs the coming-togetherness, that is the paradoxical unity of the "broken" body of Christ to demonstrate how apparently broken bodies, which are normatively signified as godless boundaries and are thus subjected to oppression, separation, marginalization, brutality, and death, are in fact consubstantial with that *bridge over troubled water* whose distinctive identity allows for the possibility of wholeness to be realized even where socio-historical realities suggest otherwise.[61]

---

[59] Eboni Marshall Turman, *Toward a Womanist Ethic of Incarnation: Black Bodies, the Black Church, and the Council of Chalcedon* (New York: Palgrave Macmillan, 2013), 5.
[60] Turman, *Toward a Womanist Ethic of Incarnation*, 14.
[61] Turman, *Toward a Womanist Ethic of Incarnation*, 165.

While Turman's project is decidedly focused on the Black church, and particularly divisions between men and women therein, her incarnational insights regarding womanist methodology in ethics ring true in the consideration of trauma and theology. It is not a passing problem, or an ancillary experience with which trauma attempts to reckon. It is, rather, a foundational consideration of the embodied reality of God, centrally expressed and alive within the body of Christ.[62]

Womanist authors demonstrate, through a focus on embodiment, that "flesh" is critical to the examination of trauma and theology—and to the ethical tasks that result, particularly those of memory.[63] Vitally, this definition of flesh is not limited to our individual iterations but is inherently social and shared. This conceptualization of flesh is drawn directly from a Christian theological orientation that is incarnationally focused. As Copeland explains,

> Humanity in all its diversity and difference is a reflection of the community of the Three Divine Persons. Their divine love constitutes the ground of our realization of the Mystical Body of Christ and our unity in it. In this Body,

---

[62] This is not to center or require pain, but rather to deal honestly with it. For a further exploration of the nature of Christianity and its intertwining with traumatic origins, see Rita Nakashima Brock and Rebecca Ann Parker, *Proverbs of Ashes: Violence, Redemptive Suffering, and the Search for What Saves Us* (Boston: Beacon, 2001).

[63] As Willie James Jennings notes, "There are, of course, great risks in holding up marginality in this way, most notably, presenting marginality as a justification for suffering or as a precursor to the glorification of subjugation or worst yet using marginality as support for forms of patriarchy. *Yet marginality constitutes more than a condition but a way of thinking that moves against its own condition.*" "To Be a Thinking Margin: Reframing Christian Intellectual Life," in *Enfleshing Theology: Embodiment, Discipleship, and Politics in the Work of M. Shawn Copeland*, ed. Robert J. Rivera and Michele Saracino (Lanham, MD: Lexington Books / Fortress Academic, 2018), 154.

each member has her and his own distinct existence; each remains herself and himself. But, even as we remain ourselves, we do not remain on our own. In the Mystical Body, we belong to God and we are for one another.[64]

The recognition of our incarnational reality determines a distinct way of being with each other. Practices as well as attitudes that illuminate the truth of social institutions, norms, and habits define our suffering as well as our healing. Through womanist theological anthropology, a vision of complex persons emerges—a vision in which whole selves are in struggle, in dynamic process rather than static hegemony.[65] As such, marked bodies are not meant to be modified or erased, but rather to be seen fully and valued for their incarnational link to Jesus Christ—not bound to eternal suffering, but destined to rise.

This recognition is valuable in its own right, but womanist theological anthropology clearly illuminates the Christian ethical task of solidarity demanded by this definition of the person. Solidarity, however, is not disembodied "good deeds," but requires mature intimacy, for "inasmuch as solidarity involves an attitude or disposition, it entails the recognition of the humanity of the 'other' as humanity, along with regard for the 'other' in her (and his) own 'otherness.'"[66] To stand with suffering others is not to subsume them into your own narrative, creating a warped version of love

---

[64] Copeland, "The New Anthropological Subject," 46.

[65] Townes, *Womanist Ethics*, 48. This also reinforces Metz's critique of the loss of subject by the deconstructionists, and the ground ceded by theology to secularism. Instead, Metz argues that Christianity must reassert its primacy in the creation of the subject in relationship with God, countering the power of society and reorienting ourselves in eschatological time. *Faith in History and Society*, 47. Metz's contribution to a further understanding of the theological anthropology presented by womanists follows in chapter 4.

[66] Copeland, "The New Anthropological Subject," 37. Not to love the other into oblivion, as Kelly Brown Douglas cautions in *The Black Christ* (Maryknoll, NY: Orbis Books, 1994), 49.

wherein people are only tools for your own self-understanding. Rather, flowing from a womanist understanding of foundational relationality and simultaneous uniqueness, solidarity requires the formation of responsible relationships rooted in the dignity of difference.[67] *Looking for* the poor, therefore, is "not to sacralize or romanticize them; it is to privilege their social location, their broken bodies, as locus of God's historical presence."[68]

For Copeland, neither identity politics nor one-upmanship reorients her theological anthropology, but a probing of the fundamental obligations that arise from this understanding of the poor, as well as "basic human creatureliness and love."[69] We must "enflesh" often antiseptic understandings of humanity to encounter the truth of incarnate personhood and the ethical implications drawn from those who "bear and face the burden of history (*her stories*) so that 'every day [is] a situation … a choice, of how to stand in relation to oppression, whether to live as subsumed by [it] or to live as active resistance towards liberation.'"[70]

Poor women of color do not choose to live as direct, felt inheritors of histories of oppression and resistance. Indeed, anyone—too often rich and white people—considering themselves outside of history is a false perception of privilege. No one is outside of history. Womanist theological anthropology

---

[67] Here I'm drawing on the work of Rabbi Jonathan Sacks.

[68] Roberto Goizueta, "'A Body of Broken Bones': Shawn Copeland and the New Anthropological Subject," in *Enfleshing Theology: Embodiment, Discipleship, and Politics in the Work of M. Shawn Copeland,* ed. Robert J. Rivera and Michele Saracino (Lanham, MD: Lexington Books / Fortress Academic, 2018), 10.

[69] Copeland, "The New Anthropological Subject," 37.

[70] Copeland, "The New Anthropological Subject," 39, citing Lewis Gordon, *Fanon and the Crisis of the European Man.* There is a very pertinent edge to this conversation that is emerging from decolonial theory. While we cannot engage the field fully here, I explore implications for trauma in Stephanie C. Edwards, "Imperialism of the Mind: Decolonial Theological Approaches to Traumatic Memory," *Political Theology* 24, no. 6 (2023): 544–569.

reveals that we must understand ourselves within history as well as through the Christian story that transcends it. To reach out from this notion of the human person toward relationship is the definition of "solidarity [that] begins in *anamnesis*—the intentional remembering of the dead exploited, despised poor peoples of color, the victims of history."[71] For Copeland and many other womanists, it is embodied memory that orients any understanding of suffering as well as any promise of hope. As Roberto Goizueta reflects on the call to discipleship based on Copeland's life and work,

> We are called to [solidarity], not just in order to imitate Christ as some extrinsic ethical role model, but in order to actually live in Christ. To put it bluntly, solidarity with the poor is not a consequence of genuine Christian faith so much as its precondition. Without a preferential option for the poor we cannot claim to know or worship Christ who has very clearly revealed where he will be found and, thus, where we must go to worship him.[72]

Humans are directly related to the Incarnate Divine, and through this are created in direct relation to the other. The Incarnate Divine calls us all toward enfleshed encounter that is simultaneously grounded in history and reaches beyond it. When persons are seen in a womanist framework, a drive to forget even the most painful experiences is risky. When memories are erased, ignored, or manipulated, experiences cannot be contextualized in history or in the Christian story. We lose the ability to learn from the actions of

---

[71] Copeland, "The New Anthropological Subject," 42. *Anamnesis* is a theological category that can potentially help evaluate trauma and is already used in related work on liturgy by Bruce Morrill, *Anamnesis as Dangerous Memory: Political and Liturgical Theology in Dialogue* (Collegeville, MN: Liturgical Press, 2000). This is also explicitly tied to the theology of Metz presented in chapter 4.

[72] Goizueta, "'A Body of Broken Bones,'" 8.

strength and agency of those most oppressed in history, potentially become unable to hold accountable those ultimately responsible for suffering, and, centrally, ignore the body of Christ present today. While this reading of womanist theological anthropology is by no means a clarion call to "bear one's cross," it is a clear demand that we must learn to hold traumatic memory rightly, as it extends beyond the individual, and even the communal, and into the Divine.

Womanist Practices of Healing: Lament, Self-Definition, and Storytelling

Much like the experiences of Coleman and Sheppard outlined above, the way into a lived womanist theological anthropology is decidedly practical. To struggle authentically with the inherent sociality of trauma, as well as of ourselves as created beings, Sheppard argues that "defilement requires *reconciliation* with God's original proclamation [in creating the *imago Dei* . . . God said *and it was good*] *and embodied practices* that repeatedly announce the goodness of all creation."[73] Rather than intentionally covering over trauma, we must simultaneously name both perpetual goodness *and* "sin as that which individually and socially blocks the way of transformation of the individual and society."[74] Here, the psychological and theological converge in womanist perspectives, as "naming" or testimonial practices that contain stories of survival as well as harm are fundamental healing tools in both fields.

There are three central practices of naming within a vision of the sociality of *imago Dei* that can support the development of an enfleshed counter-memory rooted in womanist thought: (1) lament as public prophecy, (2) personal narrative and the power

---

[73] Sheppard, "Mourning the Loss of Cultural Selfobjects," 237, brackets from 241.

[74] Sheppard, "Mourning the Loss of Cultural Selfobjects," 237.

of self-definition, and (3) intergenerational storytelling. Such practices are an example of what Copeland calls performative theo-poetics: "These movements imagine (and form) a new public space for bodily (fleshly) and embodied (enfleshed) holy connecting and touching, speaking and listening, conversation and interchange—for a range of necessary and desired healing and creative human actions."[75] Introducing these practices here gives "flesh" to the above discussions of more theoretical womanist theological insights, and suggests the initial contours of a Christian ethical response to trauma with a memory that seeks justice.

Lament as Public Prophecy

> laments mark the *beginning* of the healing process
> and people need and want to be healed
> if we learn anything from Joel
> it is to know that the healing of brokenness and injustice
> the healing of spiritual doubts and fears
> begins with an unrestrained lament[76]

Raw emotion is often an uncomfortable and circumscribed entity within mainline, white, Western Christianity. The range of practices of lament, of crying out to God, are rarely practiced at all, let alone communally.[77] For one of Sheppard's patients, whom she calls Rosie, a central experience missing from her interpretation of her life's traumas was the space for a shared truth-telling. This is particularly important to Rosie, whose "experiences reveal that the 'structural deficits' were not limited to her individual intrapsychic life—rather, her structural deficits are also communal."[78] Rosie needed to be offered the opportunity to

---

[75] Copeland, *Enfleshing Freedom*, 2nd ed., 105.
[76] Townes, *Breaking the Fine Rain*, 12.
[77] Rambo, *Spirit and Trauma*.
[78] Sheppard, "Mourning the Loss of Cultural Selfobjects," 254.

mourn not only her direct tragedies (childhood rape, prostitution, and violence) but also to mourn the failure of church to provide a space for truth-telling about her experiences and the social nature of her suffering. The fact that the church actually protected and covered up known abusers in Rosie's life (and has done so to a tragic and criminal extent in the Roman Catholic Church) requires a much broader mourning, a lament as well as actions of public prophecy—of truth telling that calls sin to account as harmful not only to the direct victim but to the entire people of God. As Sheppard identifies, "The historical, familial, and personal converge, revealing a cyclical repetition, one aspect of which includes unfinished mourning."[79]

To encounter this unfinished mourning, Townes foregrounds lament as a response to suffering, believing that the power of publicly naming experiences is one of the only paths to undoing, or at least not repeating, harms. As such, "By putting words to their suffering, the community could move to a pain or pains that could be named and then addressed. Lament is, in a word, formful. When done as communal lament, it helps the community see the crisis as bearable and manageable—in the community."[80] Viewed in such a frame, lament is inherently social rather than isolating. Although the individual(s) may feel divorced from the group, and

---

[79] Sheppard, "Mourning the Loss of Cultural Selfobjects," 254. This is also robustly explored in the field of restorative justice practices, where communities come together to recognize the harm inflicted (from the victim directly), and then recontextualize the harm within the entire group, where the perpetrator will be held accountable for reparation by the community, rather than cast out—exiled from the community such as in traditional retributive justice practices in the United States. For more on restorative justice, see Howard Zehr, *The Little Book of Restorative Justice* (Brattleboro, VT: Good Books, 2002); Rupert Ross, *Returning to the Teachings: Exploring Aboriginal Justice* (Toronto: Penguin Canada, 2006); and particularly informative for trauma, see James Ptacek, ed., *Restorative Justice and Violence against Women* (Oxford: Oxford University Press, 2009).

[80] Townes, *Breaking the Fine Rain,* 23.

from God, the opportunity for communal grief can stand in that space. As Coleman says of her healing, until she could "feel God" again, her church stood in the gap.[81] Standing with trauma is also, in itself, a countermeasure to prevailing forces that seek to silence and diminish the traumatized, because "truth-telling is what the evil bred from the fantastic hegemonic imagination does *not* count on."[82] Allowing grief to be heard is part of the prophetic forms of reconciliation demanded by traumatic experience.

One of the many harms wrought by trauma is a deep dislocation, and the power of repetitive ritual can imbue a sense of mooring within tradition, and even existence. Coleman found through her own practices that rituals "helped me integrate the trauma of rape in my life.... They helped me remember that rape is just one of my stories. It's part of who I am. But it's not all of who I am. I have other stories, and Lord willing and the creek don't rise, I will create new ones."[83] Yet to speak of trauma, in ritual or otherwise, often means to speak of something not completely understood or easily expressed. Lament can provide space for such indefinable, ineffable pain. Lament as a practice does not mandate the "facts" of a courtroom or the probing of a therapist. Instead, it calls the sufferer forward as one who remains a part of the *imago Dei* and offers the healing "gaze" of the community.[84] For victims of trauma to be able to see themselves in a new way through the practice of communal lament can provide them with an authentic response of care, rather than the often-forced explanations of suffering. Lament practiced in this way takes seriously what Elaine Scarry calls the collapse of language in the face of pain.[85] This work

---

[81] Coleman, *Bipolar Faith*, 194.
[82] Townes, *Womanist Ethics*, 162.
[83] Coleman, *Bipolar Faith*, 241.
[84] Recall Sheppard's work on mirroring.
[85] Elaine Scarry, *The Body in Pain: The Making and Unmaking of the World* (Oxford: Oxford University Press, 1985).

of lament, and of prophetic protest therein, is central not only to the Christian notion of relationship to other persons but also to our relationship with God: "Without lament, covenant is a practice of denial and pretense that sanctions social control ... loss of lament is also a loss of genuine covenant interaction with God."[86]

Agency and the Power of Self-Definition

While communal practices of naming harm and lament are crucial in the face of trauma, they do not negate or diminish the need for recovering the agential capacities of one who has suffered. Coleman recounts the process of allowing her old self to "die"—even to the extent of holding a burial service for her former self. Whereas Coleman, through the resources of doctors, therapists, friends, church, and community, was able to reconstruct herself "after death," others struggle without resolution of any kind. Yet this does not mean that such individuals are not practicing agency. As Sheppard observes Rosie, she "lived her sense of otherness, her grief, her memory—in the open. Like [her] self-portrait revealing the trauma of her life in bold red colors with her head severed, her life was a shocking and compelling attempt to give voice and meaning."[87] Finding constructive ways to foster individual agency is crucial for trauma healing, even simply seeing the person's resistant actions as related to this good, even if their content is potentially harmful.[88]

---

[86] Townes citing Walter Bruggemann, *Breaking the Fine Rain*, 24. See also Kelly Brown Douglas's account of Rachel weeping for her children in *Stand Your Ground: Black Bodies and the Justice of God* (Maryknoll, NY: Orbis Books, 2015), 228.

[87] Sheppard, "Mourning the Loss of Cultural Selfobjects," 249.

[88] This is critical in the provision of therapy and social support, calling back to the strengths-based perspective. This is not to say, however, that harmful, illegal, or even sinful acts are not to be called out for what they are, but simply to state that, for example, expressing extreme anger may not be in itself a *good* but does indicate the power of the person, who after trauma feels

Sticking with people who are processing trauma is difficult, as maladaptive behaviors are often quite impactful and disruptive. The capacity to hold this process is not, by any means, limited to or even centered in a theological or faith-based community. That said, it is also the responsibility of those communities to stand with its members, in a womanist vision of solidarity.

Coleman recognizes, "With therapists, medication, meaningful studies, a small church community, a pastor who cared, friends who understood, and a name for my condition, God was knitting me. God was knitting me back together."[89] Faith communities should not be the be-all-end-all for trauma, but if a womanist theological anthropology is taken seriously, they cannot look away. Sheppard emphasizes the centrality of community in one's self-definition—that "it is this kinship that counters the sense of foreignness and rejection. It fosters firmness and conviction of identity. The absence of deep kinship leaves one flailing."[90] Ultimately it is not that the community has to offer all the answers to the trauma survivor, but that they "show up" and assist in carrying on together. Continually showing up creates the space for, and encourages participation by, those who may consider their experiences too hard, too ugly, or simply "too much."

---

stripped of any power at all. An opposite interpretation would be to demand "strength" and "resilience" at all times, which is also an unfair burden. See Chanequa Walker-Barnes, *Too Heavy a Yoke: Black Women and the Burden of Strength* (Eugene, OR: Cascade Books, 2014).

[89] Coleman, *Bipolar Faith*, 333. Also, very practically, Coleman kept a "self-affirmations" list in her purse, ultimately to remind herself: "I am more than this," 327–328. Yet it is important to note that such a web of care, particularly of effective mental healthcare, is not the norm for African American women. This is particularly evident in the lack of clinical understanding of the role of spirituality in Black women's lives. See Corliss D. Heath, "A Womanist Approach to Understanding and Assessing the Relationship between Spirituality and Mental Health," *Mental Health, Religion & Culture* 9, no. 2 (2006): 155–170.

[90] Sheppard, "Mourning the Loss of Cultural Selfobjects," 251.

Communal presence and humility in response to trauma, which can perhaps also be seen as standing at the foot of the cross, admits to both the absurdity of suffering and the persevering *imago Dei* of the suffering person. Community can reveal to the individual the ways in which they continue to enact their individual agency, even when the darkness of their experiences threatens to hide such survival techniques from them. The "knitting together" that Coleman recounts occurs when the Mystical Body of Christ holds itself accountable for all its members. Through reclaiming herself, Coleman has the strength to discover that she does not

> want to be reduced to my symptoms and diagnosis. Tied down. I am learning the difference between captivity and rest, between illness and a condition. There's nothing wrong with me. After all this is the only me I've ever known. But sometimes I need to slow down, check to see if I'm okay; look at the emotional heap of yarn in my lap, undo a few rows, and try again. I need to know that the things I drop, the things I can't do the way I want, the hard parts of my life are not failure. They are evidence that I'm human. Not made by machine.[91]

Taking seriously her humanity is seeing the *imago Dei* incarnate within her, rather than a solely scientific accounting of her parts. This orientation of womanist theological anthropology allows for a more honest accounting of not only the harms inflicted but the continued potentiality of a person. It does not relegate traumatic experience to one incident that needs one solution, but rather embraces the intricacies of ongoing suffering and the appropriate ethical responses. As such, a womanist emphasis on agency highlights "the inter-penetration of transcendence in the flesh and

---

[91] Coleman, *Bipolar Faith,* 340.

between persons.... This breadth requires, paradoxically, greater singularity."[92] Fostering agency, and recognizing agency as ongoing within the trauma survivor, reveals ongoing goodness rather than deficiency, and individual value rather than burden.

Trauma and Intergenerational Storytelling

> No one diagnosed my great-grandfather with depression. No one diagnosed Grandma. Who's to know or care about the mental and emotional state of poor sharecroppers from South Carolina? And who can stop to think of a clinical illness when the children need to be fed? What's the difference between depression, war, being black in the Jim Crow South, and plain old hard living? Who would know to alert children or grandchildren to the slippery slope of despair?[93]

Particularly illuminated by reading traumatic experience through a womanist lens is the historical inheritance of suffering. This is not limited to the genetic predispositions to mental health issues such as depression that Coleman identifies, but also to one's expectations of healthcare itself. For Black people in the United States, a central inheritance is what Terri Laws calls "Tuskegee as *sacred rhetoric*."[94] Horrific experimentation on racial minorities, most notably in the forty years of the Tuskegee syphilis experiments, "does not end in these acts; rather its exposure is a gateway to contemporary expectations in clinical care."[95] If clinical care is feared even when

---

[92] Mayra Rivera, "Ethical Desires: Toward a Theology of Relational Transcendence," in *Toward a Theology of Eros*, ed. Virginia Burrus and Catherine Keller (New York: Fordham University Press, 2007), 256.

[93] Coleman, *Bipolar Faith*, xviii.

[94] Terri Laws, "Tuskegee as *Sacred Rhetoric:* Focal Point for the Emergent Field of African American Religion and Health," *Journal of Religion and Health* 57 (2017): 408–419.

[95] Laws, "Tuskegee as *Sacred Rhetoric,*" 413. Tuskegee is "a story of what

accessible, it is even more critical to create alternative, or rather, *expansive*, healing spaces. Intergenerational storytelling is one method that can hold both loss and strength as intrapsychic as well as social, and can include practices of lament and foster agency.[96] With Maurice Halbwachs, Townes argues that the memory that stories communicate is not possible outside of the social fabric. It is already a collective effort, where stories can be used to oppress, or "memory may serve as a corrective to dominant sociocultural and theological portrayals of history."[97] Memories within African American history are those not only of suffering, but of strength and incredible perseverance. Contextualizing traumatic experience within intergenerational knowledge has the power to resist the all-too-common cultural forgetting of suffering as well as offer broader practices of healing rooted in endemic knowledge.[98] We can reclaim individual agency through a communal refusal to forget the past, a steadfastness in understanding the larger frameworks that often enact suffering, and by announcing the positive "motherlode" of womanist inheritance.

Stacey M. Floyd-Thomas defines the components of this inheritance as radical subjectivity, traditional communalism,

---

may happen when a community of the dispossessed meets a behemothic health-care system.... The focus is on observing the disease and cataloging its effects rather than on the flesh and blood, the humanity, of those who are being 'studied.'" Townes, *Breaking the Fine Rain,* 81, 103.

[96] Sheppard, "Mourning the Loss of Cultural Selfobjects," 254, drawing on Martha M. Fowlkes, "The Morality of Loss—The Social Construction of Mourning and Melancholia," *Contemporary Psychoanalysis* 27 (1991): 529–551. See also Floyd-Thomas on the womanist inheritance of "moral tenacity" that produces "a constructive ethic that goes beyond death-dealing stereotypes and the dominant systems that perpetuate them." *Mining the Motherlode,* 169.

[97] Townes, *Womanist Ethics*, 16. For a popular account of such research, see Rebecca Skloot, *The Immortal Life of Henrietta Lacks* (New York: Broadway Books, 2011).

[98] Coleman finds healing for herself through West African dance and Yoruba religion.

redemptive self-love, and critical engagement.[99] These are the tools that must shape any practice claiming to heal trauma and must orient Christianity's overall interpretation of trauma. It is through the modes identified by Floyd-Thomas, particularly embodied in intergenerational storytelling, that Christian ethics can disentangle itself from harmful views of the person and the divine. Womanism does not present God as a "raced, sexed, embodied entity, but rather see[s] in every being's race, gender, sex, and class a voice and presence of God that needs to be heard and seen."[100] Seeing the presence of God in the traumatized person, past and present, Christian intergenerational storytelling asserts that "salvation involves learning from the lives of those who have died" and suffered, yet pushes past determinism and into possibility.[101] The practice of naming trauma in community, particularly across generations, will not mean freedom from all pain and suffering, but its practice can allow for the creation of something new and fruitful beyond the trauma itself.

Kelly Brown Douglas describes the practice of intergenerational storytelling as central to Black faith, and indeed all Christian faith. While it may be true that "Black faith cannot change the

---

[99] Floyd-Thomas, *Mining the Motherlode*, 8–14. Again I recognize that while I myself speak from white experience, I am taking up the suggestion that Black theology must shape the ways that (especially white) theology and religious institutions respond to trauma, particularly that experienced by Black bodies. See Mary C. Doak, "Cornel West's Challenge to the Catholic Evasion of Black Theology," *Theological Studies* 63 (2002): 87–106, and Christine M. Mitchell and David R. Williams, "Black Lives Matter: A Theological Response to Racism's Impact on the Black Body in the United States," *Studia Historiae Ecclesiasticae* 43, no. 1 (2017): 28–45. Or simply, as Floyd-Thomas puts it, "Womanist ethics is not only for black women or scholars but for anyone committed to the task of social justice and self-empowerment." *Mining the Motherlode*, 169.

[100] Floyd-Thomas, *Mining the Motherlode*, xiii.

[101] Monica Coleman, *Making a Way out of No Way* (Minneapolis: Fortress Press, 2008), 32.

world,... it fundamentally gives us the 'courage to be' free in a world that rejects our right to be free."[102] Stories of resistance, of fight, and of faith in the context of oppression can animate the tenacity and sense of relation that are required for the pursuit of justice. Such stories also help us understand suffering, our own and that of others. Yet finding an explanation for suffering does not in itself provide a direct route to "happiness." Instead, seeking a satisfactory theodicy primarily provides *meaning*.[103]

Meaning is the animating force of trauma healing and cultivates what Douglas calls a "moral memory" in the face of trauma. For Douglas, "Moral memory is nothing less than telling the truth about the past and one's relationship to it. Moral memory is not about exonerating ourselves for the past. Rather, it is about taking responsibility for it. To have a moral memory is to recognize the past we carry within us, the past we *want* to carry within us, and the past we need to make right."[104] Meaning is transferred through stories within the framework of moral memory, stories told by those who have "made a way of no way," stories that are a testament to endurance and gritty hope. Stories cultivate our imaginations beyond what exists, helping us all and in particular "black people to stand in the gaps between being free yet not free, without becoming lost."[105] Such contradictions—of being at once powerful

---

[102] Brown Douglas, *Stand Your Ground*, 169. As Douglas quotes James Baldwin, "History is literally *present* in all that we do." *Stand Your Ground*, 205.

[103] Peter Berger, *Sacred Canopy* (New York: Anchor, 1990), as cited by Brown Douglas, *Stand Your Ground*, 186. Paul Farmer also discusses the limits of "explanatory" power; see *Pathologies of Power: Health, Human Rights, and the New War on the Poor* (Oakland: University of California Press, 2004).

[104] Brown Douglas, *Stand Your Ground*, 221, emphasis added. As Coleman says, "Black women can take their past experiences and perpetuate them to assist in our contemporary quest for survival, life and wholeness. We may also decide that there are aspects of the past that we should not imitate. As we repeat the life-giving aspects of our past, we can help save ourselves and our communities." *Making a Way*, 103.

[105] Brown Douglas, *Stand Your Ground*, 164–165. This is explored in

and powerless—are well known to those who suffer trauma. The practice of intergenerational storytelling grounded in a womanist incarnational vision can create pathways for opening up complex spaces, across time, culture, geography, and even language (dance can tell a story!). While storytelling may, on its face, appear "small" or "simple," it is crucial that trauma healing have a place to begin, and begin again, and again. The cycles of violence and repetition of harmful patterns, both internal and external, often bind trauma survivors, and as such must be met with alternative pathways of creating knowledge, of nurturing a new story of hope, over and over, in the face of destruction.

Conclusion

With womanist theological anthropology as its foundation, enfleshed counter-memory resists Christianity's complicity in and capitulation to harmful hegemonic modes. Instead, it turns toward our incarnate, relational selves in all their complexity and messiness. It recognizes our embeddedness within our own flesh as well as how cultural constructions of health and morality act upon our bodies, creating concrete outcomes. As such, enfleshed counter-memory lives within Copeland's process-oriented task of becoming a "thinking margin":

> To be a serious thinking margin means to take up a *critical cognitive praxis*. The phrase *cognitive praxis* denotes the dynamic activity of knowing: questioning patterns and the sometimes jagged-edge of experience (including biological,

---

more detail by Alison P. Gise Johnson and Vanessa Monroe, "Excavating Darkness: Unearthing Memories as Spiritual Practice in the Service of Social Transformation," in *Walking through the Valley: Womanist Explorations in the Spirit of Katie Geneva Cannon*, ed. Emilie M. Townes, Stacey Floyd-Thomas, Alison P. Gise Johnson, and Angela D. Sims (Louisville, KY: Westminster John Knox Press, 2022), 55–66.

psychological, social, religious, cultural, aesthetic); testing and probing possible answers; marshaling evidence and weighing it against cultural codes and signs, against imperious and subjugated truths; risking judgment; taking up the struggle.[106]

Taking up the struggle through womanist practices of lament as public prophecy, personal narrative and the power of self-definition, and intergenerational storytelling, enfleshed counter-memory is neither punishing nor fatalistic. It offers an active, participatory process of co-creating a longer view of the story of the person and the community's broader responsibilities for both trauma and its healing. Decidedly practical through such lived solidarity, womanist theological anthropology also demands an honest reckoning with Christianity's own trauma experience within the body of Christ, and how our incarnational createdness must inform our approach to traumatic memory.

While by no means an easy task, the "everydayness" of the practices of memory encouraged by womanists have the power to overcome evil and empower the marginalized to re/create their own truth; and from that, a fullness of health, hope, and community.[107] In creating enfleshed counter-memory, a womanist theological anthropology asks us all to extend ourselves in love, where "the *cogito ergo sum* is replaced by the *sum amata(us) ergo sum*. The subject is 'new' insofar as she is not only constituted by,

---

[106] M. Shawn Copeland, "A Thinking Margin: The Womanist Movement as Critical Cognitive Praxis," in *Deeper Shades of Purple: Womanism in Religion and Society*, ed. Stacey Floyd-Thomas (New York: NYU Press, 2006), 227.

[107] Townes, *Breaking the Fine Rain*, 3. This is also echoed by Coleman about her healing from trauma: "Revelation did not come to me in thunderbolts. God was just there. In the hot cup of tea. In the women who gathered. In our laughter. In the knitting. God was in my uniform row of stitches. God was also in the dropped stitch that created an imperfection.... Whether I know it or not. Whether it feels like it or not. God is creating ... something beautiful." *Bipolar Faith*, 332.

but indeed reconstituted in love.... 'Being-in-love' is subjectivity transformed.' True autonomy is rooted in being-in-love."[108] In this way of constructing the human person, a dynamic, transcendent love is the basis of ourselves and our actions, always reaching outward, promising that change is possible, even and especially to the despised of history. Fundamental love in this framework is premised on justice through remembering, where the

> Christian exercise of memory feeds us and slakes our thirst, challenges us and transforms our perspectives, practices, and daily lives; memory and love require us to act and live *in* history in imitation of the gracious and healing presence of Jesus of Nazareth, who loved human beings and loved being human to the end and loves still.[109]

---

[108] Goizueta, "'A Body of Broken Bones,'" 7, working with M. Shawn Copeland, *The Subversive Power of Love: The Vision of Henriette Delille*, The Madeleva Lecture Series (Mahwah, NJ: Paulist Press, 2009).

[109] Copeland, "Memory, #BlackLivesMatter, and Theologians," 2. See also Coleman, *Making a Way*, 86.

3

THE "TRAUMATIC IMAGINATION"

Trauma as Theological Hermeneutic

Victims exist in a society that tells us our purpose is to be an inspiring story. But sometimes the best we can do is tell you we're still here, and that should be enough. Denying darkness does not bring anyone closer to the light. When you hear a story about rape, all the graphic and unsettling details, resist the instinct to turn away; instead look closer, because beneath the gore and the police reports is a whole, beautiful person, looking for ways to be in the world again.

* * *

Writing is the way I process the world. When I was given the opportunity to write this book, whatever God is up there said, *You got your dream.* I said, *Actually I was hoping for a lighter topic,* and God was like, *Ha ha! You thought you got to choose.* This was the topic I was given . . . invasion, shame, isolation, cruelty. My job is to observe, feel, document, report. What am I learning and seeing that other people can't see? What doorways does my suffering lead to? People sometimes say, *I can't imagine.*
How do I make them imagine?

—Chanel Miller[1]

---

[1] Chanel Miller, *Know My Name: A Memoir* (New York: Viking, 2019), 312, 315. Chanel's victim impact statement went viral as "Emily Doe" after it

Theology is the practice of speaking the unspeakable. We all know that, at some point, in some way, the practice of "God-talk" remains in error, or is, at best, incomplete. As Marika Rose frames the theological quest: we must admit, even from the outset, our own failure. Indeed, perhaps our goal is not "success," but, as Rose suggests, learning how to "fail better."[2] Rather than defeatist, theological work seen in this way is constituted by life-giving practices of exploration. As one of my mentors used to say, our job is to extend the edges of our own island's shores so that more mystery can lap up against us—not to chart all the waters of mystery. This practice of extension is first held within our imagination: our ability to dream, envision, and project that which is wholly outside our lived experience. Confronting the "mystery" of trauma is possible within our imaginaries, meeting Miller's question of us and uncovering what such study has to say to and with Christian theology in pursuit of an enfleshed counter-memory.

Traditionally, theology and philosophy have pursued imagination and expansion of understanding under the term "hermeneutics." Hermeneutics "explores how we read, understand, and handle texts, especially those written in another time or in a context of life different from our own."[3] Importantly for our purposes, hermeneutics is not a pure objective method; rather we

---

powerfully recounted her experiences and healing after her assault by Stanford swimmer Brock Turner.

[2] Marika Rose, *A Theology of Failure: Žižek against Christian Innocence* (New York: Fordham University Press, 2019), 177. Posited on our inability to ever reach Christ, and particularly in light of the failures of the Western church, "To love the church is to be willing to put it to death, to betray it in the name of what we love in it. It is to choose disruption over homeostasis, to confront the violence that inheres in the ordinary run of things, to refuse the lure of a peace that is not the presence of justice but the absence of disruption to our privileged lives" (178).

[3] Anthony C. Thiselton, *Hermeneutics: An Introduction* (Cambridge: William B. Eerdmans, 2009), 1. This is a great introductory volume on the history and development of hermeneutics that is broadly accessible.

are intimately involved in the process. "Hermeneutics is above all a practice," Hans-Georg Gadamer notes, "the art of understanding.... In it what one has to exercise above all is the ear."[4] Put differently, hermeneutics is the complex web of how we read a text, what we bring to the reading, how we listen to the text itself, questioning if listening to the text in its own right is even possible, and repeating this inquisitive engagement over and over.

With traumatic memory as the site of struggle, and an understanding of womanist theological anthropology as enfleshed and working toward justice, hermeneutics can help to further define how we understand trauma and its role in theology and ethics. While, of course, this chapter is only a brief introduction to the many modes and methods of hermeneutics, it undergirds how I propose we move forward in Christian ethics in relation to trauma. First, I briefly outline hermeneutics and its role in theological reasoning. Second, I delve into recent expansions of trauma theory in theology, seeing where trauma as a tool in our understanding is alive today. Third, I introduce trauma as a hermeneutic that is central to expanding our imaginations within theology. The "traumatic imagination" is a way of reading liberative theologies that has the potential to respond to our current moment, imagining new ways of understanding, speaking, and doing. While I apply this tool in chapter 4 to the work of Johann Baptist Metz, this chapter tackles trauma more broadly as a hermeneutic in theological ethics, where the current usage, application, and understanding of trauma can be applied to better understand the future of active, liberative theologies. More simply, I ask: what does it look like to do theological ethics with trauma as one's hermeneutic?

Before we begin to answer, we must reiterate that trauma as a hermeneutic for theology is not an objective or distanced act of reading. We bring our whole selves to the text, and, importantly, we are not pure, perfect, or inviolable. The pandemic years

---

[4] As cited by Thiselston, *Hermeneutics*, 2.

in particular offered explicit instruction about the gnawing, insatiable grip of pain. We have all experienced how pain, physical and mental, individual and social, holds us all in its talons. We have also learned the privileges of pain—that some of us, myself included, have survived and can survive it because of our affluence, our skin color, our geography. Yet no matter our current embodiment, years of global illness and death, political unrest, ongoing social upheaval, and widespread violence are alive in our physical, spiritual, and psychological selves. We are, collectively, exposed nerves, touching the air, pained even attempting our former, once-solid connections. Writing in the United States in early 2024, a sense of unmooring is pervasive.

How do we read, listen, imagine, comfort, or even be comforted, in this reality? How do we *look closer* in our reading, as Chanel Miller asks us to do? Here, Christian theology has a particular strength, Willie James Jennings reminds us, as we are people who "work in wounds." We direct our eyes toward suffering, recognizing its centrality in the Chistian story and the human experience. Attention is not obsession with pain but honest wrestling with reality, and the gritty, mangled aftermath that can still claim beauty and wholeness. M. Shawn Copeland defines our particular identity as Christians as at once haunted by suffering, yet emboldened by radical transformation, calling us toward justice and the promise of peace. Exploring trauma as a theological hermeneutic means confronting our classic interpretive tools from this particular vantage point, seeing what can be uncovered through the process to reread and reshape our faith and our world.

The Hermeneutical Basis for the Traumatic Imagination

At its most basic, a hermeneutic is a way of understanding, reading, and discovering that can be justified. Often simplified into the hermeneutical circle (text → context → new understanding/context), this process asks that we examine the impact of our preunderstandings and how a new context or a new text changes our interpretation of truth. How we practice our interpretation is a site of much contention. Do you stand within a certain theology? A certain politics? Are you a feminist? Foucaldian? How do *you* define the act of interpretation? Are there universal truths to be uncovered, or are we co-creating truth as we participate in the process?

Much of this complexity is rooted in the emergence of the field of hermeneutics from within biblical interpretation, where scholars were seeking to establish rules about "proper" reading of Scripture, particularly in light of rationalism and naturalism.[5] This methodology merged with later thinkers from theology and philosophy who attempted to uncover theories of "understanding" such as Friedrich Schleiermacher, Martin Heidegger, Paul Ricoeur, and Hans-Georg Gadamer. The hermeneutical waters for Christian theology became even murkier in the twentieth century as the field itself underwent marginalization within the modern academy, and "secular" hermeneutical tools were used as apologetics or seen as the mandatory mode for "true" expressions of the faith, grounded in a supposed objectivity.[6] A more generous read of the popularity of hermeneutics in theology is that, as Anthony Godzeiba and Brad Hinze name, theologians (Catholics in particular) moved toward hermeneutics in the twentieth century in response to what David Ford called the "multiple overwhelmings" of the modern world and the limitations of theology's prior tools.[7] It

---

[5] Stanley E. Porter and Jason C. Robinson, *Active Hermeneutics: Seeking Understanding in an Age of Objectivism* (London: Routledge, 2021), 1.

[6] Garrett Green, *Theology, Hermeneutics, and Imagination: The Crisis of Interpretation at the End of Modernity* (Cambridge: Cambridge University Press, 2000), 5–7. See also Porter and Robinson, *Active Hermeneutics*.

[7] Anthony J. Godzeiba and Bradford E. Hinze, *Beyond Dogmatism and Innocence: Hermeneutics, Critique and Catholic Theology* (Collegeville, MN: Liturgical Press, 2017), xii. They recognize and name the influence as well of the Frankfurt School of Critical Theory (e.g., Theodor Adorno,

could even be argued that more recent theological hermeneutics is simply a return to the beginning; as Garrett Green posits, Christian hermeneutics begins with the story of creation: a serpent questioning an interpretation of God's edict.[8]

While there are nearly innumerable ways that modern theological hermeneutics takes up this fundamental task of interpretation, three modes in particular help lay the groundwork for the traumatic imagination: liberationist, post/decolonial, and feminist/womanist. Emerging in a formal way in the mid-twentieth century, liberation hermeneutics aims to cultivate understandings of the world and God that reach beyond metaphysical definitions and into the lived, material reality of the oppressed. Premised in part on the modern turn to the subject, where assertions of truth are evaluated from the position of the person rather than a pre-given authoritative structure, liberation hermeneutics takes seriously our sense of being (ontology) and the real embodied person as central to any intellectual considerations. This work was first largely formalized under the umbrella of liberation theology emerging from Latin America, from thinkers such as Peruvian Dominican Gustavo Gutiérrez, Uruguayan Jesuit Juan Luis Segundo, Brazilian archbishop Dom Helder Camara and theologian Leonardo Boff, Spanish-Salvadoran Jesuit Jon Sobrino, and lay-led "base communities" throughout Central and South America.[9] While a wide field of thought, liberation hermeneutics centers and takes seriously the material lives and movements for

---

Jürgen Habermas), and French phenomenology and poststructuralism (e.g., Emmanuel Levinas, Jacques Derrida, Michel Foucault), as well as the need for a post–Vatican II theology to respond not only to Peter's scriptural demand to "give an account of the hope that is within us" (1 Peter 3:15) but to take seriously the end of that quote, to do so with gentleness and respect, here read as concerted effort to contend with the world that *is* and the best thinking from all sources to interpret it.

[8] Green, *Theology, Hermeneutics, and Imagination*, 1.
[9] Thiselton, *Hermeneutics*, 255–278.

justice of the oppressed, read through the redemptive claims of the gospel. Importantly, then, the "future hope" of an eschatological promise is not the only thing that is central to how we interpret. Maybe even more essentially to some, the direct, political, and embodied actions of resistance and work for liberation in the here-and-now must define how we encounter and interpret the Christian faith. The theological claim that emerges from liberation hermeneutics is seen today in diverse expressions but is perhaps best summarized by theologian and American Catholic priest Bryan Massingale: "vox victarum vox Dei"—the voice of the victims is the voice of God.[10]

Post/decolonial[11] hermeneutics also emerged in the world-shifting changes of the mid-twentieth century, gaining popularity toward the end of the century and into our current moment. Finding many of its tenets in the work of Algerian psychologist and revolutionary Frantz Fanon, it resists any essentialization of the victim-identity and any claim to external salvation narratives (a criticism of some forms of liberation models). Instead, Fanon argues that the "native" must take up responsible subjecthood and refuse to be violated—that oneself is created in concrete resistance

---

[10] He credits Matthew Lamb's *Solidarity with Victims: Toward a Theology of Social Transformation* (New York: Crossroad, 1982) as his source for this phrase, and goes on to develop it explicitly within Catholic theological ethics to challenge what the field takes as "classic" and instead push toward serious engagement with the Black experience as definitive for theological reflection. See Bryan Massingale, "*Vox victarum vox Dei*: Malcolm X as Neglected 'Classic' for Catholic Theological Reflection," *CTSA Proceedings* 65 (2010): 63–88.

[11] I include both "post" and "de" as prefix options here, as they are often used interchangeably. I have a preference for decolonial, as it indicates the process of removing colonial structures from our beings, modes, and methods, whereas "post" may simply indicate the occurrence of the thinking after the fall of a colonial power. I further explore the potential for decolonial theology and trauma in Stephanie C. Edwards, "Imperialism of the Mind: Decolonial Theological Approaches to Traumatic Memory," *Political Theology* 24, no. 6 (2023): 544–569.

and rejection of colonial powers. This includes rejection of methods of reading and interpretation from colonization. The genesis of this frame is adamantly a- or even anti-religious, rightfully naming Western Christian religious institutions as powerful hegemonic forces of colonialism and oppression in and of themselves.[12] With this in mind, can Christian theology ever claim to be decolonial? Susan Abraham argues, first and foremost, that theology cannot encounter postcolonial thinking with a competitive stance of "better than yours" truth. Instead, she takes its challenges seriously and says that, through attentiveness to the contextual thinking of postcolonial thought, Catholic theology in particular can resist the temptation to totalize experience, instead lifting up the ongoing (arguably never-ending) need for critique as well as expansion of the sacramental and salvific imagination in theological hermeneutics.[13] This focus on deconstruction and process is essential to postcolonial thinking, as there is a need to discard the binary of coloniality—us versus them— and emphasize that while we may shed prior hegemonic modes of existence, "delinking from colonial power simultaneously mark[s] both decolonizing societies and colonizing societies."[14] Through postcolonial thought, theology is made to recognize the modes of colonial hegemony upon which it depends and pushes it to shed idolatrous dependence on definitional stasis in favor of living within the constructive tension of life beyond categories of power.

---

[12] See Frantz Fanon, *The Wretched of the Earth* (1961 [French], 1963 [English]; New York: Grove Press, 2004).

[13] Susan Abraham, "Postcolonial Hermeneutics and a Catholic (Post) Modernity," in *Beyond Dogmatism and Innocence: Hermeneutics, Critique and Catholic Theology*, ed. Anthony J. Godzieba and Bradford E. Hinze (Collegeville, MN: Liturgical Press, 2017), 205. The movement toward post/decolonial methods in theology has its roots in liberation theologies, and even arguably as far back as Bartolomé de Las Casas (1474–1566); Thiselston, *Hermeneutics,* 255.

[14] Abraham, "Postcolonial Hermeneutics," 207.

Finally, and as should already be clear from chapter 2, feminist and womanist hermeneutics is foundational to my construction of the traumatic imagination. In the latter half of the twentieth century, feminist thinkers took up and expanded Paul Ricoeur's "hermeneutics of suspicion," which he coined to describe a uniting commitment he saw in the work of Marx, Freud, and Nietzsche, namely to unmask the "lies and illusions" of consciousness and seek the truth behind commonly accepted or "self-evident" meanings.[15] Feminists specifically grounded their hermeneutics in the action of consciousness raising to make active the process of uncovering how gender roles and ideologies shape whatever is being examined, as well as taking seriously the "silences" or "absences" of women's voices in particular. These were not readings for reading's sake, but, much like liberation and postcolonial thinkers, they sought a hermeneutic for ethical action toward justice and freedom. Womanists make this method explicitly intersectional, noting that much of academic feminist thought emerged from privileged spaces of whiteness that diminished or ignored the role of race, ethnicity, class, and other factors that are simultaneously definitive of Black women's lives, particularly in the United States.[16]

In theology, feminist/womanist modes encourage particular readings of Scripture and, as is central to this project, theologizing from the body in light of the Incarnation. Abraham lifts this up as the "postcolonial feminist hermeneutical lens . . . thinking by

---

[15] R. Felski, "Critique and the Hermeneutics of Suspicion," *M/C Journal* 15, no. 1 (2011): https://doi.org/10.5204/mcj.431.

[16] There is an instructive (and, for me, inspirational) record of the friendship and debate between Adrienne Rich and Audre Lorde through the 1980s and early '90s where they personally and professionally debated how the world acted upon their queer femme bodies in different ways on the lines of race, and how they defined resistance and ethical action through practical organizing, poetry, speaking, and teaching. Thiselton also provides a helpful summary of feminist and womanist development; see *Hermeneutics*, 279–305.

means of the body—the bleeding blurry borders of an Anzaldúa, straining to hear the subaltern's speech in Spivak."[17] We cannot and should not extricate ourselves from our physicality, at once crossed and marked by borders and simultaneously reaching out, yearning to hear the cries of the "other." This means that the particular body—here specifically gendered, not some universal construction—must have "necessary presence *as* bodies" in our interpretation. Our bodies mediate our understanding and carry sacramental potential: "The incarnation of God confirms the revelatory value of that vulnerable mediation."[18] Taken together, the embodied, incarnational hermeneutic from feminist/womanist theology, read with the contextual, deconstructive hermeneutic from decolonial thought, and the concrete, "bottom up" hermeneutic from liberation theology form the essential parameters for understanding the traumatic imagination.

Hermeneutics "for Life"

While exploring how we understand and interpret is a laudable goal within modern theology, there remains a bent within theological hermeneutics, including those active forms just highlighted, that is as tempting as it can be counterproductive, especially when encountering suffering: objectivity. Seeking Truth, where we begin to capitalize the "T" to indicate unassailable Reality, is not in itself a bad thing, but as Stanley E. Porter and Jason C. Robinson

---

[17] Abraham, "Postcolonial Hermeneutics," 225. Here she is referencing Gloria Anzaldúa, *Borderlands/La Frontera: The New Mestiza* (San Francisco: Spinsters/Aunt Lute, 1987); and Gayatri C. Spivak, "Can the Subaltern Speak?," in *Colonial Discourse and Postcolonial Theory, A Reader,* ed. Patrick Williams and Laura Chrisman (orig. essay 1985; New York: Columbia University Press, 1994), 66–111.

[18] Abraham, "Postcolonial Hermeneutics," 227, citing Anthony Godzieba, "Incarnation, Theory, and Catholic Bodies: What Should Post-postmodern Catholic Theology Look Like?" *Louvain Studies* 28 (2003): 229.

point out, doing so often forecloses the task of interpretation itself. "Rather than such an approach leading to hermeneutical understanding, the result has often been increased contention and disagreement and failure to communicate, such that various people within respective communities of belief simply build walls to block the opinions and methods of others."[19] Instead, a basic humility is required for the practice of theological hermeneutics. It requires, to some extent, the willingness to become what they call a "kenotic person," one who recognizes the transcendent within our midst, and, in recognition, pushes oneself toward a healthy self-emptying that can promote dialogue toward reconciliation and "new opportunities for life."[20] Such an orientation "for life" is essential to speak across any boundary of difference and, as we will uncover, is particularly essential when confronting traumatic memory, so as not to become trapped within narratives of victimhood and suffering.

Held within this life-oriented hermeneutic in the consideration of trauma is what John Caputo calls a "radical hermeneutics": a hermeneutics "from below" that does not seek relief as a surety in its conclusions that provides release; rather it aims to sit within the facticity of life, describing the irregularities, ruptures, and gaps that trauma reveals.[21] Thus, the traumatic imagination works to open space for particular expressions that cultivate meaning-making instead of reaching for and grasping tightly overarching metanarratives of understanding. My proposal here is another contribution to the work that Godzieba and Hinze

---

[19] Porter and Robinson, *Active Hermeneutics*, 7.

[20] Porter and Robinson, *Active Hermeneutics*, 140. Feminists have rightly criticized kenosis within the Christian narrative, but I find the usage of the term in this context helpful. For more, see Annie Selak, "Orthodoxy, Orthopraxis, and Orthopathy: Evaluating the Feminist Kenosis Debate," *Modern Theology* 33, no. 4 (October 2017): 529–548.

[21] John Caputo, *Radical Hermeneutics: Repetition, Deconstruction, and the Hermeneutic Project* (Bloomington: Indiana University Press, 1987), 6.

define as a "third naïveté,"[22] in which Catholic theology confronts directly the challenges of the world and brings all tools to bear on the interpretation of belief that still stands among the wastes. This is a way of reading and doing theology that is "critical and hopeful," and it is, indeed, the only appropriate theological response to the complexity and devastation of trauma.[23]

Trauma Encountering Hermeneutics

Let us recall that, at its most basic, trauma is simply any experience that overwhelms one's capacities. Trauma is thus convenient shorthand for when you might feel like life has handed you "too much" or when you're struggling to understand a complex life experience—which, though not diagnostically trauma, has become the cultural interpretation of its meaning. Medically, trauma is a defined experience that most people will have in their lifetime. As we explored in chapter 1, approximately 70 percent of the world's population has been exposed to a traumatic life event.[24] When this happens, our bodies create chemical responses to attempt to deal

---

[22] Godzeiba and Hinze, *Beyond Dogmatism and Innocence,* xviii. Caputo also adamantly resists any fall to nihilism, instead encouraging the reader to "face up to the bad news metaphysics has been keeping under cover" (*Radical Hermeneutics,* 6).

[23] Abraham, "Postcolonial Hermeneutics," 204. While this chapter introduces the broad contours of a "traumatic imagination," I am not seeking to contribute to the field of methodological hermeneutics as such, but rather attempting to take its suggestions seriously and apply them within our consideration of trauma's challenges to theology.

[24] Carolina Salgado, "Global Prevalence of Stress and Trauma and Related Disorders," Global Collaboration on Traumatic Stress, 2024, https://www.global-psychotrauma.net/global-prevalence-of-trauma. Importantly, these can and do occur within the course of everyday life. Trauma was once considered fully "extraordinary," and thinkers like Judith Herman helped to reorient the understanding that "violence is violence and trauma is trauma," such that it permeates our cultural language, as explored in chapter 1.

with the occurrence. These physical and psychological reactions to trauma are normal and are part of the way our bodies have evolved to survive extreme circumstances. When the responses do not pass, however, they become pathological and can develop into a myriad of posttraumatic disorders.

Trauma is also embedded within our overarching attitudes toward mental health and overall health, which hinge upon our understandings of morality as explored in chapter 2. These cultural and religious scripts are so deeply embedded that they often go unnoticed or are accepted as normal, right, and even just.[25] Following Emilie Townes's cultural construction of health and Cathy Caruth's naming of trauma's demands from darkness, then, we must find a new way to interpret trauma and its theological ramifications. While of course too brief, this section resurfaces three layers of trauma's operation in our current world: individual disease, the layered ethics of situational mental health, and trauma as social/structural violence. Through these layers, I establish the pervasiveness of trauma in our shared lives and reiterate the fundamental contours of this new context where theology must be read with a hermeneutic of trauma.

Trauma as Individual Disease

First, trauma operates as an individual experience that may lead to disease and, even if not a disorder, is fundamentally an experience of dis-ease. Best practices from trauma healing methods suggest that processes of integration are essential to fostering healthy resilience.[26]

---

[25] Yochai Ataria goes so far as to argue that trauma is a "black hole" around which all Western culture orbits, and our continual exposure and lack of healing attention to trauma has damaged our communities. Ataria, *The Structural Trauma of Western Culture* (Cham: Palgrave Macmillan, 2017).

[26] Juanita Meyer, "'Surviving My Story of Trauma': A Pastoral Theology of Resilience," in *Resilient Religion, Resilience and Heartbreaking Adversity*, ed. Chris Hermans and Kobus Schoeman (Berlin: Lit Verlag, 2023), 153.

Resilience is, put simply, a broad measurement of one's ability to undergo stress or harm and recover normal health. It is used as a measure in posttrauma contexts chiefly to reflect on a person's capacities, as "healing" is variously defined and, for some, may never be "completed." This *ongoingness* in a person's life is one of the powerful aspects of trauma that suggests a new hermeneutic. In fact, the process of integration toward resilience includes translation from "the" story to "my" story of trauma, where integration itself can be seen as an act of hermeneutics. Understanding how one chooses to view and narrate the experience helps a person to uncover not only potential ways they can and have shown resilience after trauma, but can also lift up moments of resistance from within suffering. Resistance is separated from resilience in this consideration because resistance is fundamentally agential, relying on a "strengths-based" vision of the self that remains active even in the most harmful circumstances.[27] Grounded in feminist/womanist hermeneutics, trauma demands attention to the centrality of the body and to its real experiences at the hands of a perpetrator, be they interpersonal or social/structural (resistance), also adding the essential vision of one whose experience of harm is far from the entire story of the self (resilience). The traumatic imagination asks that we read these "gaps"—for it can be nearly impossible for one who feels stripped of essential personhood posttrauma, such as in instances of sexual assault, to name a "strength"—as moments of incarnational solidarity. In so doing, I do not aim to diminish suffering or provide a metaphysical answer to an existential threat, but rather to break open new pathways for an individual to read their own story.[28]

---

[27] Funlola Olojede, "Resilience and Resistance in the Book of Job: An African Socio-Economic Hermeneutical Reading," in *Resilient Religion, Resilience and Heartbreaking Adversity,* ed. Chris Hermans and Kobus Schoeman (Berlin: Lit Verlag, 2023), 142. The author is presenting African biblical hermeneutics (ABH) as a distinctly decolonial act, socially engaged and attentive to moving the center of interpretation to a resistant and resilient Black theology.

[28] Jennifer Beste works on this with fundamental grace via Rahner with

Trauma as Situational Mental Health

Second, trauma reveals the layered ethics of situational mental health. By this, I mean that a trauma hermeneutic reveals complexity rather than universalizes experience. Critics of "trauma" discourse, however, rightfully name the tendency for many people to depend on it as shorthand rather than to pay attention to its diagnostic content. Dr. Allen Frances, who chaired the task force for the fourth edition of the American Psychiatric Association's *Diagnostic and Statistical Manual of Mental Disorders* (1994), says, "You can write best-sellers on [trauma] because it's an appealing model for people searching for an explanation for the distress in life."[29] This trend is particularly troubling for theologian Jennifer Beste, who calls out this universalizing behavior within the Catholic Church in response to the clergy sex abuse crisis.[30] She argues that, even though

> the narrative of a "traumatized church" can be compelling because the vivid language and images connected with trauma can resonate with many people's sense of horror at the reality of clergy sexual abuse ... it also invites hope that, given our traumatic paralysis, God will respond to

---

victim/survivors of sexual assault. See *God and the Victim: Traumatic Intrusions on Grace and Freedom* (Oxford: Oxford University Press, 2007).

[29] Ellen Barry, "She Redefined Trauma. Then Trauma Redefined Her," *New York Times*, April 24, 2023, https://www.nytimes.com/2023/04/24/health/judith-herman-trauma.html. We're now in the DSM-V (2013, revised 2022), where the conceptualization of trauma and the diagnostic criteria of trauma were adjusted significantly; see chapter 1 and Laura K. Jones and Jenny L. Cureton, "Trauma Redefined in the DSM-5: Rationale and Implications for Counseling Practice," *The Professional Counselor* 4, no. 3 (July 3, 2014), https://tpcjournal.nbcc.org/trauma-redefined-in-the-dsm-5-rationale-and-implications-for-counseling-practice/.

[30] Jennifer Beste, "Critical Reflections on the Discourse on a 'Traumatized Church,'" in *Theology in a Post-traumatic Church,* ed. John N. Sheveland (Maryknoll, NY: Orbis Books, 2023), 39–63.

our prayers to heal and redeem the body of Christ so that the church can restore its good name, integrity, and positive influence in the world.[31]

Rather than activate moral agency in response to harm, she argues, the use of "we are all traumatized" rhetoric further disempowers victims and witnesses, easing our critical assessment of guilt and culpability for laypersons, parishes, and hierarchical structures, as well as perpetrators themselves. Further, it is problematic "that our hope for healing and justice in this scenario becomes more rooted in an image of a sovereign God who can choose (or not) to have mercy and infuse us with grace, and less rooted on activism and concrete actions."[32] Such a misapplication of trauma as hermeneutic shifts us toward an acceptance of our own apathy (in the name of traumatic impairment/paralysis) as we reach toward external grace, instead of enacting already graced actions toward healing and justice. Robert Schreiter takes this a step further when he argues that the church itself must go so far as to forfeit its leadership role in any forms of reconciliation if the church itself is a part of the problem.[33] A reorientation of the traumatic imagination in theology mandates this type of radical humility rather than continued misuse of "trauma" that enacts concrete harm. This is where a proper hermeneutic of trauma must intersect with liberation hermeneutics, where the voice of the victim is revelatory of the speech of God and the focus on differentiated responsibility and material work for justice is theologically central.[34]

---

[31] Beste, "Critical Reflections," 49.

[32] Beste, "Critical Reflections," 48.

[33] Although here he is talking generally about reconciliation, not just clergy-perpetrated sex abuse (CPSA). Robert Schreiter, *Reconciliation: Mission and Ministry in a Changing Social Order* (Maryknoll, NY: Orbis Books, 1992), 64.

[34] More on justice implications emerging from trauma theology in chapter 5.

Trauma as Structural Violence

Third and finally, trauma emerges as social/structural violence. In 2023, after thirty years, Judith Herman, a founder of modern trauma theory and contextual clinical practice, published her second book on the topic. In large part, this gap in writing was due to chronic pain resulting from a broken kneecap. Her injury created so much pain, Herman says, that her life "wasn't even thinking about pain. It was being pain. One's existence was just pain.... Nothing exists outside of it."[35] After undergoing a newly developed surgery for combat veterans (Herman does not shy away from this irony) and achieving physical healing, she completed *Truth and Repair: How Trauma Survivors Envision Justice* at age eighty-one.

Crucial for Herman is resisting the cult of personality that often surrounds psychiatry and trauma. Instead, she encourages the field to move beyond the internal world of a patient and into practices of justice.[36] Unlike Bessel van der Kolk (a close colleague of Herman's, whose *Body Keeps the Score* has been a tenacious best-seller for years), Herman remains focused outside the self, moving from neurobiology and embodiment of individuals into the social sphere. Herman sees this move as necessary, even calling it a "final stage of recovery."[37] In part, this stems from Herman's commitment to reading traumatic experiences through the lens of power—a direct tie to post/decolonial hermeneutics. As such, personal suffering is never isolated. It is emboldened and enacted through structures that support such harm. She argues that coalitional organizing and community building are the only proper response to hegemonic, violent power, as they call entire

---

[35] Barry, "She Redefined Trauma." See also Elaine Scarry, *The Body in Pain: The Making and Unmaking of the World* (Oxford: Oxford University Press, 1985).

[36] Judith Herman, *Truth and Repair: How Trauma Survivors Envision Justice* (New York: Basic Books, 2023).

[37] Herman, *Truth and Repair*, 3.

communities to account and allow for contextual visions of justice that have the strength to address harm. This work will be inherently conflictual, because "When you have a movement that challenges the power structure, you're going to have a backlash," as all violence is not only the act of a single perpetrator but the result of social scripts that encourage and enable trauma, often rewarding the perpetrator and diminishing the victim.[38] The social/structural reality of trauma resonates with the "marking" of all people embedded in colonial logics, and together with postcolonial hermeneutics urges us toward delinking ourselves from social models of "power-over" and toward "power-with."[39]

Trauma as Theological Hermeneutic

With a basic understanding of the hermeneutics that inform the traumatic imagination, as well as some of the aspects of how trauma as context encounters these forms, we now turn toward building trauma as a theological hermeneutic. My proposal here is quite broad, meant to be applicable across many instances of interpretation. Just as trauma acts on multiple levels—the nuanced micro, mezzo, and macro described above—this way of imagining is similarly multivalent. No one approach works in every reading or circumstance. While I maintain that the contours I sketch are essential to reading theology rightly in light of trauma, I encourage us all to remember that the practice of this hermeneutic is just that: a practice. It is not an arrival, an accomplishment, or a completed project. Rather, the traumatic imagination is premised on continual engagement, inquiry, and renewal. Similar to healing trauma, it

---

[38] Barry, "She Redefined Trauma." Such as racism, sexism, and misogyny; see chapter 1.

[39] Olojede, "Resilience and Resistance in the Book of Job," 148—especially how the author construes Job's resilience and resistance through an African biblical hermeneutic that can engage current suffering.

asks us to be resistant and resilient. So, to address our orienting question—What does it look like to do theological ethics with trauma as one's hermeneutic?—I propose three central aspects of the traumatic imagination: time, position, and praxis. While obviously blunt tools for such a delicate task, I introduce these broad categories as a starting point for thinking together on the hermeneutical implications of trauma and the ways it might challenge us to read theology, particularly liberative theology, anew.

Time

Time is one of the most explored aspects of the relationship between trauma and theology. Whether it be liturgical, pastoral, theological, or ethical, the broken experience of time within trauma is central to its use as an interpretive key. Opposed to linear time, encapsulating discrete events that one moves through, the experience of trauma often initiates a collapse of experiences—a flow in and out of "real" time. Whether this takes its most extreme form within an individual as debilitating flashbacks or within the societal repetition of traumatic memory—often experienced by survivors of genocide or war—trauma demands that we cut through time and make the past present. Trauma reminds us, as William Faulkner's *Requiem for a Nun* is often quoted, "The past is never dead. It's not even past."[40]

Time is important to trauma because of the potential in-breaking of past pain and the fluid, omnidirectional experience of the present that it encourages. Breaking one's assumption of stasis, trauma reveals the inherent dynamism of life and its tidal flows through experience. Trauma reveals the false construct of linear, upward progress, either for our individual selves or our society, laying bare the much more true and complex intersections

---

[40] William Faulkner, *Requiem for a Nun* (New York: Random House, 1951), 73.

of our past, present, and future. Time, in the "West," is often considered an objective arbiter, a series upon which to place items in order. Trauma asks us to upend this thinking, to read time for its capacity for connection—reaching back and forward through lineages—rather than its organizing power.[41]

Time, in the traumatic imagination, does not heal all wounds, yet it offers us a new way to approach our understanding of our experiences, and how what remains can and will move throughout and potentially beyond all our lives.[42] As John Caputo puts it,

> In the thin membranes of structures which we stretch across the flux, in the thin fabric we weave over it, there are certain spots where the surface wears through and acquires a transparency which exposes the flux beneath. There are certain breaking points, let us say, in the habits and practices, the works and days, of our mundane existence where the flux is exposed, where the whole trembles and the play irrupts. Then we know we are in trouble. The abyss, the play, the uncanny—in short, all hell—breaks loose, and the card castles of everydayness come tumbling down. Something breaks through because the constraints we impose upon things break down.[43]

Rather than solely a negative experience, trauma reveals that "trouble" for structures is not necessarily trouble for the people

---

[41] Some of my other work explores epigenetics and trauma, or how our experiences are potentially passed through our families. See Stephanie C. Edwards, "'In the Bone': Race, Theological Anthropology, and Intergenerational Trauma," in *"You Say You Want a Revolution"? 1968–2018 in Theological Perspective: The Annual Publication of the College Theology Society* 64, ed. Susie Paulik Babka, Elena Procario Foley and Sandra Yocum (Maryknoll, NY: Orbis Books, 2019), 27–37.

[42] Karen O'Donnell and Katie Cross, eds., *Feminist Trauma Theologies: Body, Scripture & Church in Critical Perspective* (London: SCM Press, 2020), 169.

[43] Caputo, *Radical Hermeneutics*, 269–270.

within them. In losing our castles of everydayness and our constraints, through trauma's in-breaking we discover a level of connection across experience that can encourage collective creativity. We are then acting to address the trouble together within a deeply fecund, sometimes chaotic horizon of the possible—not an abyssal unknown.

Lutheran theologian Dirk Lange faces this horizon theologically through the concept of grace within ritual. Lange explicitly takes on the Eucharist to state that its conflation with the crucifixion is misunderstood. The ritual of shared bread and wine *breaks* the cycle of violence rather than repeating it.[44] The Eucharist can hold the absence, the unknown, the incommunicable of trauma; as ritual it makes no demands for "explanation" from those who partake. It has, as Serene Jones says, the power to speak directly into the imagination,[45] as "Our body is confronted physically by this Other body."[46] Yet Lange fully admits that such a confrontation is defined by absence, an incomplete knowledge. However,

> This absence in things does not mean that events cannot refer, nor does it imply a necessary absolutizing of meaning in order to avoid a possible dissemination. Rather, the absence, the departure, the inaccessibility that the departure enacts opens context to the possibility of something returning, of the force of a return.[47]

The move to ritual references a practice that seeks something that is not totally grasped or known.[48] Lange departs from traditional

---

[44] Dirk Lange, *Trauma Recalled: Liturgy, Disruption, and Theology* (Minneapolis: Fortress Press, 2009), 10.

[45] Serene Jones, *Trauma and Grace: Theology in a Ruptured World* (Louisville, KY: Westminster John Knox Press, 2009), 22.

[46] Lange, *Trauma Recalled*, 122.

[47] Lange, *Trauma Recalled*, 98.

[48] Lange, *Trauma Recalled,* 115: "the call of the other—the fact of

trauma theory in his faith in the return, specifically of grace, based in his reading of Luther. Also, instead of ending with perpetual repetition, Lange sees and states a clear ethical call, a "call to an impossible responsibility—to a ministry that is continually disrupting, moving out, departing toward the other because of the other, a ministry that is conformity to the cross, to the death of God."[49] This call is "not a form of *representation or mastery* but is the continual opening up to the inaccessible that returns as a force, as something uncontrollable."[50] It is precisely the *uncontrollable* that is loosed through the practice of Eucharist, the unbounded power of grace to act through the faithful, finding and uncovering Christ within meditation and within the visceral cry of the other in the world. In this way, through faith and practice, "The believer is conformed to the suffering, needy, indigent body of the neighbor" throughout history and across time.[51] This is a form of "practicing resurrection": that healing, as well as trauma and pain, is not an event, nor a codified space or a distinct encapsulated time, but is instead an ongoing, ever-developing process.[52] Time, therefore, is reread in the traumatic imagination in a necessarily expansive mode. In the individual, for the community, and even within our understanding of history, time becomes a malleable space of critical hope, necessitating a method of communication: memory. Memory is the site of ritual, of healing, and of shared testimony

---

alterity—finds expression in their writing through a reference to ritual—to the iterability of something not totally grasped or known."

[49] Lange, *Trauma Recalled*, 118.
[50] Lange, *Trauma Recalled*, 120.
[51] Lange, *Trauma Recalled*, 124. This is explored further in chapter 4 with the work of Metz.
[52] Melanie May, *A Body Knows: A Theopoetics of Death and Resurrection* (London: Continuum, 1995), 19. "Crip time" rooted in disability theology is also important here, and is further explored in chapter 5. See Madeline Jarrett, "Bodies of Hope," *Philosophy & Theology* 33, no. 1 (2021): 139–157.

that is the ground of ethical action. Time as communicated and experienced in memory is not abstract; it is fully positioned within and between persons.

Position

As such, trauma takes positionality seriously, first defining it as dedication to embodiment and second to the creation and embrace of liminal space. Embodiment may seem a basic necessity of the traumatic imagination, but we must emphasize this necessity as we often seek to relegate, divide, and displace our unruly or messy bodies. I follow the invitation of Richard Kearney and Brian Treanor's edited volume, *Carnal Hermeneutics*, where they challenge us to confront anew the enigma of the flesh:

> Above all, to realize that flesh can no longer be confined to a phenomenological account of the human body but must also be recognized as a membrane or medium connecting us to "the flesh of the world." Flesh is precisely "the edge" where the human meets worlds that exceed and entreat it— animal and environmental, sacred and profane. It is the site of endless transmissions between selves and strangers where "surplus meaning" comes to remind us that we can never be sufficient to ourselves. This surplus may be of the order of joy ... or of the order of suffering ... but both orders serve to instruct us that there is more to flesh than meets the eye—or even the tips of our fingers and tongues. Flesh raises more questions than answers.[53]

Yet the flesh is inescapable. Despite or because of its questions, flesh must be centered in the traumatic imagination. To turn away

---

[53] Richard Kearney and Brian Treanor, eds. *Carnal Hermeneutics* (New York: Fordham University Press, 2015), 11.

from the flesh would be to repeat mistakes of the past, emphasizing a spiritualism that ignores the authenticity of traumatic experience *and* denies potential ontological and ethical connections that might be cultivated through further understanding individuated as well as shared, incarnational enfleshment.[54]

Exploring her own physical brokenness, her essential embodiment, Protestant theologian Melanie May realized how her inherent physicality ("I am my body") drove her to subvert the static sense of self that was promoted by her Christianity. "Subversion has for me meant a struggle to affirm life *is* transitory, to affirm life's character *is* change, even if often in ways I would not choose. Indeed, to be alive is *precisely* to change."[55] Such change is not to be resisted but to be fully lived and interpreted through an understanding of graced incarnation and the "sacrality of moral bodies and earthly life."[56] Although, as Serene Jones puts it, "to be human is to be only a hairbreadth away from the unbearable,"[57] May believes life itself is revelatory, that "it is flesh that makes words" through which we reach out toward the Divine.[58] While such a conception is rooted in empowered participation with the Divine, it is laced with a notion of troubling divine solidarity: Not only did Jesus descend into hell, creating the Divine's witness and presence in *all* circumstances of suffering, Jesus did so *necessarily*, positioning suffering in some way as the predication for eventual redemption. Despite such a caution, May connects with the ambiguity of embodied solidarity in repetitive practices such as the Eucharist, a physical act, establishing a method of "binding and loosing, as connecting and letting go ... a rhythm of reckoning

---

[54] Abraham, "Postcolonial hermeneutics," 225.
[55] May, *A Body Knows,* 19. Also, Jones's "converted way of seeing" (*Trauma and Grace,* 11).
[56] May, *A Body Knows,* 24.
[57] Jones, *Trauma and Grace,* 18.
[58] May quoting Naomi Goldenberg, *A Body Knows,* 23.

what is life-giving and what is death-dealing."[59] Here, one's body is literally necessary for communion with God, and, as such, the body is inextricable from the traumatic imagination, giving primacy to the position of *within* even when reaching out.

Position is also defined as "liminal space" in trauma studies and often cited in trauma theology as the space at the base of the cross and the liturgical day of Holy Saturday. Within these spaces, the traumatic imagination emphasizes positions of lament, unknowing, and "keeping watch." Shelly Rambo calls this a reading "from the middle" of theology that resonates deeply with the core of Christian belief. For Rambo, trauma does not speak to theology from the outside. Trauma resonates with something very deep within the truth of Christian experience, and with trauma's insights, new meaning can be found.[60] This liminal third space—between death and resurrection—matches many survivors' experiences of posttraumatic life. Within this position, they are neither fully dead nor fully healed. In the "in-between," one recognizes that return to the person before trauma is impossible, and, even if hope for a transformed future is present, it feels inaccessible. Encouraging theology and religious leaders to recognize this space as valid and full of the Holy Spirit—rather than rush to the redemption of Easter—is the central demand of Rambo's work.

The cultivation of liminal or middle space is most helpful when understood as dynamic, what Gloria Anzaldúa called "border thinking," where porous, blurry edges are the places at which new, life-giving knowledge is found (for Anzaldúa, outside

---

[59] May, *A Body Knows*, 40. May risks in some points falling to glamorization of redemptive events in the face of pain. Also see Sharon V. Betcher, "Running the Gauntlet of Humiliation: Disablement in/as Trauma," in *Post-traumatic Public Theology*, ed. Stephanie N. Arel and Shelly Rambo (Cham: Palgrave Macmillan, 2016), 68 and passim for her discussion of disabled persons as "payment."

[60] Shelly Rambo, *Spirit and Trauma: A Theology of Remaining* (Louisville, KY: Westminster John Knox Press, 2010), 17.

of the colonial power matrix).[61] In her last work, Anzaldúa emphasized *nepantla,* a Nahuatl word meaning "in-between space," which for her can hold the potentiality of borders alongside/within the chaos, anxiety, and pain of their reality even as it underscores the ontological (spiritual and psychic) dimensions of the space.[62] Importantly for trauma, Anzaldúa's *nepantla* is suffused with spirit-force, extending within and beyond life, into death. With such destabilizing force (crossing the ultimate boundary), *nepantla* does not will loss of agency, rather some can become *las nepantleras* (threshold people), "who move within and among multiple worlds and use their movement in the service of transformation."[63] Yet even this reading of position must remain critical, as scholars of color have critiqued modern trauma theology for its overemphasis on psychological middle space, forgetting the very real suffering that results from "remaining" in oppressed, liminal positions, or "keeping watch" from privileged, removed ones.[64] Still, the deeply incarnational vision of humanity, and the ethical extension of the work of theology into healing solidarity in border/*nepantla* space, is essential to the traumatic imagination.

Here, Mayra Rivera's postmodern exploration of our entangled enfleshment can help overcome the separation that lingers in our consideration of positionality. Rivera posits that flesh *as a concept* "accents the complex textures of those [material and religious] relations—their inherent multiplicity; the sedimentation of past

---

[61] Abraham, "Postcolonial Hermeneutics," 221.

[62] AnaLouise Keating, "Editor's Introduction: Re-envisioning Coyolxauhqui, Decolonizing Reality: Anzaldúa's Twenty-First-Century Imperative," in Gloria E. Anzaldúa, *Light in the Dark / Luz en lo Oscuro: Rewriting Identity, Spirituality, Reality* (Durham, NC: Duke University Press, 2015), xxxiv.

[63] Keating, "Editor's Introduction," xxxv.

[64] Anthony Reddie, "Why Black Lives Still Don't Matter," in *Bearing Witness: Intersectional Perspectives on Trauma Theology,* ed. Karen O'Donnell and Katie Cross (London: SCM Press, 2022), 23.

events; the constant flow of elements in and out of bodies."[65] Flesh reveals what it is to be human, and encourages an orientation of dynamism rather than stasis, based on the ever-moving connections between us that exist at/on our very edges. Flesh is both embodied individually and the substance of the space that is shared among all humanity. Rivera recognizes the power of Christ's Incarnation in this view of the flesh, stating that, by "focusing on the circuitous paths of flesh—connecting past and present, spirit and earthly elements— the incarnation brings to mind and may help us reevaluate carnal/ earthly bonds as grounds for a commitment to a shared life."[66] Viewing the Incarnation as central, she finds that our potential moments of healing encounter are not limited to spoken words as is generally accepted in trauma treatment. Healing encounter can come between bodies, in acts of art and ritual, the power of which is being reified by ongoing trauma healing research.

Further, reading Maurice Merleau-Ponty and Frantz Fanon in conversation, Rivera creates a vision of the positive disruption of the flesh as an entity that undoes rational discourse but disrupts to reveal the only thing that can potentially bind us. With Fanon, she explores how his narratives constantly attempt to place him, a Martinique-born, Afro-Caribbean psychiatrist and philosopher, within the world. The only site upon which he lands is his body itself. While Fanon deconstructed this location, specifically for the ways society, culture, and religion acted upon it, Merleau-Ponty attempted to vocalize affirmations of fleshly experience.[67] Rivera holds in tension, yet always together, these two strands of the body's interactions with society. Both the deconstructive and the positive are essential when considering trauma in its harms and in the resilient and resistant humans who survive. Even as Fanon

---

[65] Mayra Rivera, *Poetics of the Flesh* (Durham, NC: Duke University Press), 12.

[66] Rivera, *Poetics of the Flesh*, 155.

[67] Rivera, *Poetics of the Flesh*, 119.

struggles, he concludes asking that his body continue to *make* him, "to keep him open toward the world."[68] Taking seriously such a request means creating theology that centers the flesh—that does not leave bodies, in all their particularity, complexity, and capacity for connection, at the door. The traumatic imagination, therefore, centers the position of entangled enfleshment as liminal space. Within as well as between bodies, we re-member, we seek to heal in recognition of how tenuous as well as precious our enfleshed selves are created. In concept as well as material reality, enfleshed liminal space is the site of individual and communal memory, essential to trauma as a hermeneutic.

Praxis

While time and position are both practical as well as conceptual within the traumatic imagination, they can fall prey to abstraction that does not serve the task of theological ethics. And, although one in seven patients who seek medical care every day in the United States will engage with a Catholic provider, theology is not mental healthcare provision.[69] What, then, is a proper, active theological response to trauma?

---

[68] Rivera, *Poetics of the Flesh*, 130. Often these connections between bodies are created through our emotions, making it necessary not just to create or recognize liminal, enfleshed space but also to cultivate right feeling within them. See Sue L. Cataldi, *Emotion, Depth, and Flesh: A Study of Sensitive Space, Reflections on Merleau-Ponty's Philosophy of Embodiment* (Albany, NY: State University of New York Press, 1993).

[69] Corporate Overview, Catholic Health Association of the United States, accessed May 28, 2024, https://www.chausa.org/docs/default-source/default-document-library/cha-corporate_overview-022322.pdf?sfvrsn=ad52e5f2_10. Here, there are strains of my attempt to hold together Aristotle's three basic human activities: *theoria* (thinking), *poiesis* (making), and *praxis* (doing), with the goals of truth, production, and action, respectively. I focus on the last here as, of course, all three are intertwined but ethics is often distracted by the first two that become de facto "doing" rather than actual action.

From Judith Herman on, the emphasis on community and its power to hold and even somewhat heal trauma is central. Thus, a dynamic theology, a theology of praxis, of encounter, is essential. Within hermeneutics, this move is grounded in the work of Emmanuel Levinas and John Caputo, where the "face" of the other, particularly in suffering, "opens the way to the recess, the 'ground' of the soul, its most hidden chambers."[70] While calls for and necessary action of justice remain important, I draw from these two thinkers in consideration of praxis to uncover how embodied and engaged the traumatic imagination must be, especially in light of the prior reflections on how trauma shapes time and position.

Any abstraction from the persons, the "faces," of trauma creates objective distance that simply cannot exist within this hermeneutic. We are all intertwined within our seeing of the other, our own faces simultaneously witnessing and being witnessed. For both Levinas and Caputo, these encounters are anything but theoretical; they are lived, embodied connections. The face is not a "thing," but the site of communication and language:

> In short, the face is one of those places of opening (Heidegger) and break-through (Eckhart), where the bottom drops out, where the surface opens up, where shadowy formation replaces the rock-hard identities of being and presence (Derrida). One begins to sense the abyss within, the unmanageable flow which inhabits it, that one has to do here with deep waters and with who knows what.[71]

Tamsin Jones argues that such essential "face-to-face" encounters with the "other"—which, for Levinas, create ethical responsibility—are also always haunted with divine encounter and thus

---

[70] Caputo, *Radical Hermeneutics*, 272.
[71] Caputo, *Radical Hermeneutics*, 274.

constitutive of the self. Yet Jones does not fall to the passive creation of the person by outside forces. Instead, she argues that, although we need the other, the traumatic lens can recover the self in the postmodern context. Trauma mandates attention to the *whole* person—mind *and* body, autonomy *and* relation—that forms the totality of the responsive and response-able self. In this way, she argues, our telling and our listening must be endless, that "the self of the retelling is neither the old self restored, nor a new self realized apart from the 'death' of the assault, but instead one of relationality and attempted integration."[72] This creates a necessary "violence" to the event itself, in that the fullness of experience can never be understood, but truths about it can be uncovered, and must be, to survive and live beyond the trauma. Such a "combative epistemology," as Jones terms it, posits that truth can still be found and does matter, although the resolution per se is fruitful ambiguity rather than decided facts. As Rambo states regarding her construction of witness: "Instead of simple knowledge between persons, there is a transmission of what is unknown and what could not be contained in the past."[73] Such a relational and complex self, practicing responsiveness and responsibility to the unknown within personal discernment and in communal "face-to-face" praxis, must be centered within the traumatic imagination.

Focusing on "the face of suffering" in particular reveals the tension that must remain within the praxis of the traumatic imagination: the cry for meaning and healing, with the simultaneous "refusal to be saved."[74] The postcolonial hermeneutic that informs our turn to trauma emphasizes the complex cry for meaning, healing, *and* refusal as the necessary ground of self-empowering

---

[72] Tamsin Jones, "Traumatized Subjects: Continental Philosophy of Religion and the Ethics of Alterity," *The Journal of Religion* 94, no. 2 (April 2014): 155.

[73] Rambo, *Spirit and Trauma*, 36.

[74] Caputo, *Radical Hermeneutics*, 272.

action that resists disempowering models of external salvation, hesitating to locate central or essential meaning from within pain. Porter and Robinson lift up the necessary practice of this encounter within theology, as

> active kenotic hermeneutics seeks a new form of dialogue in which the basis of reconciliation is a shared religious feeling.... [And yet] reconciliation is not agreement of belief and/or perception—there is no erasure of the self to secure immutable facts—but a shared experience ... typified by the acceptance of ignorance and of a shared interest in the good.[75]

Thus, praxis within the traumatic imagination emphasizes that we are not isolated brains. We are deeply embedded, fully embodied, agential, and responsible persons. Our encounter with the face of the other is centrally an *experience*, wherein we share ourselves and our stories as fundamentally relational and ever-mysterious, always reaching toward the good.[76]

Such a view demands a broader vision of the causes and impacts of trauma that expand beyond an individual right to treatment and into communal responsibility for harm, thus revealing the necessity of multivalent justice praxis—individual, communal, and social—in the traumatic imagination. Importantly, this is still rooted in Caputo's radical hermeneutic:

> a radically interpretive gesture, which consists not in finding meaning but in dealing with the breakdown of meaning, the shattering and foundering of meaning. It is not a hermeneutic which finally fixes meaning and truth once and for all but a hermeneutic fired by the

---

[75] Porter and Robinson, *Active Hermeneutics,* 177.

[76] That is, where the concern for justice is always present, but must be so contextual that the traumatic imagination need not (and cannot) define the specifics of justice for each circumstance.

dissemination and trembling of meaning and truth. It is a hermeneutic of the *ébranler,* possible only when the whole world trembles.[77]

This trembling is a call to external engagement rather than a plunge into an internal spiral. Trauma and all suffering pull us toward engagement with our irreducibility, "the face of the one who suffers is itself, but it is also essentially more. And it is the sense of this 'more' which radical hermeneutics wants to cultivate."[78] Beyond engagement, the traumatic imagination as hermeneutic does not result in a fall to negative theology: the still-powerful but, in light of trauma, often unsatisfying *via negativa.* Trauma, as outlined here, is an ethical demand that requires engagement with this "more" in practical work for justice alongside its interpretive power.

Here, memory understood in the traumatic imagination is a key tool for such justice. As Episcopal priest and theologian Flora Keshgegian emphasizes, memory is not only a *problem* for survivors. It is a *resource.*

In her work, Keshgegian helps survivors name and claim their experience as multifaceted: as memory of (1) suffering and loss, (2) resistance and agency, and (3) connection with life and wholeness that is not defined by their suffering.[79] Memory understood in this way can orient us to discover tools of resistance to understand more fully the harm experienced individually, the structures that often support ongoing oppression, and the enduring claim for life beyond pain. This is especially necessary as "most people with painful memories ... would rather not have them, and if they blame anyone they tend to repeatedly blame themselves."[80] As

---

[77] Caputo, *Radical Hermeneutics,* 279.

[78] Caputo, *Radical Hermeneutics,* 287. I also agree with Caputo about his assessment of radical hermeneutics not resting in negative theology, but where he does not provide the next ethical step, I attempt to do so here.

[79] Flora Keshgegian, *Redeeming Memories: A Theology of Healing and Transformation* (Nashville: Abingdon Press, 2000), 121.

[80] Charles Whitfield as cited by Keshgegian, *Redeeming Memories,* 52.

such, the communal, historically situated, incarnationally defined orientation of the traumatic imagination beyond individual harm is critical. It offers a new way of reading one's experiences and one's theology "for life."

Yet, as Keshgegian readily admits, the process of claiming and reintegrating painful memories is one of long-term struggle.[81] The practice of trauma memory must be tempered with an awareness of the potential instrumentalization of suffering, in which one is asked to carry forward the burden of an experience "for" the community (e.g., the seeming mandate of survivors to tell their stories publicly and act as humanity's conscience). This, too, must be resisted, as the one who suffers owes nothing to those who witness. The sufferer's experience calls the community to greater responsibility. Now what?

The traumatic imagination emphasizes the importance of the "counter-story" or counter-memory that demands concrete justice for persons and simultaneously does not reduce the person to an isolated experience of trauma. It urges us to see that an individual who tells their story is not simply defined by one event. "There is a need to keep telling the world that something remains," that they are much more than their wounds.[82] As such, the theological traumatic imagination reads time, position, and praxis differently and importantly as a type of memory—a re-membering that seeks to put back together what has been ruptured, to sit within as well as seek to balm the wound, to move within and across boundaries—all in memory of the in-breaking of Christ and the gospel promises of justice.

---

[81] Seen also in the stories of Monica Coleman in chapter 2, and in May, *A Body Knows*, 67.

[82] John Swinton, *Dementia: Living in the Memories of God* (Grand Rapids: William B. Eerdmans, 2012), 66. However, as a friend recently expressed, "I do not owe anyone my wounds." This is also profoundly true in trauma treatment, and not often a right of survivors that the world at large respects.

Conclusion

So, once again, back to our orienting question: what does it look like to do theological ethics with trauma as one's hermeneutic?

A partial answer: the traumatic imagination helps us to read and act with a particular preunderstanding of time, position, and praxis that can open spaces to co-create new ways of being and being-with that strive toward flourishing.

Exploring trauma as a hermeneutic uncovers how we might follow trauma's demands from darkness, from the at-once viscerally known and the simultaneously deeply unknown.[83] While this may sound neat and tidy, tied up with an academic bow, we return as we began to the heartrending reality of this way of reading the world. Anyone who has looked into eyes filled with tears, a face breaking in grief, in hunger, and in pain, need not be reminded of the difficulty of this task.

The traumatic imagination challenges every single one of my first instincts: asking me to look past outbursts and disruptive behavior, "abnormal" or even amoral actions; to overcome my own urge to look away, to dismiss, to extricate myself from responsibility. The traumatic imagination asks me instead to practice "withness," to read beyond the presenting behavior to understand what is missing, what has been taken, what is screaming out for healing, where I become myself with and for the "other." With John Caputo, I believe the traumatic imagination asks us to "try not to make things look easy ... [to instead practice] hermeneutics as an attempt to stick with the original difficulty of life, and not to betray it with metaphysics."[84] In this mode, enfleshed counter-memory as Christian social ethic is grounded in the traumatic imagination, revealing the fluidity of time, the enfleshment of position, and the praxis of memory as essential to theological ethics.

---

[83] Here, I am leaning on Caruth from chapter 1.
[84] Caputo, *Radical Hermeneutics*, 1.

4

READING LIBERATIVE THEOLOGIES WITH A TRAUMA LENS

Metz and Trauma's "Dangerous Memory"

Towards the end of the Second World War, at the age of sixteen, I was snatched out of school and conscripted into the [Nazi] army. After a hasty training in the barracks at Würzburg I arrived at the front, which by that time had already advanced over the Rhine into Bavaria. My company consisted solely of young people, well over a hundred of them. One evening the company commander sent me with a message to battalion headquarters. I wandered during the night through shattered, burning villages and farmsteads, and when next morning I returned to my company I found only the dead: dead bodies, overwhelmed by a combined fighter-bomber and tank attack. I could only look into the still, dead faces of all those with whom on the previous days I had shared the anxieties of childhood and the joys of youth. *I cannot remember anything but a silent cry.* {I strayed for hours alone in the forest. Over and over again, just this silent cry! And up until today I see myself so.} I can still see myself there today, and my childhood dreams have collapsed before that memory. A great gap had been torn in my powerful Bavarian Catholic socialization with its well-knit trust. What happens if one does not go to a psychologist, but into the church, and if one cannot be talked out of such unreconciled experiences either by the church or by theology, *but together with them wants to believe and together with them wants to talk about God?*

—Johann Baptist Metz[1]

To this point, I have largely focused on the survivors of harm, but what are the costs—practical and theological—if perpetrators of violence "forget" their actions or are encouraged to do so? While Metz's short service in the Nazi army ended without his personal commission of violence, the experience shaped the rest of his life. Seeking an answer to his own question, he became a Catholic priest and studied under Karl Rahner, with whom he formed a deep relationship. Metz's eventual break from his formation in the Rahnerian transcendental method had everything to do with the massive, systemic killing of the Shoah in which he marginally participated. Living through the communal formation of memory in the aftermath of the war, Metz was disappointed by his fellow

---

[1] Johann Baptist Metz, "Johann Baptist Metz," in *How I Have Changed: Reflections on Thirty Years of Theology*, ed. Jürgen Moltmann (Harrisburg, PA: Trinity Press International, 1997), 31. Emphasis added. Bracketed addition from Metz's telling of this story in Metz, "Communicating a Dangerous Memory," in *Communicating a Dangerous Memory: Soundings in Political Theology*, ed. Fred Lawrence (Atlanta: Scholars Press, 1987), 40. This is reminiscent of Friedrich Nietzsche's observation, "Gradually it has become clear to me what every great philosophy so far has been: namely the personal confession of its author and a kind of involuntary and unconscious memoir." *Beyond Good and Evil*, trans. Walter Kaufmann (1886; New York: Vintage, 1966), as cited by Susan Brison, *Aftermath: Violence and the Remaking of a Self* (Princeton, NJ: Princeton University Press, 2002), 23. See also Dorothee Soelle, *The Silent Cry: Mysticism and Resistance* (Minneapolis: Fortress Press, 2001).

theologians' lack of explicit attention to the devastation of the Shoah, arguing that one cannot do theology with one's back to Auschwitz.[2] In this chapter, I engage Metz through Armenian American Episcopal priest and theologian Flora Keshgegian to apply the three dimensions of a theological hermeneutic of trauma: time, position, and praxis. Applying this "traumatic imagination" to Metz reveals new gifts in his work and demonstrates how theological ethics might be constructed with trauma at the forefront, namely with an emphasis on the mystical-political that reaches beyond individualism and into contextual, entangled enfleshment. Metz's work supports a moral mandate for those who witness trauma to counter the demands of the powerful who manipulate persons, spaces, and memories to fit within their designs. The answer Metz offers to the risks of traumatic memory, writ large, is the necessary cultivation of a subversive hope rooted in the dangerous memory of the life, death, and resurrection of Christ. This practice of "dangerous memory" can interpret trauma for the individual as well as the community, and embolden an ethic of resistance to the causes of suffering throughout the world.[3]

First, I specifically engage Metz's theological anthropology, comprising the co-constitutive concepts of memory, narrative,

---

[2] James Matthew Ashley, *Interruptions: Mysticism, Politics, and Theology in the Work of Johann Baptist Metz* (Notre Dame, IN: Notre Dame Press, 1998), 158. Metz himself states that his encounters with the Frankfurt School (especially Ernst Bloch) "politicized me out" of transcendental theology. See Johann Baptist Metz, *A Passion for God: The Mystical-Political Dimension of Christianity*, trans. J. Matthew Ashley (New York: Paulist Press, 1998), 3.

[3] Johann Baptist Metz, *Faith in History and Society: Toward a Practical Fundamental Theology*, trans. J. Matthew Ashley (1979; New York: Crossroad, 2011), 88. Also, although I don't agree with his conclusion, this is echoed by Stanley Hauerwas in "Remembering as a Moral Task: The Challenge of the Holocaust" (1981) in *The Hauerwas Reader,* ed. John Berkman and Michael Cartwright (Durham, NC: Duke University Press, 2001), 327–347, where he argues that Christians must be a "community of remembrance" that resists "abstract universalisms of mankind."

and solidarity.[4] Metz's understanding of the human person in this tripartite form holds direct relevance to the traumatic experience and further expands our enfleshed, womanist thinking developed in chapter 2. I then turn to a brief exploration of trauma as "dangerous memory," revealing how Metz's concepts of *interruption* and *forward memories* create the basis for a mystical-political interpretation of trauma and a Christian ethical mandate of remembrance in a liberative key. As Metz's work is largely theoretical, I conclude with Keshgegian, whose own use of what I term the traumatic imagination to read Metz demonstrates concrete life-giving practices of dangerous memory for and with trauma survivors.

Metz's complicated personal history and subsequent dedication to theological reasoning from its echoes throughout his life illustrate the way trauma shapes the self *and* emphasizes the broader context in which any trauma must be read. As this book has stressed, trauma is inherently communal and, as such, must be seen in its particularity as well as its universality. As Metz emphasizes, although not in these exact words, the personal *is* political.[5] Insisting that theology attend to the person *in history*, Metz reveals yet another layer of the challenge of traumatic memory: *the danger of its memory for us all.*[6] Direct survivors, their families, and their faith communities are not the only responsible actors within our trauma-addled world. *All of*

---

[4] These three concepts make up the last three chapters of *Faith in History and Society*, but as Ashley argues, they are the interpretive framework of all Metz's work. See J. Matthew Ashley, "Introduction: The Path to *Faith in History and Society*," in Metz, *Faith in History and Society*, 3.

[5] Metz, *Faith in History and Society*, 178. The phrase I use here was coined during the student movements and second-wave feminism in the United States in the 1960s.

[6] Not all memories are dangerous, as reviewed in the trauma context in chapter 1. Here, I focus on subversive memories of the victims of history, those whose recollections run counter to the dominant history written by the victors. This idea was coined by Herbert Marcus in the Frankfurt School, then taken into theology by Metz.

us must do the hard work of understanding ourselves within the web of human suffering. Christian enfleshed counter-memory must include survivors, perpetrators, and outside witnesses—and must wrestle with the complex truth that we often embody aspects of all such identities simultaneously. While such a metanarrative must be approached with caution, so as not to collapse our thinking into false universalisms, Metz inspires a necessary prophetic edge essential to positive action in the face of trauma. Through Metz's thought on metahistory and our roles therein, this chapter asks: If Christianity bears the promise of freedom to followers of Christ, what does freedom mean when faced with the devastation of trauma? How can a call "to remember" be understood without further burdening the victim/survivor, functioning instead as a call to the broader community to foster a greater sense of responsibility? What if we take our unreconciled experiences to the psychologist *and* to the church?

Theology from Catastrophe

Metz's theology is far from systematic. Rather, it is a constellation of writing that coalesces around a major theme: How does one talk about theology from the place of catastrophe? James Matthew Ashley, a leading Metz scholar, argues that Metz resists systemization because of the abstraction he sees in transcendental theologies: that while claiming to be historically based, they pay no attention to the real suffering of the world. Concrete suffering is disruptive. It fundamentally resists categorization, and its meaning is always outside our grasp. Catastrophe, from its Greek root, means an overturning, an upending of existence defined by tragedy. Thus, for Metz, theodicy is the animating principle of theology as it gives us the right questions, rather than the right answers.[7] It

---

[7] "Questions That Irritate," from Ashley, *Interruptions,* 160. See also Johann Baptist Metz, "Suffering from God: Theology as Theodicy," *Pacifica* 5 (1992): 274–287.

is the fundamental human questioning of the goodness of God, embodied within Jesus's "impassioned cry of Mk 15:34, 'My God, my God, why have you abandoned me?'"[8]

Doing theology from the reality of catastrophe means that "the eyes of theology" must point directly at the truth of lived experience, because "if theology becomes obsessed only with the coherence of its concepts, or their collective correspondence to a reality 'out there' then it risks losing its eyes for the new movement of the Spirit in our midst."[9] Our eyes are not to be focused on a spiritualized abstraction obsessed with orthodoxy, but onto the body at the center of the faith, those whose suffering echoes it, and the creativity of the Spirit that endures within and beyond the devastation. Metz reinforces this orientation, what he calls a "mysticism of open eyes," by focusing on the parable of the Good Samaritan:

> The story of his eyes, of attentiveness to the suffering of others, the readiness to listen more to the authority of a sufferer than to the call to the temple ... One can learn from Jesus: I've often called it a mysticism not of closed eyes but of open eyes, capable of perceiving the suffering of others, and if we're already speaking of the memory that has been preserved in the church, then this memory must beyond question always be an essential part of the memory of suffering, quite unsentimental, focused on the suffering of others.[10]

---

[8] Ashley, *Interruptions*, 160. Theology itself is practical and personal: "God simply cannot be thought without this idea irritating and disrupting the immediate interests of the one trying to think it." Metz, *Faith in History and Society*, 62.

[9] Ashley, *Interruptions*, 201.

[10] Metz in Hans Norbert Janowski, "Television Discussion," in *How I Have Changed: Reflections on Thirty Years of Theology*, ed. Jürgen Moltmann (Harrisburg, PA: Trinity Press International, 1997), 100.

Mysticism in this sense is not a practice divorced from reality, where one seeks to escape the world's pain, but is rather melded directly with our lives as they are. "For Metz, a true mysticism, one in which a person enters the mystery of their own existence as a subject in God's presence, is always a mysticism that sees more of life and not less."[11] While Metz focuses on suffering in particular, his call is toward a broader awareness, the capacity to see pain as well as the activity of persons and the Spirit to survive and to heal.

This practical mysticism is not only about how we see each other but also about how we see God. Liturgical theologian Samantha Slaubaugh points out that while Christ's life, death, and resurrection are *dangerous* as they offer a direct, contradictory story to that of the powerful of history, it also troubles the image of a detached divinity so often accepted by the faithful. It asks us to recognize God in our midst, because "as dangerous as this memory is—for it takes one away from the safe, distant God who has little practical impact—it is fundamentally a liberative memory. The ability to remember this dangerous narrative of God coming into the world, suffering, and rising again frees one to see with open eyes the very narrative itself in one's own particular social and historical context."[12]

As such, Metz centers the person in his thought, reacting against the ruling framework of the bourgeois person: shaped by instrumentalism, used within consumer principles of exchange, and anonymized via hyperprivatization. The person *as subject*, contra object as in the bourgeois frame, is the locus of suffering and, as such, must be the focus of liberation.[13] Emphasizing

---

[11] Samantha Slaubaugh, "A 'Liturgical Mysticism of Open Eyes': Johann Baptist Metz, Caryll Houselander, and Pandemic Liturgy," *Religions* 12, no. 9 (2021): 685.

[12] Slaubaugh, "A 'Liturgical Mysticism of Open Eyes,'" 685.

[13] Metz raises this concern in response to both capitalist and communist structures of societies in the mid-twentieth century. Metz, *Faith in History and Society*, 181.

theological anthropology also speaks to Metz's concern with theology's sublimation into evolutionary, "modern" time, where the cogs of history grind ever forward, with no concern for persons and no hope for liberation. The Christian story stands in opposition to this version of time. It instead promises a full end to time and the capacity for ultimate transformation in the vision of an apocalyptic spirituality.[14] Within this framework, Christianity values and uplifts the particular, unique creation of each and every person—indeed, all of existence. To understand the promise of fulfilled time and its relation to trauma, it is helpful to outline the three co-constitutive elements of Metz's theological anthropology: memory, narrative, and solidarity. These three elements provide the building blocks for reading trauma as "dangerous memory," where embodied memory can be a tool for resistance, narrative is the process of cultivating memory, and solidarity is the necessary ethical outcome when theological anthropology is understood as a political pursuit grounded in collective memory.

Memory

Memory, for Metz, is the essential core of the human person: memory is the action of "a reason that intends to become practical as freedom."[15] As this definition indicates, memory is never a purely internal pursuit, but has direct, external impacts. The person, as

---

[14] Metz, *A Passion for God*, 14. Where *eschatology* is a broad term that deals with "last things" such as the immorality of the soul and the end of time, *apocalyptic* "means revelation or unveiling and normally refers to the kind of writing that gives a revelation of hidden knowledge, particularly of God's control over when and how history ends [e.g., divine intervention specifically in cataclysmic events]." Everett Ferguson, *Backgrounds of Early Christianity* (Grand Rapids: William B. Eerdmans, 1987), 377. This does not mean a spirituality hyperfocused on the end of the world, but rather one that recognizes the unique, revelatory, and ongoing role of God in our lives.

[15] Metz, *Faith in History and Society*, 171.

such, is outward-facing. Indeed, for Metz the person is essentially constituted in relation to the other, particularly the suffering or death of the other, and this relationship is held in memories. This fundamental relatedness is rooted in the ultimate relatedness of humanity with God, and the impossibility of truly isolated existence based in our created nature. Humans *are* because of others and God as ultimate other. In this ontology, memory forms the basis of our relational being as an action, not a static category. Memory's essential action is the pursuit of liberation via two components: memory of freedom and memory of suffering.[16] Both are required to ensure that the past—even or especially of suffering—is not relegated to meaninglessness, and to resist the modern mentality of constant progress that, for Metz, offers only repetition rather than liberation.[17] Metz stresses that the function of memory is the empowerment of those who suffer (indeed, all of humanity) to continue the struggle for freedom. This is not to say that all memory, prima facie, is empowering or liberative, but that memory rightly understood is freeing. Metz was not ignorant of memory's manipulation or misuse, but wanted to call Christianity to account for forming right memory as central to our created nature as *imago Dei*. What forms the content of "empowering" memories is the *memoria passionis*. The story of Christ's passion "is a radical biblical category, [and as memory] becomes a universal category, a category of rescue."[18] As such, right memory is inherently "dangerous," as it keeps open the possibility that things can be different from their current state—even radically so, as demonstrated by the gospel.

Memory of Christ's passion is central, as it testifies to resurrection not bound by earthly constraints, of healing that is literally impossible without God. Suffering is irredeemable and

---

[16] The ability to name suffering as such is to recognize that it is not "normal" and there exists another way; in this sense, for Metz, a memory of suffering already implies a memory of freedom.

[17] Metz, *Faith in History and Society*, 177, and Ashley, *Interruptions*, 116.

[18] Metz, "Communicating a Dangerous Memory," 43.

cannot be erased, as seen on the risen body of Christ, and our concepts and rationalizations fall short in its wake. Indeed, "in the last resort, no happiness enjoyed by the children can make up for the pain suffered by the fathers, and no social progress can atone for the injustice done to the departed. If we persist too long in accepting the meaninglessness of death and in being indifferent to death, all we shall have left to offer even to the living will be banal promises."[19] Memory of the passion and the resurrection resists meaninglessness and is practiced for Metz in the Catholic liturgy. Liturgy exemplifies the redemptive action of dangerous memory, when ordinary time (*chronos*) enters into eschatological encounter with God (*kairos*).[20] At this moment, God's preferential option for the poor and suffering, exemplified by God's self/child on the cross embodied in the bread and wine of the Eucharist, is remembered and given the future promise of resurrection. This is the specific hope of the vanished, the dead of history. As Ashley frames it,

> Because their future is still outstanding, the memory of the promises made to those who have suffered and disappeared in the past projects a future that is more than a mere extrapolation of the present, because it cannot be encompassed by the history of success that culminates in what exists in the present. This gives these memories their disturbing, dangerous character. It also gives them their power to break through the systematically managed totality of present society, with its pregiven agenda of what a "reasonable" person ought to desire, hope for, and struggle for.[21]

---

[19] Metz, "Communicating a Dangerous Memory," 43, quotation from "Our Hope: A Confession of Faith for This Time," *Study Encounter* 12, no. 1–2 (1976): 70. See also Metz, *Faith in History and Society*, 125.

[20] For a thorough treatment of the liturgical practice of anamnestic reason, see Bruce Morrill, *Anamnesis as Dangerous Memory: Political and Liturgical Theology in Dialogue* (Collegeville, MN: Liturgical Press, 2000).

[21] Ashley, *Interruptions*, 117.

Thus, memory is constitutive of our very selves and is also the tool of the vanquished, the way in which one must read history to find the ultimate truth, rather than merely the stories of the victors. This stress on "truth" over "fact" is echoed by many trauma survivors, and is nurtured by fostering and supporting dangerous memories. While not falling prey to counterfactual lies, seeking the whole truth of trauma means tracing its ripples throughout individual lives and communities.[22] These memories of the truth of the trauma experience often run up against accepted power structures that are supported by complexes like racism, sexism, homophobia, and classism that seek to justify the suffering of the oppressed and reason away their pain as earned through their actions.

Resisting this social impulse to forget suffering, and driven by the victims of history, the cultivation of dangerous memories leaves open paths of hope for all—including, somewhat challengingly, perpetrators. Perhaps this stance stems partially from Metz's own experience as a sixteen-year-old conscripted, yet still complicit, German soldier, but it is also grounded in his view of the comprehensive nature of salvation and God's promise of universal redemption. Although excluding no one, the challenge of a dangerous memory is not confronted easily, and requires a willing entry into discomfort, pain, and doubt that the modern, particularly Western, person is culturally trained to ignore or repress. Yet, as Metz's colleague Lutheran theologian Dorothee Soelle argues, the desensitization that the drive for freedom from suffering involves is at its root the inability to perceive reality, as "freedom from suffering is nothing other than a blindness that does not perceive suffering. It is the no longer perceived numbness to suffering. Then the person and his circumstances are accepted as natural, which even on the technological level signifies nothing but

---

[22] As discussed in chapter 1, this is not that facts do not matter, but that the existential components (the "truths") of trauma often exceed their bounds and are unaccounted for in traditional justice practices.

blind worship of the status-quo: no disruptions, no involvement, no sweat."[23] Memory is therefore an essential aspect of the person as well as an ethical mandate. Where society may urge a false sense of complacency and flight from the inescapable nature of suffering, dangerous memory requires work: the essential work of uncovering the challenging reality of God's kingdom, which is already—but not yet.[24]

Narrative

The method of work for cultivating a dangerous memory is that of narrative, or "dangerous stories" of suffering. Narrative is the mechanism that, for Metz, attends to the dangers of universal approaches and does not "fall victim to a flat relativization of cultural worlds: emphasizing respect for and obedience towards the authority of those who suffer. For this authority [of those who suffer] is the only authority in which the authority of the God who judges manifests itself in the world for all men and women."[25] As such, narrative is "selectively and symbolically engaging rather than aiming at being exhaustive," and helps illuminate the critical functions of memory as not only existential, but also ethical, apologetic, and prophetic.[26] Thus, although the *method* of cultivating dangerous narratives as stories that push against prevailing oppressive structures through the memory of those who suffer and

---

[23] Dorothee Soelle, *Suffering* (Philadelphia: Fortress Press, 1975), 39.

[24] God's in-breaking into history in Christ creates a type of theological tension, often termed a "realized eschatology." Such language is often used as the root of liberative theologies, and Metz was deeply informed by the theological work of Latin American priests whose work forms the corpus of Catholic liberation theology.

[25] Metz, "Johann Baptist Metz," 35.

[26] Fred Lawrence, "Dangerous Memory and the Pedagogy of the Oppressed," in *Communicating a Dangerous Memory: Soundings in Political Theology*, ed. Fred Lawrence (Atlanta: Scholars Press, 1987), 20.

are fighting for freedom in the promise of Christ is universal, the *content* is deeply personal, individual, and context-dependent. The universality of narrative is present in its form, in the recognition of God made real through our willingness to look directly at suffering through interpretive storytelling, speaking and listening to the stories of persons who struggle for freedom.

Importantly for trauma, narrative is a fundamental form of expression for those seeking healing. The field of trauma studies holds a general consensus regarding the power of testimony in reestablishing or creating meaning, even or especially in the face of the amorphous nature of biological human memory and its capacity for change throughout the lifespan. The seminal study by Dori Laub and Shoshana Felman states of testimony recorded of survivors of the Shoah:

> While historical evidence to the event which constitutes the trauma may be abundant and documents in vast supply, the trauma—as a known even and not simply as an overwhelming shock—has not been truly witnessed yet, not taken cognizance of. The emergence of the narrative which is being listened to—and heard—is, therefore, the process and the place wherein the cognizance, the "knowing" of the event is given birth to. The listener, therefore, is a party to the creation of knowledge *de novo*. The testimony to the trauma thus includes its hearer, who is, so to speak, the blank screen on which the event comes to be inscribed for the first time.[27]

The stories we tell are not simply stories but convey fundamental truths of our self-identity. As Felman and Laub point out, narrative reaches beyond data and into meaning-making, structuring how

---

[27] Shoshana Felman and Dori Laub, *Testimony: Crises of Witnessing in Literature, Psychoanalysis and History* (New York: Routledge, 1991), 57. This is what Metz calls a "narrative depth structure." *Faith in History and Society*, 186.

we understand, interpret, and *know* not only the events of our lives but how they shape our very selves. Within narration of our painful memories we can and do push on border limits, on definitions of "normal" or "expected" or "sensical" that are destroyed by trauma experience. Through broader contextualization of experience in the narrative of one's life, these definitions are revealed to be socially constructed and enforced, rather than natural.[28] Just as trauma itself pushes past our capacities, in narration we exceed such predetermined bounds, creating new stories that can form new selves in response. When practiced with dangerous memory at the forefront, narrative is the method that can facilitate the formation of integrated selves grounded in a hope that far exceeds what existing hegemonic forces present as possible.

We, in a vital way, become fully authentic selves when we narrate our memories. We also create a marking, an inscription, on the other who hears the events of our lives—particularly those of suffering. Where Laub and Felman describe those who listen as blank screens, they are vitally present and participatory. Those who listen may be "other" or "blank" as they sit fully outside of the experience being narrated, but they maintain integral selfhood. Here, the act of communication not only constitutes *one* self, but reveals our fundamental relationality—that we need each other to exist fully. One cannot speak alone, lest one be lost to delusion. The process of narrative cannot happen in a vacuum; it requires a witness, a hearer of the word, particularly holding the speaker in beloved community.[29] The practice of narration—

---

[28] Recall our work with Emilie Townes's cultural production of health in chapter 2.

[29] These communities do not have to be permanent or hyperpersonal, but can be constituted of people of goodwill who seek to understand "the other." For example, while imperfect, many global truth and reconciliation commissions are premised on this type of loose community that reaches for narrative encounter to create peace. For the potentials and pitfalls of communal narrative formation see Stephanie Edwards, "Creating a Multidirectional Memory for Healing in the

to speak, be heard, be understood, and then to do the same for another—is a uniting insight between trauma healing and Metz's theological anthropology. As such, narrative practice makes a direct impact on our theology, that the "functioning-in-the-face-of bestows on theology traits of narrative and memory . . . [and that narrative] heightens its sensitivity to the concrete responsibility encountered in controversial talk about God."[30] Metz pushes the role of narration beyond self-actualization and into the embodied, relational ethics at the heart of God-talk.

For Metz, the three existential categories of the authentic human person—memory, narrative, and solidarity—are necessarily related, intertwined, and truly co-constitutive just as persons themselves are related, intertwined, and truly co-constitutive with other persons. There is not a direct, linear procedure through which one cultivates memory, practices narrative, and then enacts solidarity although it may function in that manner. The process is a circular, dynamic, even haphazard entrance into the true messiness of life. And yet, rather than be overwhelmed by chaos, Metz finds meaning, and God, within this process.[31] The "other" to which we speak is not just our fellow persons, it is a suffering unto God (*Leiden an Gott*) that animates us, a practice of narrative seen in the paradigmatic Job: the person should not give in, even to God, but "rather [as Job] suffers, he stands, he complains, he battles."[32] This is a practice that reaches toward answering Metz's question: taking one's unreconciled experiences to Godself, telling unflinching

---

Former Yugoslavia," in *Healing and Peacebuilding after War: Transforming Trauma in Bosnia and Herzegovina*, ed. Marie Berry, Nancy Good, and Julianne Funk (New York: Routledge, 2020), 89–105. For Metz, precision of form/practice is missing in his work as he remains largely theoretical in his construction.

[30] Metz, "Communicating a Dangerous Memory," 38.

[31] See Metz, *Faith in History and Society*, chapter 12, especially p. 200, on mystagogy for all and on the necessary nature of the "everyday."

[32] Soelle, *Suffering*, 112. Also explored within the cry of Israel for Metz. See Ashley, *Interruptions*, 127.

truth, struggling, and forging new meaning. Such an orientation complements trauma studies, which finds that even the confusing, inconsistent, and unformulated story of the trauma victim is an authentic expression of their pain and of fundamental truth.

Even inchoate narrative begins healing, for, as Soelle puts it, "The cry coming in the midst of pain is already in itself a physical easing of pain, since the crest of the pain wave moves along with a form of activity, however slight, as it comes to expression in protesting, facial contortion, groaning or screaming.... Nothing can be learned from suffering unless it is worked through."[33] Narratives encourage such a working through that turns toward God as well as the other. The dangerous stories offered by all humanity take seriously, and value, a spirituality of complaint that does not rest in platitudes but extends a concrete demand upon the human community and upon God to offer restoration.[34] However, these stories only *work* "to the extent that we do enter into them, allow ourselves to be taken up by them and transformed by hearing or reading them.... In them we resist the urge to make clean, black-and-white divisions in history, placing blame on 'the other,' whoever that might be."[35] While the nuance encouraged by narratives of trauma does not mean that responsibility for concrete suffering, the work of justice, is not to be pursued, it does expose a level of complicity and connection within our global community that is often overlooked. Indeed, for many sufferings of the world, we are all in some way responsible.[36] To hold this truth,

---

[33] Soelle, *Suffering*, 126. Further, for Metz, "In every thing there is always a loud, or at times a silent, cry. This is what led me not long ago, for example, to ask Jürgen Habermas in a friendly way whether it has really been settled once and for all that the meaning of human language is rooted in communication and not, perhaps, in that cry." Metz, *A Passion for God*, 5.

[34] Ashley, *Interruptions*, 166.

[35] Ashley, *Interruptions*, 121 and 131.

[36] I am drawing a distinction here between the narratives used in more amorphous community spaces, such as those presented through womanist thought in chapter 2, rather than the more exacting accounting for harm that

narratives within the work of Metz ask that within the vision of eschatological time, Christians see the redemption of all creation, and in the present are called to work for the tangible liberation of those who suffer.

Solidarity

For Metz, any theological anthropology reflects the human community and its liminality. Humans understand what it means to *be* through the death of the "other"' because, as humans, we understand what it is to exist.[37] As such, theological anthropology is a political pursuit: we are created in fundamental solidarity with all other humans. Metz posits two essential definitions of solidarity: the concrete-particular and the universal-mystical. The first calls us toward solidarity with the victims of history—to seek out and correct injustices to the extent possible, and then extend ourselves further, to the point that we appear fools in the eyes of society. Solidarity in this mode requires real risk, modeled on the life of Jesus, for "really there is no suffering whatsoever in the world that does not concern us."[38] In this way, "Love does not 'require' the cross, but *de facto* it ends up on the cross."[39] The second formulation of solidarity

---

is pursued, say, by the criminal justice system. Yet this does not mean that communities and individuals will not explicitly name and claim particular wrongdoing on the part of certain individuals, groups, and systems, but that (particularly for Metz) our connections to suffering are much more global and metaphysical than regularly understood.

[37] Ashley, *Interruptions*, 147 and 159. This extends beyond the I-Thou-Neighbor, and reaches into the entirety of the world. Metz, *Faith in History and Society*, 209.

[38] Janowski, "Television Discussion," 101. This attitudinal stance also resists the "natural" state of suffering, that falls before evolutionary cycles and accepts suffering as immutable. Metz, *Faith in History and Society*, 229. It also refuses to "pass off the subject that has already been social empowered as 'the' religious subject" (213).

[39] Soelle, *Suffering*, 163. As Metz quoted in *Our Hope*, "Jesus was neither a

is universal-mystical, where positioning solidarity in reflection of Jesus's life and death illuminates Metz's view of the person as subject, where the transcendental subject "is related from its very roots to the other."[40] However mysterious in its existential dimension, universal-mystical solidarity is also essentially bound to the practical task of becoming ourselves. Through the practice of solidarity, "in believing that others can rely on them, in communicating to others and hoping them 'for others,' they belong to oneself as well. Only then."[41] Believers are nourished by this imitation of Christ, by "bringing Jesus's love and partiality for the marginalized into the political and social structures in and through which we create and recreate ourselves."[42] In its fullness, solidarity makes memory and narrative practical, ensuring that we are tied directly to life in the here-and-now as well as the hereafter.

These three components—memory, narrative, and solidarity—compose for Metz what it means to become an authentic human in relationship with God: "Our being is meaningful in terms of the past which we remember, it is meaningful in terms of the community in and with which we hope and labor for a future, and all of this is primarily present to us in an open, never fully thematizable mode of being that can only be adequately captured narratively."[43] As victims of history, we do not remember to dwell in pain or seek redemption in it, just as witnesses or perpetrators on any level do not remember to drown in guilt.[44] All of humanity

---

fool nor a rebel: but He could obviously be mistaken for either.... Anyone who follows him ... must allow for the same possibility of being the victim of such confusion." Metz, "Communicating a Dangerous Memory," 45.

[40] Ashley, *Interruptions*, 198. This is a "reciprocal recognition" (Metz, *Faith in History and Society*, 211). As Soelle points out, this is also solidarity without condition, that is, the total affirmation of reality as described and experienced (e.g., parent/child). Soelle, *Suffering*, 92.

[41] Ashley, *Interruptions*, 52.

[42] Ashley, *Interruptions*, 130.

[43] Ashley, *Interruptions*, 153.

[44] For Metz, guilt properly understood is taking responsibility as

remembers dangerously together to drive us to "a critical and liberating response that is justified and required by the apocalyptic character of our situation."[45] With Rahner, Metz argues that the experiences of everyday believers are essential, that interpretations of life are not "pour[ed] out 'from above' into bewildered souls; rather ... [there is] an invitation to a journey of discovery into the virtually uncharted territory of one's own life."[46] While the defining characteristic of Metz's theological anthropology is the lens of suffering rooted in Christ's passion, this orientation is not meant to glorify pain. Metz emphasizes that "suffering isn't fantastic, isn't a sign of love. Suffering is painful, and it leads to nothingness."[47] Instead, the universal character of suffering is an invitation to uncover the "right questions" offered by the exploration of theodicy and the reality of humanity as bearers of dangerous memories, tellers and hearers of dangerous stories, and actors of personal and communal liberation.

Trauma as "Dangerous" Memory:
Reading Metz with a Traumatic Imagination

The dynamic action around which Metz's theological anthropology, theodicy, and indeed his entire body of work orbits is the spirituality of *Leiden an Gott*—suffering unto God. A "spirituality of complaint," this animating principle drives all Metz's theology, revealing a political, praxis-oriented anthropology that emerges from

---

Homo peccator, particularly because we always try to exculpate ourselves of responsibility for the existence of suffering. *Faith in History and Society,* 119.

[45] Ashley, *Interruptions,* 124, and Metz, *Faith in History and Society,* 154. Both Ashley and Metz repeat with Jon Sobrino that the only goal of all this talk is to remove the crucified people of the world from the cross.

[46] Metz, *A Passion for God,* 13.

[47] Hartmut Meesmass, "An Account of the Symposium," in *How I Have Changed: Reflections on Thirty Years of Theology,* ed. Jürgen Moltmann (Harrisburg, PA: Trinity Press International, 1997), 123.

a lived, spiritual stance first, rather than "pure" intellectual categories.[48] Suffering unto God is also a resonant and helpful orientation of spirituality in response to trauma. The goal of such a spiritual practice is not to determine universal answers, or force "accepted" models of healing, but rather to cultivate spaces of ongoing complaint and transformative praxis. Such a commitment to protest does not dwell within its own bounds, simply repeating pain again and again, nor does it settle with the complaint being the only solution. Instead, a spirituality of suffering unto God reaches outward, in the belief that voicing of experience can reveal and build a way forward within community. Together "we turn toward God, not in a trusting surrender, but in a complaining, expectant interrogation of God."[49] Through this type of narrative we resist the movements of technological advancements of modern society that often make us anonymous to each other and force an unbounded understanding of history without end. Metz argues that these movements constantly seek to strip us of awareness, of a sense of time, and have succeeded in creating a global society as we are today: we have no memories of "why" but only of "that."[50] Often this stripping of memory is a tool

---

[48] Ashley, *Interruptions*, 170. However, this spirituality should not be disembodied. Just as for womanist scholars, the concrete body is central to Metz's construction of this practice; Ashley, *Interruptions*, 85. As Ashley describes, we are "*being* a body.... In [Metz's] usage our embodiedness means not only having a physical body, but also being situated in history at a particular time, in a particular culture, thus linked with other persons in a particular way" ("Introduction," 6). In other words, "it tries to hold on to a permanent, integral dual structure, a mutual priority of subject and society/history." Metz, *Faith in History and Society*, 73.

[49] Ashley, *Interruptions*, 163.

[50] Metz, *Faith in History and Society*, 54. Here he is exploring the phenomenon of authority, and arguing that in the post-Enlightenment era it is only important that one *is* an authority, rather than that one *has* authority. He is teasing out the differences between social and political uses of power, versus the orienting power/authority of concepts such as freedom and the experience of suffering.

of the powerful, to repress the memory of suffering in particular, and to make its occurrence something tied to nature—a mere fact of life that no one can avoid. Alternatively, cultivating bonds of suffering, of trauma as dangerous memory, across experience creates an intimacy that does not threaten one's own healing but rather emboldens it with new possibilities.

Metz's theology of *Leiden an Gott* offers the context for a truly new narrative for trauma victims/survivors that contextualizes their experience and calls for a communal ethical response. Here, trauma scholar Michael Rothberg's concept of "multidirectional" memory is illustrative of how desperately we need authentically new ways forward. Rothberg offers a reflection upon W. E. B. Du Bois's 1949 visit to Poland and his subsequent article, "The Negro and the Warsaw Ghetto." Du Bois was distinctly moved by his time in Warsaw, reflecting on the disturbing echoes of suffering between the Jewish people and Black Americans. On this site, he saw the production of "biopolitical" space that revealed racialized thinking and state violence enacted on bodies.[51] A "double vision" of uniqueness as a well as similarity emerged, and became central to all Du Bois's work, balancing both the extreme particularities of a context while simultaneously recognizing commonalities. In this way, a multidirectional memory becomes the condition for authentic solidarity, not a false "unity" that only supports the political priorities of the powerful.[52] Standing in the rubble of Warsaw, Du Bois uncovered a relational view, that the "experience of particular suffering can be brought into dialogue with each other."[53]

Such a "counterdiscourse" can only be found, however, if groups as well as individuals embrace Rothberg's proposition of

---

[51] M. Rothberg, *Multidirectional Memory: Remembering the Holocaust in the Age of Decolonization* (Stanford, CA: Stanford University Press, 2009), 115.

[52] Rothberg, *Multidirectional Memory,* 12 and 121; Rothberg uses the word "colonial."

[53] Rothberg, *Multidirectional Memory,* 131.

noncompetition. Only when "one is willing to give up exclusive claims to ultimate victimization and ownership over suffering" can new narratives be created.[54] It is not that metaphorical "real estate" and concrete physical space do not matter, but that both can be resisted, reinterpreted, and brought under the greater goal of a relational effort toward mutual understanding and peace. For example, Rothberg would agree that Black Americans need particular physical spaces to tell their stories, that the historical harms of chattel slavery require particular remedies, and that we must eliminate the more amorphous social programming, such as that performed through stereotypes in culture and language, that continues to damage Black people. Rothberg is attempting, however, to encourage a broader framing of experience, the type of noncompetitive connection rooted in the experience of suffering that he sees within Du Bois's essay—a wider sense of lived solidarity. In recognizing connection, it is clear that all people are "implicated subjects, beneficiaries of a system that generates dispersed and uneven experiences of trauma and wellbeing simultaneously."[55] In very real ways, histories are "implicated in each other," and it is impossible to maintain a wall between them, even if desired. As Du Bois testified while standing in Warsaw, "The only way forward is through . . . entanglement."[56]

This is a powerful example, but one with limited efficacy. Understanding one's context in light of the other requires some form of contact, "open eyes" as emphasized by Metz, as well as a truly new frame in which to interpret the relationship. A powerful

---

[54] Rothberg, *Multidirectional Memory,* 132. Although beyond the scope here, this process must also include expanded religious narratives and visions.

[55] M. Rothberg, "Preface: Beyond Tancred and Clorinda—Trauma Studies for Implicated Subjects," in *The Future of Trauma Theory: Contemporary Literary and Cultural Criticism,* ed. Gert Buelens, Sam Durrant, and Robert Eaglestone (New York: Routledge, 2014), xv. See also Rothberg, *Multidirectional Memory,* 310.

[56] Rothberg, *Multidirectional Memory,* 313.

and compelling answer—one that can resist the fall to abstraction to which Rothberg's interpretation of Du Bois is prone—is Metz's positioning of human history within the apocalyptic time of the Christian narrative, and the communal practice of *Leiden an Gott* that leads to a truly political theology. While of course not applicable to everyone, transforming Christian ethics in this way grounds the real work of the faithful in light of trauma. First, Christianity centers on a memory of suffering that reveals our bond within a "history *ex memoria passionis* as a history of the vanquished."[57] This memory is practiced within the community, and focuses on cultivating individual and group connection to the divine. With Metz, cultivating memories in this frame also focuses on narratives of lived suffering and liberation, emphasizing the sociohistorically shaped, embedded nature of reason—that, even while reason remains constitutive of our personhood, it is neither objective nor pure in the traditional sense. Memory as the action of reason is grounded in the senses, passions, and emotions much more so than rational "facts," as modern neuroscience attests. Our expressions of pain, frustration, and joy are rooted in shared contact with others, where we work to build relationships that can hold the detail of all our stories, rather than merely the broadest contours of them.[58] Further, practices of Christian memory, of remembering Christ's life and death, position all memories within a divine sense of time that offers a hope that chronological time cannot.

---

[57] Metz, *Faith in History and Society*, 107.

[58] This is reminiscent of Townes's call to let "dirt in our nostrils" or Pope Francis's mandate for believers to be "shepherds with the smell of sheep." Townes, *Womanist Ethics,* 30; Pope Francis, "Address to the World's Priests at the Chrism Mass on Holy Thursday," March 28, 2013. As disability theologian Molly Haslam emphasizes, a primacy of participation rather than any essential capacity (reason or otherwise) is primary here when applying to trauma, to hold the multitude of God's creation within and beyond whatever form a body or mind may take. *A Constructive Theology of Intellectual Disability: Human Being as Mutuality and Response* (New York: Fordham University Press, 2012).

Still, hope for the practices of trauma as dangerous memory is not confined to the fulfillment of time promised by God. Instead, Metz desires to bring all theology into its particular context, to view the world as history and thus illuminate the nature of theology as inherently political—in the here-and-now.[59] Within this mystical-political framework, *Leiden an Gott* is essential to enacting trauma as dangerous memory, enfleshing memory toward justice.

Without the larger context of *Leiden an Gott* enacted through solidarity, trauma—indeed all suffering—in Christianity becomes overly privatized, the realm only of interpersonal dispute. With Metz's mystical-political views of suffering, trauma is revealed instead as structural as well as personal sin, and demands personal as well as structural healing. Such a move resists the continuing privatization of religion, what Metz delineates as the "problem of the bourgeois man," which has created "man" as the absolute center, and reduced praxis to private morals within systems of exchange.[60] Metz does not want to eliminate the individual, but rather to question whether the "principle of individuation *by itself* is adequate or strong enough to achieve the task that is given to religion: to stand up so that all persons might be subjects in solidarity, just as much when confronted by violent oppression as in the face of the caricature of solidarity found in forced massification and in institutionalized hatred."[61] Metz answers that individuation is insufficient; insufficient not only to resist overt violence but also because people alone are incapable of revealing the truth of one's circumstances and providing fuel for resistance. Reaching beyond the individual and toward the communal is central to Christian enfleshed counter-memory— not to rest in recognition of connection but to reach beyond into action for justice.

---

[59] Metz, *Faith in History and Society*, 12–13, 15, 17.

[60] Metz, *Faith in History and Society*, 43, 49. Using "man" as Metz's original usage, translated from the German by J. Matthew Ashley.

[61] Metz, *Faith in History and Society*, 59.

In this spirit, Metz sees Christian political theology as the appropriate orientation of the believing community. Political theology is a primarily threefold social praxis that is ethically defined, historically grounded, and rooted in a *pathic* structure.[62] A *pathic* structure attends to the history of suffering in the world, and does not relegate any of the dead to meaninglessness. Seeing with "open eyes," Metz takes power into the experience of suffering, stating that it must be seen as a mode of resistance.[63] From this orientation of resistance, the co-constitutive aspects of memory, narrative, and solidarity that form one's anthropology are also *fundamental categories of salvation*, and as such must be fostered. Practices of resistance via the memory of suffering within Metz's political theology must be global, communal, and democratizing—"from below." The call to memory does not mean suffering will be given a pat reconciliation, or a "manageable unity." Instead, to some extent the memories will remain unintegrated, but "the essential dynamism of history is the memory of suffering as a negative awareness of the freedom that is to come, and as a stimulus to act within the horizon of this history in such a way as to overcome suffering."[64] Suffering as such has no "goal" or even essential meaning. Yet when it is contextualized in Christ's passion, it has a future.[65] It is only through practices of memory, and particularly memory of suffering and trauma as dangerous memory, that practices can "for brief moments illuminate, harshly and piercingly, the problematic character of things we made our peace with a long time ago and the banality of what we take to be 'realism.'"[66]

---

[62] Metz, *Faith in History and Society*, 67.

[63] Metz, *Faith in History and Society*, 67. Recall Sheppard's client Rosie in chapter 2.

[64] Metz, *Faith in History and Society*, 104. Metz shows similarities here to the work of Edward Schillebeeckx's "negative contrast experience."

[65] Metz, *Faith in History and Society*, 104. "Rather, salvation history is the world's history in which space is made for defeated and repressed hopes and suffering to have meaning" (109).

[66] Metz, *Faith in History and Society*, 105. Also, "Human experience of the

Traumatic Memory in a Mystical-Political Framework

While this chapter has shown how memory forms an essential part of the human person, and how trauma as dangerous memory holds potential for recontextualizing suffering, practical questions remain for those who suffer. The second half of this chapter addresses the ethical practices that correspond to these claims of the value of memory, and how to approach cultivating traumatic memory within Metz's mystical-political framework. This work falls within what Ashley terms Metz's political hermeneutic of danger.[67] By remembering from the vantage point of the suffering, this orientation interrogates the motivation of the world's powerful, implicates the status quo as something other than "natural," and reminds all humanity of ultimate vulnerability—essential moves when contextualizing lived traumatic experience.

The type of political action that constitutes this work is inherently dangerous, conceptually as well as literally. Resisting socially accepted or forced interpretations of suffering has real outcomes on real bodies. From destabilizing one's inner world to the myriad outcomes in one's interactions with church, family, community, criminal justice, schooling, and so on, dangerous memory is disruptive.[68] Simultaneously, however, it offers a way forward that encourages a type of healthy, generative memory rather than a repetitive, damaging cycle.[69] This section explores the

---

other within a personal with-world is for Metz the only adequate context within which to develop an understanding of historicity." Ashley, *Interruptions*, 81.

[67] Ashley, *Interruptions*, 143.

[68] See the many stories of resistance to prevailing stories of suffering, including Chanel Miller, *Know My Name: A Memoir* (New York: Viking, 2019); Patrisse Khan-Cullors and Asha Bandele, *When They Call You a Terrorist: A Black Lives Matter Memoir* (New York: St. Martin's Griffin, 2017); and Valerie Kaur, *See No Stranger: A Memoir and Manifesto of Revolutionary Love* (New York: One World, 2020).

[69] For Metz, these actions of practical solidarity are also reflected in a mystical connection with the dead of history, those whose stories have been

mystical dimensions of traumatic memory in the Christian context, read with the traumatic imagination's components of position, time, and praxis. I then connect this framework to an embodied ethic of what Metz terms "interruption" and "forward memories." Interruption and forward memories provide the foundation for Keshgegian's work expanding Metz's categories within the lives of trauma survivors. Keshgegian's critiques and modifications of Metz give us essential tools to evaluate traumatic memory and then to construct an ethic of enfleshed counter-memory in the next chapter.

Position in the Wound:
Reading Christ through a Trauma Lens

First, a way to read the mystical side of dangerous traumatic memory is through Christ's wounds, explored in the work of theologian and trauma scholar Shelly Rambo. In *Resurrecting Wounds,* Rambo examines the Gospel of John's account of the risen Christ's return to his disciples bearing the wounds of his crucifixion. She focuses particularly on Thomas, who interacts directly with Christ's wounds, still present on Christ's resurrected body.[70] Taking to task her Calvinist inheritance, Rambo argues that, for reasons of polemics as well as true belief, Calvin glazes over or downright ignores the visceral and deeply upsetting imagery of Thomas probing Christ's wounded flesh. While Calvin may want to turn his followers' gaze away from bodies—even or especially the wounded divine body and onto the "word"—Rambo argues that John's telling of Thomas's and Christ's interaction speaks directly to life in the aftermath of trauma—namely through

---

forgotten or covered over, or who have no possibility for redemption in this world. This can rarely be made "real," as it is inherently a mystical experience, but it can perhaps be revealed through practices of ancestral connection, such as some rituals of Indigenous American and African American spiritualties.

[70] Christ's wounds are explored in a different key in Roberto S. Goizueta, *Caminemos con Jesús: Toward a Hispanic/Latino Theology of Accompaniment* (Maryknoll, NY: Orbis Books, 1995).

"bodily markings, an awareness of multiple witnesses present, and the status of death within this precarious sphere of life."[71] Specifically, Rambo is concerned with the pressure to erase wounds, a pressure we see in the Christian narrative that effectively says, "Life, if it is to triumph over death, must not retain the marks of death. Wounds must be erased."[72] Such erasure is particularly complex in the aftermath of trauma, where people are fundamentally changed in ways that can never be eliminated.

Like Metz, Rambo sees wounds not as stumbling blocks to salvation but as generative categories of Christian life on earth. Instead of the antiseptic triumphalism too often represented through Christ's resurrection, Rambo focuses on how the Holy Spirit is "engrafted" into Christ's wounds, and as such how those wounds display a potential entry for resurrection within normal human life. While she by no means glorifies the wounds, she does deliberately recognize their endurance. Rambo makes clear not only the fact that wounds remain on Christ's risen body but also that the wounds are the site of extreme intimacy between Thomas and Christ.

Rambo is seeking what she calls "ways of resurrecting" through the gospel by inviting ghosts into the Upper Room—not just the Holy Ghost, but all those specters connected to events we would rather forget.[73] She argues that something fundamental can be reclaimed through the sense of haunting that pervades John's account: "Ghosts signal unsettling memories coming forward ... [But] ghosts [also] do important work of resurrecting pasts in order to heal them."[74] Reading haunting in this way empowers the faithful with a task: with the Holy Spirit, there exists the

---

[71] Shelly Rambo, *Resurrecting Wounds: Living in the Afterlife of Trauma* (Waco, TX: Baylor University Press, 2017), 10.

[72] Rambo, *Resurrecting Wounds*, 36.

[73] This is akin to Metz's mystical focus on "the dead." Rambo, *Resurrecting Wounds*, 8–9.

[74] Rambo, *Resurrecting Wounds*, 37.

power to change, not erase, even the most horrific experience. The Holy Spirit within wounds attests a something-to-be-done, from within and without. Resonant with Metz's approach, this does not mean constructing a comprehensive account of suffering, as "the presence of absurdity and evil in our midst makes any comprehensive attempt to make sense of things absurd or even obscene."[75] Instead, meaning "must be introduced and 'described' by the intelligible power of Christian action itself": comforting the sick, visiting the prisoner, feeding the hungry.[76] It is through these practices that we realize the mystical vision of trauma as dangerous memory, an *imitatio Christi* that provides practical movement toward healing in the present, and initiates an awareness of the mystical connection between all those who suffer throughout human history. Such imitation is not limited to a particular goal of healing or ultimate resolution, but rather refers to the empowerment of all persons to continue the struggle of life and create sustainable hope for a transformed future. For Metz and Rambo, meaning is eschatological but can be fostered by mystical as well as ethical action from the position of the wound:

> According to this imagery, the person does not finally arrive at a pure, unmediated bliss of union with God that sidesteps the finitude, fragility, and sinfulness of our present existence. Rather, the union with God in this life, which adumbrates that final consummation of all things that has been won in the cross and resurrection, occurs within a dark cloud of unknowing. The weakness, pain, and longing of this life are not left behind but become the very medium

---

[75] Ashley, *Interruptions*, 144. Rambo argues, "As the wounds of history return, reappearing in the present, Christian theology might offer a vision of resurrection that addresses these wounds, precisely because the wounds return." *Resurrecting Wounds*, 14.

[76] Ashley, *Interruptions*, 144. This is also resonant with Latin American liberation theology.

in which God is found. It is entirely appropriate to tarry in this "dark cloud," and in certain circumstances it may be the one thing necessary.[77]

Interrupted Time:
Traumatic "Interruption" as Ethical Demand

Such a willingness to "tarry in this dark cloud" is only the result of allowing oneself to be interrupted: disturbed, challenged, and upset. Traumatic experience is an ultimate interruption. It stops us in our tracks, laser-focused on suffering's presence, and reaches out across time, seeking resonance. While I am not arguing for the victimized to stay within harmful patterns, trauma does have the power to positively interrupt those outside of the experience, those of us who witness. The goal of Metz and this project is, as the saying goes, to "comfort the afflicted, and afflict the comfortable."[78] Yet this goal is not meant to instrumentalize suffering or to mandate any action by those who experience trauma. Rather, I focus on the mandate for response from those who witness. Despite being outside of a particular event, we are not called to be neutral. In fact, for Metz and womanist thinkers in particular, neutrality is not an option, because neutrality often reflects a willful ignorance of suffering that undercuts an authentic faith.[79] Most essentially, if God is revealed within the dark cloud, whose promise of ultimate redemption interrupts and "thereby continually nourishe[s us with] a *question*" and a hope, we must meet God there.[80]

---

[77] Ashley, *Interruptions*, 194.

[78] This was originally attributed to writer Finley Peter Dunne in an 1893 newspaper column, where it was said in regard to the role of the press. See David Shedden, "Today in Media History: Mr. Dooley: 'The Job of the Newspaper Is to Comfort the Afflicted and Afflict the Comfortable,'" *Poynter*, October 7, 2014.

[79] See the reflections of Townes and Walter Brueggemann in chapter 2.

[80] Metz, *A Passion for God*, 18.

The question found in this engagement pushes us to acknowledge "the other as other, endeavoring to uncover the *traces of God* in the experience of the other's alterity."[81] An individual's trauma can never be fully known to a witness. That is not the goal. The goal is to recognize both the complete "otherness" of another's pain, and for one to detect similarities across suffering rooted in hope. As Ashley states,

> To those who are not the direct victims of history's negativities, to the degree that they have not been stripped of their identities by them, it offers the capacity to continue to affirm and to live, in the face of guilt: the guilt of complicity that comes by means of the ambiguous societies and histories in and through which we gain our identities, or even the guilt of surviving. But it is a capacity that requires of us conversion, a continual turning toward those endangered points in our world and our history which most clearly disclose the incompleteness, the frightening vulnerability, and the endangered fragility of our identities as subjects.[82]

In this frame, trauma interrupts to make an ethical demand: not to forget. It instead encourages the fostering of "irritating" moments that refuse to be systematized. We must allow ourselves to be *moved* by suffering, bothered by it—not to become "voyeurs of others' suffering and consequently of our own dissolution as responsible subjects."[83]

---

[81] Metz, *A Passion for God*, 27.
[82] Ashley, *Interruptions*, 164. Metz states, "Metanoia, conversion, and exodus are not just purely moral or pedagogical categories; rather, they are thoroughly noetic [relating to mental activity / the intellect]." *Faith in History and Society*, 62.
[83] Metz, *Faith in History and Society*, 36.

This task is deeply personal and individual, yet in Metz's methodology is also a political question: "It is not concerned first with my individual death [or suffering] but with the deaths of others, and the ways in which I am implicated in those deaths in and through the social and political histories which are constitutive for the meaning of my present existence."[84] Therefore, responding to Christ's preferential option for the poor—or, for Metz, "the authority of those who suffer"—means that religion should itself function as an interruption, "as necessary prelude to action" that inspires the kind of prayer and reflection that reveals one's social and historical role to imitate Christ.[85]

Praxis of Memory:
Cultivating "Forward Memories"

Taking the position in the wound and the interruption of trauma seriously requires an ethical response: the cultivation of *forward memories*. Such memories reflect the promise of God, and as such are full of anticipatory content and utopian orientation.[86] However, this utopian orientation does not negate actions for emancipation, but instead places such actions within the story of redemption. Important for Metz is to not collapse emancipation (earthly) and redemption (heavenly), where emancipation requires self-liberation (not the paternalism so rampant in the "bestowal" of rights) and redemption requires God's power within the fullness

---

[84] Metz, *Faith in History and Society*, 159.

[85] Metz, *Faith in History and Society*, 195. Metz "is less interested in developing concrete suggestions for action than he is in creating the sense of urgency, of danger, that will move Christians to act" (*Faith in History and Society*, 195). He quotes Bertolt Brecht: "When atrocities happen it's like when the rain falls. No one shouts 'stop it!' anymore" (Metz, *Faith in History and Society*, 157). Therefore, no matter where trauma interrupts time (either historical suffering or current local to global violence), Metz argues we must reach across and act.

[86] Metz, *Faith in History and Society*, 112.

of time.[87] Such a vision of history is not just about "tacking on" Christianity to what already exists but, rather, is a true hope in a new or renewed vision of history.[88]

Forward memories are not the salvation of the memory itself, nor valuing the suffering that it represents, but rather creating a "memory with future content" that has the potential for salvation and can be redeemed in the sense of apocalyptic time. For those who suffer now, forward memories provide a new way of seeing all experiences, including trauma, and as such are the foundation of true hope, where actions for both emancipation and redemption are taken up as the ethical task of Christian community:

> The process of remembering, that is, of actualizing a *memoria* that transcends the present and breaks it open, really cannot be initiated and carried through today solely or even primarily by the individual.... [The] genuine Christian character is the critically liberative but also redemptively dangerous way that [the Christian dangerous memory] introduces the remembered message into the present, so that "it will shock people and yet overcome them by its power."[89]

Groups must hold the process of memory together—as Monica Coleman's community did by "standing in the gap" until she was prepared to take up the task of her own emancipation. In Christian community, the shock of Christ's passion should infuse forward memories with the promise of salvation for the living and to remind

---

[87] Metz, *Faith in History and Society*, 114–115. Importantly, emancipation and redemption are distinct but not fully separate. This is also resonant with decolonial thought, which interrogates the enduring colonial, white supremacist, white savior complex—particularly active still in global Christianity.

[88] Metz, *Faith in History and Society*, 117.

[89] Metz, *Faith in History and Society*, 184. Here he is addressing the potential power of Christian dogma, where dogma is framed as practical memory. Metz was particularly influenced by Ernst Bloch and his positive teleology.

us all that the passion includes Christ's descent into hell, and thus a solidarity with the dead; that *no one* is forgotten or cast aside being a preoccupation of Metz and a commitment of this project.

This framework for understanding Christianity's dangerous memory is the interpretive key to seeing trauma differently in our theology. Only a soteriology that takes responsibility for the dead does not attempt to exculpate itself from the stories of history's failures, and instead seeks a full response within God's promise of redemption.[90] In this hope for others, most extremely demonstrated in a hope for the dead, we dare to hope in what God may offer others, and therefore ourselves. In this vein, Metz includes those who commit harm within his framework, albeit somewhat obliquely. Even though Metz asks, "Is not the substance of an integral freedom always bound to the powerless, those who have no power above and beyond the power of love, and no ally other than the dangerous memory of an unrequited hope for freedom?" he does not ignore the complexity of personhood and our capacity to embody both victim and perpetrator, flawed and saved.[91]

---

[90] Metz, *Faith in History and Society,* 120. Also, "The basic theological question—and theology is a culture of questions, not of answers—is not 'Who saves me?' but rather, 'Who saves you?' ... A basic form of Christian hope is also determined by this memory.... To dare to hope in God's Kingdom always means entertaining this hope for others and therefore also for oneself. Only when our hope is inseparable from hope for others, in other words, only when it automatically assumes the form and motion of love and communion, does it cease to be petty and fearful." Metz, "Communicating a Dangerous Memory," 40, including quotation from "Our Hope," 77. Metz sees our current state in the way he attributes to Teilhard de Chardin: "We keep on insisting that we are vigilant and waiting for the master. But if we were really honest would we not have to admit that we don't expect anything at all anymore?" Metz, *Faith in History and Society,* 165.

[91] Metz, *Faith in History and Society,* 93. Metz also sees the church as the venue for fostering such a "critical freedom" and considers that doing so is the only way truly to hear the challenge of Christ. The church must seek to foster the challenges that arise from freedom, turning toward the people (a church

Rather than collapsing experiences or ignoring necessary practices of justice, reading trauma as dangerous memory in Christian theological ethics situates faith as *memoria* in the concrete "understanding and appropriating [of] the 'already' within the 'not yet,' taking up the givenness of salvation in hope."[92] This frame resists the instrumentalization or reduction of people, their memories, their actions, and their healing. Trauma, memory, and the persons who are their locus are not "things" to be used but full subjects in history with fundamental relatedness to others and to God. With Metz, we must embrace the tension of "already but not yet" through the practices of dangerous memory, dangerous stories, and universal and particular solidarity. "Christianity is no ideology for apathy in which all suffering is reified into the kind of pain that can be done away with," Metz insists.[93] Embracing trauma as dangerous memory calls community to account—that, as church, we bear a memory not of victory but of the vanquished. Christianity "does this not with an abstract countercult of suffering, but rather by enabling men and women to go through other people's suffering by virtue of their own capacity to suffer, and precisely in this way to draw near to the *mysterium* of his Passion."[94] Our dangerous memory boldly confronts the

---

of people, not just *for* people). *Faith in History and Society,* 94–95, 128–129. I see resonances of Metz's commitment to all persons in the work of restorative/transformative justice; see the work of Robert J. Schreiter.

[92] Metz, *Faith in History and Society,* 182.

[93] Metz, *Faith in History and Society,* 134. As Metz summarizes, "The faith of Christians is a praxis in history and society that understands itself as a solidaristic hope in the God of Jesus as the God of the living and the dead, who call all to be subjects in God's presence." *Faith in History and Society,* 81.

[94] Metz, *Faith in History and Society,* 134. See also Metz, *Faith in History and Society,* 37. For more on Metz's resistance to any form of instrumentalization, see Metz, *Faith in History and Society,* 210, and Ashley, *Interruptions,* 36. Importantly, "Only cynics can interpret [suffering] as something noble and virtuous; it leads people to self-rejection and self-hatred. There is a suffering

triumphal narratives of perfection, embracing complexity and resilience instead.[95] In this framework of reading Metz through the traumatic imagination, we co-create generative practices within communities that face the reality of harmful memories and the struggle to believe *with* them.

Bringing Metz to "Life"

Although Metz offers a compelling theological and conceptual ground for the evaluation of trauma, his practical engagement with explicit cases of those who suffer is limited. Even his own practice of narrative is limited to brief snippets, and is most often found in compilations of speeches rather than as a foundational core of his theological work. As a German theologian, albeit inspired by the practices of Latin American base communities, he is not embedded in the theological praxis with the oppressed persons that he describes; at least his own or their direct narratives do not appear as central in his most popular published materials. Keshgegian takes up this critique in her work of practical theology, and explicitly engages with Metz's thought in conversation with her work with trauma survivors and her own history as the child of Armenian genocide survivors. Specifically helpful for building a Christian enfleshed counter-memory are her proposals of (1)

---

that forces whole peoples to lead a life without any affirmation, in which they seek out affirmation at best in a bottle, and a simulated sense of identity. This suffering is not a remembering of God. There isn't any remembering in it at all, and thus no hope either." Metz, *Faith in History and Society*, 135.

[95] Metz, *Faith in History and Society*, 169. For Metz's "world-facing" ethic, see "Facing the World: A Theological and Biographical Inquiry," *Theological Studies* 75, no. 1 (2014): 23–33, specifically John K. Downey's Translator's Note: "Metz proposes that the logos of theology move beyond a theoretical mediation of religion and human experience toward a ground in critical and reflective praxis, that is, in thoughtful and transformative action," 24. See also Ashley, *Interruptions*, 196.

practices of complex narrative, (2) decentering the cross, and (3) multiple memorative practices. By seeing where Keshgegian pulls at the threads of Metz's thought, it is evident just how difficult, even harrowing, the task of traumatic memory is for survivors as well as witnesses. Without understanding the gut-wrenching intimacy of working toward healing through traumatic memory, any call to "remember," based in Christian theology or otherwise, easily becomes callous and presumptive, if not outright harmful.

Practicing Complex Narratives

First, Keshgegian explores the complexity of traumatic memory itself and the potential for practices of narrative that Metz suggests. Remember: trauma overwhelms a person's capacities and compromises biological memory functions. Additionally, trauma occurs within a sociopolitical-historical context that not only shapes the violence itself but also influences the interpretation of the trauma as well as the pursuit of healing, personally and communally. Keshgegian argues that stories of suffering, indeed all stories, are subject to external as well as internal threats that can distort memories. She uses case studies of childhood sexual abuse and the Shoah to illustrate her argument: that it is critically important to define what we "remember *for*." In trauma healing in particular, we must remember "for life" and the search for justice, over and against any other modes or practices that would encourage memory for political gain or solely utilitarian purpose, *even the enlightenment of others to our cause*. She particularly critiques Metz on this last point: that his theology appears to depend upon the suffering of others—and thus falls into the trap of instrumentalization that he tries so hard to avoid. While she agrees with Metz "that human existence and reality are constituted narratively," and narrative is the mode of communicating dangerous memories, she argues that his construction does not interrogate the role of power within this practice and that it maintains, rather than challenges, the societal status quo—as in his use of the language of "option" and "preference" that positions those "outside" of suffering to choose, or ignore, pain.[96]

As an alternative, she offers the language of "withness": "such witness [withness] is rooted less in moral choice and more in recognition and affirmation of a common, yet multiple humanity. The mystery of grace, offered by God in creation and redemption, is that we are all profoundly and inextricably interconnected one to another."[97] The practices of "withness" do not require any particular action or narrative from the victim/survivor, but rather seek to ensure that they are heard on their own terms and in their own time, and that they honor the risk taken in practicing narrative. Keshgegian points out that "as we have learned from those who study trauma, the 'danger' contained in the return and interruption of memories may be necessary for healing and may carry the potential for redemption, but such danger is not good."[98] Therefore, the practice of "dangerous" traumatic memory must maintain the balance of seeking healing for the wounded and calling witnesses to be transformed. Keshgegian argues that Metz, overall, does not focus enough on transformative historical possibilities and instead risks reifying the tendency of victim narratives to become mixed with a "bent pride" in their stories of suffering. As she reflects on her own family and

---

[96] Flora Keshgegian, *Redeeming Memories: A Theology of Healing and Transformation* (Nashville: Abingdon Press, 2000), 155. Metz's self-identified task was somewhat different than what practical theologians or pastoral ministers may want to conclude from his thought. He saw his task primarily as transforming Christian theology itself, and the task of defining and initiating political theology could well be argued to be necessary to support the practice of narrative within its framework. At its heart, Keshgegian's critique of his thought appears to be one of method: while encouraging "bottom-up" practices, Metz remains a "top-down" theoretician, at least in his most influential works.

[97] Keshgegian, *Redeeming Memories*, 155.

[98] Keshgegian, *Redeeming Memories*, 143.

cultural inheritance, Keshgegian illuminates the risk of this type of narrative, where "the last defense against annihilation became oddly the stories of annihilation, and the proof of our existence lay in the repetition and the remembering of our victimization."[99] Dangerous traumatic memory, without lived healing and empowered witness, becomes pathology and can inhibit the possibility for true flourishing. Therefore, in practices of dangerous traumatic memory, narratives must embrace complexity and dynamism but always seek to answer "for justice and hope" to the question "Why do we remember?"

Decentering the Cross

An explicit theological move for Keshgegian in constructing this type of response to trauma is to decenter the cross. She rightly identifies the centrality of the crucifixion of Christ for Metz's thinking, and uses feminist/womanist, postcolonial, and African American theologians to demonstrate how such a focus can harm rather than heal. Similar to the womanist thought presented in chapter 2, Keshgegian lifts up instead the value of an incarnational view, one that expands our vision of "Christ with us" into Jesus's life and ministry, not bound to or even located on the cross.[100] With Metz, Keshgegian agrees that the cross and resurrection are definitional. These two moments of Christ's life attest that "Life is always possible, even if one's personal life comes to an end. Such life is not triumphant in a dominant sense, but it does celebrate resistance and resilience."[101]

However, this story is incomplete, she says. Focusing only on the cross and resurrection can and indeed has been read in reductive and manipulative ways that support harmful

---

[99] Keshgegian, *Redeeming Memories*, 12–13.
[100] Keshgegian, *Redeeming Memories*, 184.
[101] Keshgegian, *Redeeming Memories*, 180.

sociopolitical structures. Rather than focus on a spiritual practice with God, such as Metz's *Leiden an Gott*, Keshgegian argues that an ethical response to trauma is rooted in embodied reclamation of power. This is a practice of remembering for re-membering, bringing back into relationship what has been torn apart: "re-membering is envisioned as a process of incarnation, which is to say that redemption is participation and incorporation. Through the narrative of Jesus Christ we can not only encounter God, but also participate in the divine. This is the work of the Spirit."[102] The Incarnation attests to a broader, deeper vision of "God with us" that permeates human practices of "withness." Practicing an Incarnation-focused theological and ethical response to trauma demands an attention to life and flourishing for the victim/survivor, not only the hope in eschatological time.

With Delores Williams, Keshgegian points out that in the wilderness, Jesus conquered sin in life, not death.[103] By focusing

---

[102] Keshgegian, *Redeeming Memories*, 194. Also, "re-membering is most fundamentally a process of claiming and exercising power, in relation. It is grounded in witness" (195). This is supported by the work of "minority" theologians who help to re-vision the Godhead to upend colonial, white power structures: "To envision Jesus in particular cultural forms or through experiences that support our humanity is to live into the promise of the incarnation—that the divine becomes one with our humanity, concretely and specifically in history" (189). While I take her point, she seems to gloss over the praxis-orientation of Metz's suffering unto God.

[103] Keshgegian, *Redeeming Memories*, 185. She further illuminates her soteriology: "Remembrance of and witness to Jesus Christ's saving action ought to be guided by such principles that (1) affirm our being human as the site of redemption; (2) declare God to be on the side of redemption in and through humanity; (3) see the goal of redemption as wholeness and integrity, right relation and full humanity; and (4) recognize redemption as political, meaning it is in history and involves community and relationships, as well as the exercise of power. Finally, to be human is to be embodied, so redemption is in and through bodies, individual and corporate. The story of redemption is about embodied, historical remembrance, which is to say, we are saved by the Body of Christ" (190).

on the Incarnation, Keshgegian again troubles Metz's focus on the death/suffering of the "other" as being central to salvation. She reminds us that "'crucified peoples participate in salvation because of their humanity, not their oppression."[104] In this way, the focus of re-membering can move from emphasis on the wound to moments of resistance. It matters what we remember, and what we narrate. If the wound, exemplified in her thought in the cross, is the focus, then the cross, the pain of trauma, will remain strong. If the story told and remembered is concerned primarily with moments of resistance, of humanity, then the hopeful vision of the Incarnation and the promise of God's deep relationality with us will be further realized.[105]

Multiple Memorative Practices

Finally, Keshgegian attempts to illuminate what she calls "multiple memorative practices" that can properly address trauma in a theological context. She examines the mystically gathered Christian church as a locus for the communication of memory and, as such, a potential site for healing practices. However, despite her critique of Metz, she too remains abstract in her prescriptions: "No one narrative can tell or hold the full story of remembrance. Narrative adequacy and effectiveness are to be measured by a

---

[104] Keshgegian, *Redeeming Memories*, 173.

[105] Remember strengths-based assessment from chapter 1. Many practitioners believe this approach to result in higher levels of healing and "success" as measured by quality of life. For a popular accounting of this phenomenon with particular regard to trauma, see Jim Rendon, *Upside: The New Science of Post-Traumatic Growth* (New York: Touchstone, 2015). It is also important to note that Keshgegian further aims to decenter the resurrection and even the figure of Jesus Christ to a degree that I do not. Instead, with liberation theologians such as Jon Sobrino, I see the cross as not being salvific without the resurrection, and that "living as risen beings" in light of the resurrection is the meaning of Christian life.

narrative's ability to communicate multiple and even conflicting remembrances; and to do so in the face of threats," internal to the person and external to the event, where "bearing witness is the faithful and ongoing practice of remembering as preserving, resisting, and connecting in full awareness of the complex and conflictual narrative field in which we remember."[106]

From this broad outline, we can discern that *preserving, resisting,* and *connecting* are central steps to enacting the multiple memorative practices essential for Keshgegian's focus on remembering for redemption. Preserving calls us to remember the event as it occurred, in the telling of the victim/survivor(s); resisting calls us to remember the actions of agency and survival enacted by the victim/survivor(s); and connecting calls us to remember the ways in which such trauma is intimately related to all suffering throughout history. Importantly, these three modes are not sequential and do not replace one another. Similar to Metz's theological anthropology of memory, narrative, and solidarity, they are co-constitutive rather than linear. Keshgegian uses the metaphor of weaving to illustrate how seeking to remember rightly through multiple memorative practices requires us to "pluralize the process of remembering," and in so doing seek life-transforming dangerous memories.[107] She admits this lack of precision is purposeful: that in response to the instability of trauma, remembering for hope must embrace ambiguity. Within the complexity of traumatic memory, she argues, "Ambiguity is not the enemy of hope; finality and certainty are."[108]

In part, this embrace of opacity is Keshgegian's recognition of the imperfection of victims/survivors, as well as the complexity of healing and the potential use/abuse of memories of suffering by both personal and political entities. She resists any romanticization

---

[106] Keshgegian, *Redeeming Memories*, 154.
[107] Keshgegian, *Redeeming Memories*, 152–153.
[108] Keshgegian, *Redeeming Memories*, 181.

of the suffering person, and readily admits that such framing of the "pure" victim only reifies the "victim role" she is attempting to challenge. Maintaining memory as a victim only, and not seeking transformative justice as a survivor as well, is potentially damaging and unquestionably limits the possibilities for change both individually and socially. Keshgegian posits that, much like Metz's broad category of narrative, multiple memorative practices are judged by their efficacy, rather than aligning with a set of predetermined rules for content or structure—"ultimately, the liberating and transformative potential of remembering is measured by what that remembering makes possible."[109] Taken together, these three moves—practicing complex narratives, decentering the cross, and multiple memorative practices—provide necessary critique to the work of bringing Metz's thought into practical application for a Christian enfleshed counter-memory.

Conclusion

This chapter outlined the major theological contribution of Johann Baptist Metz that can be helpful in the evaluation of post-traumatic memory and the potential for a Christian enfleshed counter-memory. Namely, Metz's concepts of memory, narrative, and solidarity as co-constitutive of theological anthropology provide a nuanced vision of the human person and the central role of memory in identity. This adds more texture to the explicit attributes of the person as incarnate *imago Dei* from womanist thought, particularly in relation to traumatic memory and its

---

[109] Keshgegian, *Redeeming Memories,* 158. For Keshgegian, it is also important that God remains free and noninstrumentalized, even in the construction of pathways to freedom. She states that God cannot simply be "recruited" to this task, as this is exactly how oppressors use the divine (159). Instead, God's presence on the side of the victim can be known in and through the gospel, but it can always be more than can be known, and as such holds true the promise of ultimate transformation beyond human history.

healing. Further, Metz's work on dangerous memory provides an alternative framework for the conceptualization of trauma, both for the individual and for the ethical role of the broader community. Finally, his attention to the interruption of suffering and the cultivation of forward memories provides theoretical and theological grounding for an ethic of a Christian enfleshed counter-memory. Keshgegian's critiques add the important correctives of power analysis, what we are remembering *for*, and the necessary ethical claim for practical transformation that trauma demands.

Traumatic memory is incredibly complex, and "remembering [i]s both a problem and a resource for those struggling for life."[110] Even so, the practice of memory is "tested and made true by what it makes possible," aimed ultimately at not only the alleviation of suffering but also the broader flourishing of the person and the world.[111] As various scholars of womanist thought demonstrate, healing, integration, and flourishing are not an isolated pursuit. With regard to trauma, and perhaps all human action, "Agency is not located in an individual actor, but is a function of the ability of a person to interact with and among a web of relations."[112] The sociality of the person demonstrated by Metz and our communal responsibility for historical transformation presented by Keshgegian are essential as we move into the explicit construction of an ethic of enfleshed counter-memory.

---

[110] Keshgegian, *Redeeming Memories*, 16.
[111] Keshgegian, *Redeeming Memories*, 235.
[112] Keshgegian, *Redeeming Memories*, 158.

5

CHRISTIAN ENFLESHED COUNTER-MEMORY

"Boy, did I have a bomb when I was 10. That was quite an explosion. And I learned to love it. So that's why. Maybe, I don't know. That might be why you don't see me as someone angry and working out my demons onstage. It's that I love the thing that I most wish had not happened."

I love the thing that I most wish had not happened.

I asked him if he could help me understand that better, and he described a letter from Tolkien in response to a priest who had questioned whether Tolkien's mythos was sufficiently doctrinaire, since it treated death not as a punishment for the sin of the fall but as a gift. "Tolkien says, in a letter back: 'What punishments of God are not gifts?'" Colbert knocked his knuckles on the table. "'What punishments of God are not gifts?'" he said again. His eyes were filled with tears. "So it would be ungrateful not to take *everything* with gratitude. It doesn't mean you want it. I can hold both of those ideas in my head.... It's not the same thing as wanting it to have happened," he said. "But you can't change everything about the world. You certainly can't change things that have already happened."

— Interview with Stephen Colbert[1]

---

[1] Joel Lovell, "The Late, Great Stephen Colbert," *GQ*, August 17, 2015.

When comedian Stephen Colbert's father and two brothers were killed in a plane crash in 1974, he was only ten years old. That event has shaped his entire life and his search for purpose through art and performance. As a practicing Catholic, he eloquently reflected on his eventual adulthood acceptance of this early trauma in a cover story for *GQ* magazine, stating, "I love the thing that I most wish had not happened." This seemingly impossible sense of peace was fostered initially through the model of his mother's faith and perseverance through her husband and children's deaths, and later through Colbert's own pursuit of meaning. While his conclusions about his experience are not universal, they do indicate the potential for reframing and reinterpreting trauma that many survivors report after various therapies, spiritual investigations, and additional life experiences. Colbert admits that he is not himself without the trauma; he is who he has become because of it.

This echoes what Flora Keshgegian urges us to consider regarding the potential good of fostering memories of severe traumatization: what are we "remembering *for*?" If we are remembering for *life*, then our pursuit of an ethic of traumatic memory can be framed in ways that alleviate as much suffering as possible and encourage positive individual growth, while simultaneously calling communities toward relationship and responsibility. Colbert's integration is one way of processing trauma, but it is neither the only nor the necessary way to translate experience. Emphatically and continually resisting the centrality of any form of trauma in self-identity—a stance held by many people who, for example, have been raped—is another, completely valid mode of processing. Enfleshed counter-memory, as developed here, resists the demands for a singular, authoritative solution to processing trauma. Instead, I carve a middle path between two existing extremes: the ease with which some overly medical views seek to eliminate trauma from memory[2] *and* the ease with which some overly spiritualized views

---

[2] While bioethics is not the focus of this book, it is important to note

of trauma-via-redemptive-suffering seek to retain painful memory at all costs.

Insidiously, these ways of forgetting—forgetting the memory and forgetting the present self, respectively—are often used by people in power to reify a status quo that serves their position. For example, and central to my positionality, this includes those in the magisterial Catholic Church who "literally 'cut off' documentation of the trauma" of clergy-perpetrated sex abuse, at best making healing the realm of private life with minimal communal responsibility.[3] Enfleshed counter-memory stakes its claim in opposition to such sinful behavior, holding to the prophetic center of the faith: the incarnate, active, and risen Christ. Enfleshed counter-memory as a term is intentional: "enfleshed" in relation to the focus on complex and incarnational embodiment drawn from womanist thought; "counter," as the memory of trauma often runs up against the sociocultural status quo of silence and forced forgetting of complicated pain, here drawn from Johann Baptist Metz; and "memory" as the essential category that unites considerations of trauma with Christian theology. An ethic of enfleshed counter-memory is enacted in the pursuit of justice in response to trauma, the practices of which are teased out at the end of this chapter. Through this framework, it is clear that both the enfleshed individual and the broader Body of Christ are

---

that I (and many others) explore how all medicine, even that which claims to be purely secular, makes metaphysical claims regarding what should be treated, why, and toward what end. My dissertation delves in detail into proposed pharmaceutical "forgetting" treatments for PTSD and lays the initial groundwork for this book. For a summary version of this research, see Stephanie C. Edwards "Pharmaceutical Memory Modification and Christianity's 'Dangerous' Memory," *Journal of the Society of Christian Ethics (JSCE)* 40, no. 1 (Spring/Summer 2020): 93–108.

[3] If any is taken at all; see Jennifer E. Beste, "Discourse on a 'Traumatized Church,'" in *Theology in a Post-Traumatic Church*, ed. John Sheveland (Maryknoll, NY: Orbis Books, 2023), 46.

harmed by trauma, and actions for healing of both are necessary, even if they are not "successful."[4] While a seemingly simple turn of phrase, easily written off as a disembodied theological "solution," enfleshed counter-memory is meant to encourage concrete, even revolutionary, action that meets the challenge of trauma with committed hope and endurance.

As a social ethic, enfleshed counter-memory here described will be quite "thin."[5] Yet throughout this final constructive chapter I weave in snippets of poetry, stories, and lived testimony that bring us back to ourselves, our communities, and our connections to the entire created world. This "conclusion" functions more as an invitation: to engage, to question, to seek. If, to return to our orienting question from Ruby Sales, we must explore "where it hurts," we must also actively cultivate ways to listen and feel rightly.[6] To understand why I avoid the triumphal conclusion of complete healing so often sought by those who encounter suffering, I first engage disability theology. Disability scholarship provides the nuanced, embodied, care-focused, and justice-oriented theology that is essential to ground the components of

---

[4] Without the balance offered by both perspectives, the particular and the universal, the consideration of trauma becomes overindividuated and/or overly abstract. Enfleshed counter-memory expands our framework for understanding trauma healing (especially stretching beyond only direct experience / individual healing) and resists reductive communal approaches, especially Christianity's "rush to redemption" that harms as it attempts to heal (see the work of Shelly Rambo).

[5] Thin description is used in ethics to describe basic parameters for thinking and acting. In response to the multiple complexities of treating trauma writ large, as this book has explored, it is appropriate as a social ethic to suggest directions and contours, rather than overly precise prescriptions or plans.

[6] As John N. Sheveland reminds us, we (particularly Catholics) are stuck in a condition of the "inability to feel rightly" in a culture of abuse, and we must find a path forward in light of the gospel. "What Is Redemption?" in *Theology in a Post-Traumatic Church*, ed. John N. Sheveland (Maryknoll, NY: Orbis Books, 2023), 72.

enfleshed counter-memory. Following this brief summary, I place enfleshed counter-memory in the lineage of Christian liberation psychology, in the tradition of Jesuit and Salvadoran martyr Ignacio Martín-Baró. From this foundation I parse the components of an enfleshed counter-memory, and how each expand traditional parameters of ethical evaluation of trauma essential to a Christian response.

Finally, I explore how enfleshed counter-memory is co-constitutive with the work of justice, illuminating practices that fall into three general realms: (1) empowerment of individual agency and integrity as self, (2) community support and participation in re/integration of persons, and (3) solidarity and the preferential option for the poor. Without justice, the work of enfleshed counter-memory could remain circumscribed to individuals, unable to claim its full transformational power as a social ethic. Justice work demands that we understand ourselves beyond the limited identities of victim, perperator, or outsider so readily applied to trauma. We are all, as Michael Rothberg puts it, *implicated subjects,* where we occupy complex positions within regimes of domination, participants in history entangled with its everyday injustices.

As such, a social ethic of Christian enfleshed counter-memory reaches toward action based in the understanding of our intertwined moral agency, how we may be implicated, "how we are 'folded into' (im-pli-cated in) events that at first seem beyond our agency as individual subjects."[7] This is a lifelong practice, developing what activist and author adrienne maree brown calls *emergent strategies* that demand we not only deconstruct and understand the suffering of the world, but that we act to build new worlds of justice and peace in recognition of our entanglement. As brown reflects on this shared task,

---

[7] Michael Rothberg, *The Implicated Subject: Beyond Victims and Perpetrators* (Stanford, CA: Stanford University Press, 2019), 1–2.

It is so important that we fight for the future, get into the game, get dirty, get experimental. How do we create and proliferate a compelling vision of economies and ecologies [and theologies] that center humans and the natural world over the accumulation of material?

We embody. We learn. We release the idea of failure, because it's all data.

But first we imagine.

We are in an imagination battle.

... Emergence emphasizes critical connections over critical mass, building authentic relationships, listening with all the senses of the body and mind.

... The crisis is everywhere, massive massive massive.

And we are small.

But emergence notices the way small actions and connections create complex systems, patterns that become ecosystems and societies [and theologies]. Emergence is our inheritance as part of this universe; it is how we change. Emergent strategy is how we intentionally change in ways that grow our capacity to embody the just and liberated worlds we long for.[8]

Enfleshed counter-memory is, I hope, a part of this work: providing new ways to imagine our being that centers our contingent, entangled selves; encouraging practices of lived solidarity that challenge oppressive structures *and* provide soul-filling connection; and, ultimately, creating a way to intentionally hold trauma memory rightly in the Christian ethical life.

---

[8] adrienne maree brown, *Emergent Strategy: Shaping Change, Changing Worlds* (Chico, CA: AK Press, 2017), 18, 3. Note: brown styles her name all in lower case, and I follow her chosen grammar.

Disability Theology and the Fundamentals of Ethics in Healing

At the outset of our imagining together, it is important to name a current that flows underneath work in trauma and theology: a debate concerning constructions of "cure" and "healing." Whether you entered this book searching for one or the other, or you seek a more nebulous goal following the model of Jesus's social ministry, it is essential to recognize that, on some level, many of us want to fix what is broken—in ourselves, in our families, in our world. This instinct toward wholeness is by no means a warped desire, but it is often more complex than we recognize.

For clarity, I address medical methods of confronting suffering as "cure" or "curative," and all other methods (e.g., therapeutic, spiritual) as "healing." Take the example of an organ donation recipient: while the transplant of an organ (hopefully) cures a patient's presenting medical need, the process itself can cause depression, anxiety, and a myriad of other lifelong struggles. In this case, the organ saves the physical life of the patient and cures a physical malfunction—but it does not necessarily heal the whole person, and perhaps even causes or exacerbates further suffering. The complex interplay between our bodies and minds, medical treatments and "healing," are, as Deborah Beth Creamer identifies, ultimately issues of self-understanding.[9] This self-understanding is complicated by our universal somatic contingency (we are malleable, uncontrollable, mortal bodies). As such, we often seek healing through methods larger than strictly curative medical settings and ask questions that exceed a purely curative narrative about our bodies and minds.

---

[9] Deborah Beth Creamer, *Disability and Christian Theology: Embodied Limits and Constructive Possibilities* (Oxford: Oxford Scholarship Online, 2009), 4. A paradigmatic work on this topic is Nancy Eiesland, *The Disabled God: Toward a Liberatory Theology of Disability* (Nashville: Abingdon Press, 1994). For a modern Jewish theological approach to disability, see the work of Julia Watts Belser.

Whether an external, apparent difference (e.g., wheelchair use), or an internal, often "hidden" one (e.g., trauma), all bodily aberrations present difficult questions to a world in which the presumption of "normalcy" is embedded within our discourse and our environments. Whether it is race, gender, sexuality, or ability, the white, cis-gendered, heterosexual, able-bodied male dominates our imaginative landscape.[10] We see ourselves in direct relation to this image, and often shape our choices in alignment with its contours. As Creamer states, "Disability is not an object—a woman with a cane—but a social process that intimately involves everyone who has a body and lives in the world of the senses."[11] Echoing Emilie Townes from chapter 2, it is *how we are* that shapes what injuries we perceive and what healing we seek.

Disabled as a category is far from static. It is extremely malleable, as it is one into which all of us enter, and may leave, at various points in our lives, from temporary injury to chronic illness. Therefore, questions of dis/ability[12] are not limited to those for whom the label is often readily applied, such as the profoundly mentally ill or a person who permanently uses a mobility aid. Disability must instead be understood as a universal aspect of human life experience, defined by socially constructed impediments as well as the physical and/or mental limitations in themselves.[13] In this understanding

---

[10] Creamer, *Disability and Christian Theology*, 16.

[11] Creamer, *Disability and Christian Theology*, 5.

[12] Labels are an essential yet controversial aspect of this conversation. The "/" used here indicates the balance between recognizing that persons contain and maintain their abilities despite their limitations, although maintaining the "dis" that indicates at the same time an essential difference (difference *not* error) in their particular embodiment. See Creamer, *Disability and Christian Theology*, 4. More recent disability theology boldly claims the label "disabled," expanding into "crip" and the reclamation of other "offensive" labels. See, for example, Miriam Spies, "From Belonging as Supercrip to Misfitting as Crip: Journeying through Seminary," *Journal of Disability and Religion* 25, no. 3 (2021): 296–311.

[13] Jerome E. Bickenbach in Christopher A. Riddle, *Disability and Justice: The Capabilities Approach in Practice* (Lanham, MD: Lexington Books, 2014),

of disability, *cures* may not be possible, but *healing* continues to be available. For example, although fighting societal constructions of limitations, many disability advocates find their differences to be strengths, and continue to challenge cultural assumptions placed upon them.[14] They argue that they do not need to be cured, but rather that society needs to expand its notions of access, justice, and healing to better care for all its members.

The struggle led by disability advocates to modify our understanding of disability and our related language is central to a Christian enfleshed counter-memory. Though theologian and disability scholar John Swinton explores such language in relation to dementia, his findings can be readily applied to all issues of compromised memory, including trauma:

> The global and rather vague ascription of "impaired thinking" provides a negative hermeneutic that will inevitably prime a person to see some things and to omit others. Bearing in mind that, at least within the West, thinking has come to be conceived of as a central dimension of the structure and function of the mind—and, indeed, of what is essential to our humanness ("I think; therefore I am")—ascribing impaired thinking to a person with dementia has quite particular connotations: *dementia = deprived of mind = deprived of humanness*.[15]

Our language primes us to frame a certain attribute or experience in a specific way, and through this language (and the assumptions it contains) our communities determine our morals, our morals

---

ix. Note: This definition of disability is not meant to conflate all disabilities, as the experience of each individual is distinct and nuanced, but there are essential central themes that emerge in the conversation.

[14] For example, disability advocates who established many fundamental access rights in San Francisco (1977), and protestors/advocates for the Affordable Care Act and universal healthcare in Washington, DC, like Ady Barken.

[15] John Swinton, *Dementia: Living in the Memories of God* (Grand Rapids: William B. Eerdmans, 2012), 58, emphasis added.

shape society, and society determines (to a large extent) the treatment, perception, and dis/empowerment of all our bodies. If one is deprived of mind, one does not have full access to humanity, and therefore should be "cured" to restore not only one's mental functioning but one's return to full humanity. Swinton clearly shows how persons with dementia suffer specifically from this construction and how, like trauma, these distinctly social and communal attributes of the disease are ignored.[16] For Swinton and other Christian scholars of disability, our bodies are inherently ethical, and to treat them otherwise does a disservice to our incarnate createdness. Therefore, it is not only a social justice issue when persons are shunted aside because of their disability, but a fundamental matter of salvific consequence.

Standing on the shoulders of disability theology, if I am not arguing for a blanket cure to traumatic memory, then what is healing? For it remains true that, particularly in the Christian worldview, there persists a call to alleviate suffering wherever possible (modeled by Jesus's healing ministry).[17] Rebecca Leah Levine argues that even progressive models of human development and societal care overemphasize "improvement" of the patient in order to gain ethical status rather than empower the person as they are.[18] This is a concern for disability studies in general, whose scholars caution against proposing "perfection" or "healing" as a mandate for just action and the consideration of disabled persons

---

[16] E.g., high social abandonment rates that cause only strangers to interact with the person, exacerbating their disease.

[17] However, there is complexity here, for in the Gospels Jesus seems to cure or fix physical ailments to bring one closer to God, but also shows that disability is not a block to grace. Passages such as the story of the ten lepers (Luke 17:11–19), the bleeding woman (Matt 9:20–22; Mark 5:25–34; Luke 8:43–48), and the Gerasene demoniac (Mark 5:1–20; Matthew 8:28–34; Luke 8:26–39) all have potential significance for further complicating this discussion.

[18] Such as Martha Nussbaum's capabilities approach. See Rebecca Leah Levine, "Disabling the Patient by Incorporating the Capabilities Approach into Person-Centered Care," *The American Journal of Bioethics* 13, no. 8 (2013): 55.

as a category.[19] Mandates for a certain state of health do not value the person as such, and premise the good of their complete healing, whether possible or not. While, of course, bodily integrity and health are a *good,* it becomes very risky when applied to persons with disabilities. The construction of a "perfect" body and mind—which are in themselves fallacies—leads to a circumstance in which one's validity as a moral agent deserving of equal regard is stripped and depends solely on one's ability to present as "normal."

Healing trauma, then, must be an act of process that resists a drive to "normalcy," rather than an accomplishable goal of a particular outcome. It must hold people as they are, both their physical/psychological realities and their dignity that exceeds any such definition. Healing in this mode rejects the necessity of cure or centrality of perfection so frequently embedded in our approaches to healing. Instead, healing is a "noun of process" in which an individual's integration of memory is not necessarily met and maintained, but includes the many states through which the person, and their communities, may vacillate throughout their lifetimes. The healing I suggest is possible through enfleshed counter-memory is centrally focused on fostering the self-understanding clarified by disability scholarship, alongside a renewed commitment to direct community/social support grounded in our shared liminality of the flesh. It does not require a particular capacity but is premised on participation in "responsive relation."[20] We continually heal together, again and again, in recognition of our movement in and out of "ability" and in the hope of a fully liberated future.[21]

---

[19] Creamer discusses this phenomenon in her third chapter, specifically with regard to the ingrained treatment of disability/suffering as a deserved result of sin (in the Christian framework).

[20] Molly C. Haslam, *A Constructive Theology of Intellectual Disability: Human Being as Mutuality and Response* (New York: Fordham University Press, 2011).

[21] This thinking is influenced by Stephen Long's approach to culture, where the original meaning is tied to cultivation, specifically of crops, and

Christian Liberation Psychology and Enfleshed Counter-Memory

January 6, 2006: Twelfth Night ... Poets resow themselves into home. Poets resew themselves into home. The metaphors of planting and stitching sound trite, mundane, anti-poetic. The poets resent themselves into home. By way of a creative misreading, the word "resew" became "resent." There is strength in error. Am I feeling a loss of nerve, the result of ingesting fear of error? Is that why I want to hang on to the lifeline that having an apartment in Vicksburg has come to represent? Confess. Otherwise, the talons of the Holy Ghost will tear out your liver. O.K. Yes, fear has become or is becoming more real. I can touch it, just as I can touch the surface of the desk. I do not want to pass my hand over the textures of fear. I don't want to have those blues. None of us who survived the hurricanes want those blues. We will not want to be roaches in a red light seeking darkness. We will not want to be lunatics by Lundi Gras. Witnesses of nightmare. Like thunder the feeling is frightening. Whom can I beg to rescue me?

Jerry W. Ward, Jr.[22]

---

includes a position of ongoingness and change. D. Stephen Long, *Theology and Culture: A Guide to the Discussion* (Eugene, OR: Wipf & Stock, 2008). Healing together is anything but simple, as caregiving itself is also socially constructed. For a recent theological engagement with this topic, see Kristin Heyer, "Enfleshing Social Production: Gender, Race, and Agency," *Journal of Moral Theology* 12, Special Issue 1 (2023): 81–107. Sample practices that can cultivate this culture of healing are included in the justice section of this chapter.

[22] Jerry W. Ward, Jr., *The Katrina Papers: A Journal of Trauma and Recovery* (New Orleans, LA: UNO Press, 2008), 70.

What might it look like to run our hands over fear, to resew our way home into empowered, enfleshed counter-memory? Christianity has an extended lineage, for good and ill, of intervening in bodies and brains—from hospitals to refugee camps to education to psychological services. While the role of Christian healthcare is often (rightfully) questioned for ties to colonial modes of power, as well as overly spiritualized responses, the work of Spanish Jesuit and psychologist Ignacio Martín-Baró offers an alternative for understanding enfleshed counter-memory in a Christian view of psychology. Liberation psychology, as defined by Martín-Baró, locates psychological experiences within their context, directly naming the sources of oppression and injustice that suffocate the possibility of genuine flourishing and often determine mental health or disease.[23] Resonant with the view of the person in enfleshed counter-memory, Martín-Baró adamantly maintained the biopsychosocial-*spiritual* model of psychological practice, where one's entire being is centered, not relegated for consideration in different spheres. For, as Swinton observes, "if we truly are relational, dependent creatures, created by a God who remains steadfastly at the helm of creation, moving it toward its final destiny, then a person's neurobiological state is not a-theological, and scientific explorations of that neurobiology are not pre-theological. In a real sense, *neurology is theology.*"[24]

---

[23] Wayne Dykstra, "Liberation Psychology—A History for the Future," *The British Psychological Society,* November 14, 2014, https://www.bps.org.uk/psychologist/liberation-psychology-history-future. See also Martín-Baró's own account of the development of the field of which he is considered the founder in Ignacio Martín-Baró, *Writings for a Liberation Psychology,* ed. Adrianne Aron and Shawn Corne (Cambridge, MA: Harvard University Press, 1994).

[24] Swinton, *Dementia*, 8. "It makes a world of difference to suggest that dementia happens to people who are loved by God, who are made in God's image, and who reside within creation. The task of theology is to remind people of that distinction and to push our perceptions of dementia beyond what is expected, toward the surprising and the unexpected."

Important for Martín-Baró's context in mid-twentieth-century El Salvador, this meant transforming social psychology from a colonial mode of external study to a position of listening to the expressed "needs, aims, and experiences of the oppressed," the poor who his liberation theology centered.[25] Such listening was not passive for Martín-Baró. He reached beyond the individual psychological task, instead advocating for a collective response in light of what was heard, "requiring the restoration to the community of a 'historical memory' as well as the development of popular forms of political organization and action."[26] Here, forming/recovering memory is a process of contextualization of experience toward empowerment of self and community. This memory is active, revealing the social construction of our circumstances and their psychological impacts, resisting what many consider the "natural" way of things. Memory in this form resists the hyperpersonalized approach of psychology that often reduces whole persons to events: "a still shot, it captures a moment and calls that Us, making it seem that what we are during some frozen, circumscribed moment is all that we can or will ever be." Instead, it surges forward into praxis, "not an account of what *has been done,* but of what *needs to be done.*"[27]

Martín-Baró did not exclude himself from the call to action of his approach. He saw himself as living in a limit situation,

---

[25] Elliot G. Mishler, "Foreword," in *Ignacio Martín-Baró: Writings for a Liberation Psychology,* ed. Adrianne Aron and Shawn Corne (Cambridge, MA: Harvard University Press, 1994), x.

[26] Mishler, "Foreword," xi.

[27] Adrianne Aron and Shawn Corne, "Introduction," in Aron and Corne, 5–6. For a more recent account of this process in action, see Rosa Lia Chauca-Sabroso and Sandra Fuentes-Polar, "Development of a Historical Memory as a Psychosocial Recovery Process," in *Psychology of Liberation: Theory and Applications,* ed. Maritza Montero and Christopher C. Sonn (New York: Springer, 2009), 205–219.

at an important boundary that marked the limits of human possibility: limits not in the sense of an end of possibility; limits rather as markers of the place where all possibilities begin. This is not the division line between being and nothingness; it is the frontier which separates *being* from *being more*.... [He] dared to immerse both himself and his chosen profession in the process of *posibilitar,* making possible.[28]

Here, justice and memory are linked, each requiring the other to approach the limit of trauma and seek what is possible. What is *possible* is inextricably linked to Martín-Baró as priest, living and dying with the Jesuits at the Universidad Centroamericana José Simeón Cañas (UCA) and his Salvadoran community. "Padre Nacho," as his parishioners called him, cried out for justice until his last breath, believing in a God and a people of liberation. Looking straight at his executioner, shouting over the gunfire directed at his close friend Ignacio Ellacuría, Nacho exclaimed, "¡Esto es una injusticia!"[29]

In this lineage of a theologically informed, radically engaged liberation psychology, enfleshed counter-memory can function as a new script for Christians to engage trauma. As created beings, the task of enfleshed counter-memory is cultivating memories for life (Keshgegian) *and* "dangerous" memories (Metz) that counter social structures that create suffering, viewing all persons through

---

[28] Aron and Corne, "Introduction," 7–8.

[29] Daniel J. Gaztambide, "Ignacio Martín-Baró," in *Encyclopedia of Psychology and Religion,* ed. D. A. Leeming, K. Madden, and S. Marlan (Boston: Springer, 2010), 544. Martín-Baró was executed alongside five of his fellow Jesuits, their housekeeper, and her fifteen-year-old daughter by a US-trained Salvadoran death squad on November 16, 1989, just after his forty-seventh birthday. For a comprehensive account of this community and its work, see Robert Lassalle-Klein, *Blood and Ink: Ignacio Ellacuría, Jon Sobrino, and the Jesuit Martyrs of the University of Central America* (Maryknoll, NY: Orbis Books, 2014).

an incarnational theological anthropology rooted in relationality (womanist thought). When "viewed and redescribed from the perspective of the strange biblical world," the metaphysical claim of Christian enfleshed counter-memory is of a hope and time beyond secular conceptions of cure or healing.[30] As theologian Melanie May states,

> We are living between the times and the orders of things. We are privileged to witness and to participate in a passing away and a coming to be. There is never one without the other. We can, of course, choose to keep company with those preoccupied with survival and shoring up sagging structures. We can also choose the ways we can greet the future that *is* coming, with or without us.[31]

The harm caused by trauma does not ask us to "shore up" sagging structures. It demands a language of abundant flourishing, not of mere survival. Christian enfleshed counter-memory is this language and embodied practice, living out the reality of remaining woundedness simultaneous with ongoing, joyous life coursing out from a gritty hope.

The Ethical Expansion of Christian Enfleshed Counter-Memory

> I hoped the perpetrator in uniform would be brought to justice this time, but hope died. I hoped history would stop repeating itself, but hope died. I hoped things would be better for my children, but hope died.
>
> So I have learned to not fear the death of hope.... The death of hope begins in fury, ferocious as a wildfire. It

---

[30] Swinton, *Dementia*, 19.

[31] Melanie May, *A Body Knows: A Theopoetics of Death and Resurrection* (New York: Continuum, 1995), 98.

feels uncontrollable, disastrous at first, as if it will destroy everything in the vicinity—but in the midst of the fury, I am forced to find my center. What is left when hope is gone? What is left when the source of my hope has failed? Each death of hope has been painful and costly. But in the mourning there always rises a new clarity about the world, about the Church, about myself, about God.

... And so, instead of waiting for the bright sunshine, I have learned to rest in the shadow of hope ... knowing that we may never see the realization of our dreams, and yet still showing up.... It is working in the dark, not knowing if anything I do will ever make a difference.

—Austin Channing Brown[32]

Trauma and unfulfilled healing ask us to rest in the type of hope that Channing Brown describes. Resting in this sense, however, means learning to do good work in the dark rather than be preoccupied with the search for sunlight. Through this image Channing Brown asks us to sit in the real, in the messy shadows, and continue to show up with the clarity of knowledge that the world can and will be other than its current state—as the Oscar Romero prayer says, "We are prophets of a future not our own."[33] Within the context of enfleshed counter-memory, working in the shadow of hope is the reminder of the realism necessary to stay with trauma and its long-term consequences, avoiding both the

---

[32] Austin Channing Brown, *I'm Still Here: Black Dignity in a World Made for Whiteness* (New York: Convergent, 2018), 178–181.

[33] "Prophets of a Future Not Our Own" was written as a poem by Ken Untener in 1979, but is commonly known as "Oscar Romero's Prayer." I became familiar with its text through the hymn by Gregory Dale Schultz, often sung at Santa Clara University, "We Are Prophets," https://gregorydaleschultz.bandcamp.com/track/we-are-prophets.

dismissive "grin and bear it" survivor model *and* overly idealistic attitudes that often permeate justice work. Working within and through unfulfilled hope has unique force when grounded in Christ, as we are a people who wait in hope at the foot of the cross, and this "hope cannot simply be given a nod of recognition, for it demands not only a contract from us, but also a covenant and a commitment."[34] This covenantal orientation defines enfleshed counter-memory as a social ethic as well as a sacred relational agreement between persons and for humanity with God.

Where disability theology helps us to think in innovative ways about the individual evaluation of somatic experience, and liberation psychology reorients how we imagine what healing trauma looks like, these fields do not account for all the questions raised from the perspective of incarnate personhood presented by a womanist theological anthropology, or by the inherently mystical-political nature of the person and their experiences situated in eschatological time presented by Metz. Severe trauma "demands a language of life that can account for the ruptures of experience and history without succumbing to despair."[35] Enfleshed counter-memory, as a language of life, specifically expands the traditional, atomistic medical and spiritual modes of encountering trauma. Examining each part of the phrase—enfleshed / counter / memory—with its ethical correlate, this section demonstrates how enfleshed counter-memory serves as a shorthand for a comprehensive way of thinking about and approaching trauma that serves its covenantal orientation.

---

[34] Emilie Townes, *Womanist Ethics and the Cultural Production of Evil* (New York: Palgrave Macmillan, 2006), 164.

[35] Shelly Rambo, *Resurrecting Wounds: Living in the Afterlife of Trauma* (Waco, TX: Baylor University Press, 2017), 5.

Beyond Autonomy, toward "Enfleshment"

While autonomy is not an unimportant ethical category when considering trauma, it is insufficient for a Christian ethical response. Autonomy in the US context is wrapped up in cultural hyperindividualism and the primacy of independence as the highest good of social life. Enfleshment as a concept used throughout this book recognizes the importance of our bodies themselves and reaches beyond individual iterations of flesh and into flesh as a shared, connective, ethical tissue. Enfleshment reminds us, as Shawn Copeland states, that "the body is no mere object—*already-out-there-now*—with which we are confronted: always the body is with us, inseparable from us, *is* us."[36] While the body is us as individuals, it is also shared and holy—an intimate connection to God the creator and Christ the incarnate within all persons. Enfleshment resists the tendency to define autonomy narrowly, because "when autonomy is narrowly construed in terms of total self-reliance, personal preference and self-assertion, it can compound the burdens of frailty and sickness."[37] Viewing persons through the lens of the Incarnation and creation as *imago Dei,* as do the womanist thinkers in chapter 2, we expand the realm of potential healing: enfleshment contains the individual, our connection to the Divine, and our interconnection as humanity.

Enfleshment allows for and even demands that the messy complexity of the body, mind, and liminal existence itself be seen as whole, good, and ultimately mysterious. Enfleshment resists the

---

[36] M. Shawn Copeland, *Enfleshing Freedom: Body, Race, and Being* (Minneapolis: Fortress Press, 2010), 7.

[37] Based in the myth of individual independence as the measure of self-worth, see Margaret Farley, *Compassionate Respect: A Feminist Approach to Medical Ethics and Other Questions,* Madeleva Lecture Series (Mahwah, NJ: Paulist Press, 2002), 29.

drive toward order and control that dominates healing narratives that seek to define the body as a straightforward system rather than in its chaotic truth. Enfleshment attests that the truth of irreducible unruliness is divine. Though medical categorization of trauma and its focus on patient-centered autonomy are helpful, using them as a "primary interpretative principle," especially within theology, misses "any emotional, spiritual, or social aspects [that] are presumed to be epiphenomenal to the central neurological root," rather than central to the trauma experience.[38] Psychologist Steven J. Sandage of Boston University's Danielson Institute argues that trauma is *always* existential, yet, in initial emergency interventions, a traumatized person often cannot access such questions. Later, in ongoing traditional treatment (if they can access it), they are not invited to engage such questions.[39]

It is the particular role of Christian ethics, and an enfleshed counter-memory in particular, then, to center these existential aspects of trauma, to cultivate expansive healing paths, and to address the social sin of cultural constructions of disease that lead to the malignant social positioning of those who suffer. Enfleshment pushes beyond clinical autonomy, and clarifies our ethical connection to the "excess disability" often placed on those who are labeled with illness—and those who never get the privilege of care—and calls us all toward a greater sense of lived responsibility beyond individual experience.[40] Finally, taking

---

[38] Swinton, *Dementia*, 52–53.

[39] Steven J. Sandage, "Trauma and Spirituality," Boston University School of Theology, April 1, 2024. See also E. G. Ruffing, C. A. Bell, and S. J. Sandage, "PTSD Symptoms in Religious Leaders: Prevalence, Stressors, and Associations with Narcissism," *Archiv für Religionspsychologie / Archive for the Psychology of Religion* 43, no. 1 (2021): 21–40.

[40] "Excess disability relates to manifestations of incapacity that do not relate directly to any physical damage that might have occurred to an individual. So, for example, the social isolation and exclusion that come from being labeled 'schizophrenic' emerge not only from the condition itself but from people's

incarnate enfleshment seriously in Christian ethics uncouples salvation from any measure of medical or bodily functioning, freeing us all to recognize our shared liminality in the imperfect Body of Christ. As Channing Brown might say, in this way we live through the death of hope of pure health, but we enflesh our connection through imperfection and show up to do the work together that reaches toward ultimate healing.

Beyond Non-maleficence and Beneficence, toward "Counter"

The traditional metric from medical ethics applied to intervention in presenting conditions is to "do no harm" (non-maleficence). While, similar to patient-centered autonomy, this is a laudable maxim, non-maleficence is so deeply linked with autonomy that when enacted often directly leads to isolation and abandonment in the name of "personal freedom." Sometimes, in the rare US circumstance that someone can afford and access all necessary treatments as well as lives with all necessary social-emotional supports, this negative ethical injunction is paired with its more active partner: beneficence—acts that seek the good, or at least the better, in a given circumstance. These tenets are not fundamentally in error, but they remain limp responses to the demands of trauma on Christian ethics, often only appearing in their lowest form as guidance for individual action that avoids damage rather than cultivates flourishing.

What is needed instead is the "combative epistemology" teased out in chapter 3: a way of knowing embedded within committed acts of resistance and resilience, as well as memories of the same.[41]

---

reaction to the label." Swinton, *Dementia*, 87.

[41] "Counter" also becomes very real as systems often favor perpetrators, especially if they hold positions of power, where they enact "DARVO"—Deny, Attack, Reverse Victim, and Offender—and further harm the traumatized. Judith Herman uses Brett Kavanaugh's Supreme Court confirmation hearing as a textbook example of this behavior against Dr. Christine Blasey Ford. See

Centrally, such acts are never only individual; they are held, pursued, and remembered by community, a community that is itself responsible, implicated, and intertwined with suffering as well as hope for transformation. This way of knowing and doing even exceeds the limited bounds of beneficence (as understood in most trauma treatment settings), bringing *all of us* into responsibility for creating flourishing together. A resistant and resilient orientation is foundationally corporate and, through communal cooperation, seeks to counter the drives for efficiency over care, freedom over dependence, and purity over culpability.[42] Commitment to resistance and resilience pushes back on the overwhelming orientation of Catholic healthcare guidelines, which are dominated by an obsession with "noncooperation" with so-called evils, rather than beginning from a place of enmeshed resistance.[43] An active cultivation of memorative, justice-oriented practices, on the other hand, is defined by its desire for the flourishing of all, not only avoiding harm and seeking individual good.

From its "counter" position, enfleshed counter-memory requires an understanding of Christian time read with the traumatic imagination, where hope is founded, as Metz would say,

---

Herman, *Truth and Repair: How Trauma Survivors Envision Justice* (New York: Basic Books, 2023), 67.

[42] Resisting our cultural existence as *Homo economicus,* and moving toward a vision of agential dependency, see Heyer, "Enfleshing Social Production," 94, 99. This is also a component of hospitality, which is internal to each person as well as external to others. As May puts it, drawing on the thought of Julia Kristeva, this hospitality is not easy and lies at the root of our being: "we will never be able to live well with the strangers appearing around us unless we are able to live well with the strangeness—the otherness—in ourselves." May, *A Body Knows,* 57.

[43] While recognizing a social responsibility, the official guidelines for Catholic healthcare emphasize a regulation-focused theological interpretation of care, rather than an interdependent one. See USCCB, "Ethical and Religious Directives for Catholic Healthcare," 6th ed., 2018, https://www.usccb.org/about/doctrine/ethical-and-religious-directives/upload/ethical-religious-directives-catholic-health-service-sixth-edition-2016-06.pdf.

in memories with future content. Here, beneficence expands to include a view of human flourishing beyond the curative and into a hope for healing at once within human life and beyond it. While not excusing one's suffering—like telling the suffering to "await your reward in the Kingdom of Heaven"—enfleshed counter-memory does encourage a view of beneficence rooted in the real experience of chronic pain and suffering that may not be healed within strict medical parameters, but that can potentially be held, honored, and eventually liberated by God and our own graced actions. Through the lens of trauma, non-maleficence and beneficence rightly understood necessarily lead to seeking relational justice, for "bearing witness is revelatory, not regulatory."[44] Surging forward with Martín-Baró, such actions of enfleshed counter-memory are communal, people drawing together to weave a fabric of compassion in times of crisis.

In the decades-long Colombian conflict, for example, Christian Justapaz (Justpeace) groups not only practically protected persons targeted for assassination, they "transformed moments of crisis into epiphanies of grace.... There is no way to speak of what the community has done to neutralize torment, relieve pain, and to risk everything to protect and heal."[45] They risked everything to not only ensure no further harm came to their members, but they cultivated peaceful actions in a thoroughgoing culture of violence, in a view of sacred time beyond any imminent threat. This dedication to relational justice (running "counter" to any formal authority), cultivates resistance and resilience as acts that seek the good for all. These communities epitomize how, despite very real constraint, Christian notions of time and liberation draw

---

[44] May, *A Body Knows*, 73. Although concrete laws and regulations may be the outcome of effective justice work in response to trauma, the point here is that enfleshed counter-memory pushes us toward a thoroughgoing conversion of our way of thinking, seeing, and responding to suffering.

[45] Janna L. Hunter-Bowman, *Witnessing Peace: Becoming Agents under Duress in Colombia* (New York: Routledge, 2022), e-book Introduction.

us deeper into entanglement, rather than divorce us from history, and how persons continue to act for the good and avoid harm in even the most extreme circumstances.[46]

Beyond Distributive Justice, toward "Memory"

Finally, distributive justice, understood as fair allocation of resources, is markedly expanded by enfleshed counter-memory. This traditional ethical category is often discussed but rarely taken seriously in response to trauma, particularly in the American healthcare context with its lack of mental health resources for most of its citizens. Justice, however, is co-constitutive of enfleshed counter-memory and exceeds the bounds of simple calls for more funding/programs/access or individual resources. Justice within enfleshed counter-memory is as practical as it is memorative, fulfilling Keshgegian's call to a communal life of multiple memorative practices (preserving, resisting, and connecting) that can truly hold trauma. These practices intertwine concrete efforts with the simultaneous reckoning with the existential force of trauma, moving an understanding of justice away from solely policy and into right memory that has the power to change people, communities, and systems.

Centrally, with Margaret Farley, justice as memorative practice asks, "What does compassion require?" Especially for those who bear witness and accompany those who suffer, it is not enough to *feel* for someone (from the root meaning of compassion—to suffer with). Farley's proposal for medical ethics combines compassion with respect, where our intimacy with a particular iteration of

---

[46] Hunter-Bowman highlights that her emphasis is on moral agents under duress, but not from the classic, liberal "negative" orientation (where we focus on freedom *from*), but rather she highlights how groups and persons act despite constraints (in their ongoing freedom *to*). This approach connects with the strengths-based orientation of this book.

suffering does ignite empathetic feelings, but also demands that the cause of the violation be righted to respect the person in particular and any others in a similar position.[47] It is only such an engaged orthopathy, where feelings of mercy and love are matched by appropriate action, that justice as memory reveals its full force.

Within enfleshed counter-memory, work for justice also maintains a realistic and pointed attentiveness to power that is both a theological and ethical criterion, in tandem with embodied compassion.[48] Power is present throughout all human interactions, including efforts in theology and ethics. Without a keen eye toward the presence and function of power and privilege, enfleshed counter-memory can easily be coopted to support the status quo or the desires of those who hold social/political/religious authority (think of the recent expansion of the US criminal justice system into "restorative" justice and the currently disappearing diversity, equity, and inclusion [DEI] offices created after the June 2020 uprisings). While there is still healthy debate surrounding the nuanced balance between compassionate care and the need for justice, Christine Gudorf points out that proposing an "ethic of care" is not a substitute for principles such as justice, but rather acts as a corrective to their implementation. Often associated with feminist ethics, an ethics of care is based on determining the correct *response* to a situation in recognition of our interrelatedness, rather than sole reliance on predetermined rules.[49]

---

[47] Farley, *Compassionate Respect*, 42, 79: "Compassion sheds light on the individual patient in her concrete situation in all of its particularity and complex embodiment, ... the situation of sickness, ... the form of relationship needed ... [whereas] the norms of respect, in the affirmation of the well-being of others and ourselves, shed light on what compassion will require.... Genuine human mercy is made true by its justice."

[48] Nicholas Wolterstorff as quoted by M. A. Stenger, "Justice as a Theological and Ethical Criterion in Relation to Power and Love," *International Yearbook for Tillich Research* 9, no. 1 (2014): 164.

[49] Christine E. Gudorf, "The Need for Integrating Care Ethics into

Compassion, respect, justice, and responsive care constitute the parameters for the relational, memorative actions that expand our vision of and action toward right memory in response to trauma. For example in their years of work with seminary students and clergypersons, researchers at the Danielson Institute in Boston noticed a worryingly high occurrence of trauma, depression, and anxiety in their studies. In a 2022–2023 national study, one-third of Abrahamic faith leaders expressed suffering from traumatic stress—a rate higher than the US military.[50] In response to and operating from a framework resonant with the parameters of an enfleshed counter-memory, the Danielson is currently piloting CHRYSALIS (Catalyzing Helping professionals' Resilience, vitalitY, and Spirituality for Authentic Living and Inner Strength). It consists of groups of helping professionals meeting regularly with clinicians to process the existential impacts of their work, develop personal and culturally embedded capacities toward thriving, and "interrogate and resist personal, relational, and systemic pressures that are counter to your well-being, while working toward systemic change."[51] While primarily a randomized psychological study testing

---

Hospital Care: A Case Study," in *Medicine and the Ethics of Care*, ed. Diana Fritz Cates and Paul Lauritzen (Washington, DC: Georgetown University Press, 2001), 69–101. See also Farley, *Compassionate Respect*, 32.

[50] Steven Sandage as quoted by Giovanna Dell'Orto, "Clergy Burnout Is a Growing Concern in Polarized Churches, A Summit Offers Coping Strategies," Associated Press, October 9, 2023, https://apnews.com/article/clergy-burnout-church-mental-health-summit-570e71ec96575abc92865ad5baf491e6.

[51] The Albert & Jessie Danielson Institute at Boston University, https://www.bu.edu/danielsen/center-for-the-study-of-religion-and-psychology/peale-project/. The pilot year of 2023–2024 is ongoing, with preliminary efficacy data showing positive quantitative and qualitative results: L. E. Captari, E. J. Y. Choe, S. A. Crabtree, S. J. Sandage, J. A. Gerstenblith, L. B. Stein, K. R. Hydinger, and G. Stavros, "The Development and Feasibility of a Novel Group Intervention to Support Helping Professionals in Metabolizing Suffering and Engaging Strengths: The CHRYSALIS Program," *International Journal of Group Psychotherapy* 74, no. 2 (2024): 177–216.

an intervention model, this group-based work is rooted in similar insights to the necessary ethical expansions outlined earlier: the need to move from "self-care" to holistic formation, from individualism to relationality, from self-blame to existential grounding. Overall, the program aims to cultivate tools for engagement versus tools for withdrawal, understanding that the root cause of clergy's presenting challenges is deeply tied to the systems in which they operate and the intimacy with violences that their work entails. As well as successfully addressing a population in need, CHRYSALIS is working toward the type of integration of trauma—an enfleshed counter-memory beyond the parameters of strict distributive justice in mental healthcare—that can become a memory for life.

Enfleshed Counter-Memory as the Work of Justice

If traumatic disorders are afflictions of the powerless, then empowerment must be a central principle of recovery. If trauma shames and isolates, then recovery must take place in community.... If trauma is truly a social problem, and indeed it is, then recovery cannot be simply a private, individual matter. The wounds of trauma are not merely those caused by the perpetrators of violence and exploitation; the actions or inactions of bystanders—all those who are complicit in or who prefer not to know about the abuse or who blame the victims—often cause even deeper wounds. These wounds are part of the social ecology of violence, in which crimes against subordinated and marginalized people are rationalized, tolerated, or rendered invisible. If trauma originates in a fundamental injustice, then full healing must require repair through some measure of justice from the larger community.

—Judith Herman[52]

---

[52] Judith Herman, *Truth and Repair*, 3.

Enfleshed counter-memory is not just memory for memory's sake. As contextual and historically situated people, enfleshed counter-memory is always positioned as a memory *for*—a memory that considers real persons as ends in themselves as well as within situations that have specific purposes and ends for memory. Positioned distinctly within a Christian worldview, "we are each a whole world in ourselves yet always beyond ourselves, 'ends' because our center is at once beyond us and within us."[53] As a response to trauma, as described by Herman, enfleshed counter-memory is also not a response for response's sake but exists within the search and work for justice. Enfleshed counter-memory is the theoretical ground for the work of justice, and the work of justice is constitutive of enfleshed counter-memory. In short, it is impossible to merely talk *about* enfleshed counter-memory; instead it is established and created by concrete action.[54]

Much like the praxis circle, enfleshed counter-memory is rooted in a continual process of action/theory/reflection in whatever order the steps occur—it is a *practical* theology. It takes seriously the demand of trauma to imagine expansively, read critically, and harness our "prophetic fury" toward sinful powers that attempt to destroy right memory.[55] As such, the

---

[53] Farley, *Compassionate Respect*, 37.

[54] To ignore the practical nature of enfleshed counter-memory is to misunderstand its purpose, and cooperates with structural and personal sin that encourages trauma. See Flora Keshgegian, *Redeeming Memories: A Theology of Healing and Transformation* (Nashville: Abingdon Press, 2000), 152. Also, as it addresses trauma in particular, mental illness "*is the product of both damaged neurons and the experiences of particular forms of relationship and community.*" Swinton, *Dementia*, 107. Again, this section does not provide an instruction manual for all necessary skills, like Psychological First Aid (PFA) or how to write a crisis plan, but instead offers practical frames for discernment of individuals within communities to structure potential relational responses.

[55] Townes, *Womanist Ethics*, 164. Importantly, such practices are rooted in an ethic of care based in the "praxeological" framework (practical theology, an action/reflection methodology) proposed by Townes, *Breaking the Fine Rain*

work for social justice is essential to a Christian enfleshed counter-memory and inherently part of its definition. For our consideration here, justice falls within three major realms, from micro to macro: (1) empowerment of individual agency and integrity as self, (2) community support and participation in re/integration of persons, and (3) solidarity and the preferential option for the poor.[56]

It is from gritty, committed, shadowed hope that I propose this three-part structure be taken up as a framework for persons and communities themselves to expand. Just as the practices suggested in chapter 2 are presented, these are intentionally broad, evocative suggestions for communities to add texture and detail as needed by their context. As repeatedly stressed through this volume, trauma is painfully particular as well as almost banally

---

of Death: African American Health Issues and a Womanist Ethic of Care (Eugene, OR: Wipf and Stock, 1998).

[56] While these are by no means definitive of all possible routes, they are inspired by Judith Herman's three broad phases of individual trauma healing: safety and stabilization, remembrance and mourning, and reconnection and integration (see *Trauma and Recovery*). It also follows the three broad layers of trauma's operation I sketch throughout this book: as individual disease, layered ethics within situational mental health and suffering, and trauma as social/structural violence. Finally, they reach back to Thomas Aquinas's reclamation of Aristotle's spheres of political community. Copeland references these levels of action: "One cannot say I love God whom I cannot see but fail to love the brother and sister whom one does see. This is the real grounding of Christian living. This starts in the home where one learns how to be attentive to the other person, to a significant other or spouse or partner or children, then moves out to wider concern for others. This is learned behavior. Jesus also learned to reach out to the concerns of other groups and individuals from other cultural groups. Consider his encounter with the Syrophoenician woman who had pestered and argued him to act. Jesus demonstrates for us it is possible to learn, it is possible to change." Saracino and Rivera interviewing Copeland, "An Interview with M. Shawn Copeland," in *Enfleshing Theology: Embodiment, Discipleship, and Politics in the Work of M. Shawn Copeland*, ed. Robert J. Rivera and Michele Saracino (Lanham, MD: Lexington Books / Fortress Academic, 2018), xxvii–xxviii.

universal. With both of these poles in mind I attempt to frame the work of enfleshed counter-memory. The common root is found in a vision of covenantal relationship, where the work for justice within enfleshed counter-memory has the potential to assist individuals, communities, and Christian theology itself to live into a deeper and more robust understanding of and engagement with the ongoing suffering of our world and ourselves.

Empowerment of Individual Agency and Integrity as Self (Micro)

> The truth is none of us are enough enough. But you know this already.
>
> The truth is I came here hoping for a reason to stay.
>
> Sometimes those reasons are small: the way you pronounce spaghetti as "bagheddy."
>
> It's late in the season—which means the winter roses, in full bloom along the national bank, are suicide notes.
>
> Write that down.
>
> They say nothing lasts forever but they're just scared it will last longer than they can love it.
>
> Are you there? Are you still walking?
>
> They say nothing lasts forever and I'm writing you in the voice of an endangered species.
>
> The truth is I'm worried they will get us before they *get us*.
>
> Tell me where it hurts. You have my word.
>
> —Ocean Vuong[57]

---

[57] Ocean Vuong, *On Earth We're Briefly Gorgeous* (New York: Penguin Press, 2019), 176.

Just as Ruby Sales helped us begin our exploration with the question "Where does it hurt?" Ocean Vuong follows it with a commitment: "You have my word." As he reaches out toward his interlocutor, Vuong reminds us of the space we share: the brittle, forever-passing-away present. He also pushes us toward recognition of those who have been violently forced to the margins, feeling hunted for a perceived difference rather than sought out for their particular revelation of the creative power of existence. Here, this reflection reminds us that, while we begin with individuals as the agential powers of human creativity, autonomy and self-integrity are by no means fostered, sustained, or lived in a vacuum.

The foundational, and most particular, component of justice in an enfleshed counter-memory is empowerment of individual agency and honoring the integrity of self. As Eboni Marshall Turman points out, because subjugated people (for her, Black women) have been defined solely by their relation to "the other" for so long, the inherent dignity of the person remains unseen or ignored, usually to the benefit of oppressive social structures. The starting point for any ethic of justice, she argues, must be a rootedness in the *incarnate a priori*.[58] Seen from this vantage point, our unique enfleshments are primary for any justice pursuit that claims to be Christian. While our selves are multidimensional, three aspects emerge from such an understanding of the person, and lie at the core of enfleshed counter-memory as enacted on the micro level: first, agency, understood as the capacity to act, particularly to act for the good; second, integrity of self, understood as the healthy acknowledgment of all parts of our story; and, third, empowerment as a practice cultivated through community (from Martín-Baró).[59]

---

[58] Eboni Marshall Turman, *Toward a Womanist Ethic of Incarnation: Black Bodies, the Black Church, and the Council of Chalcedon* (London: Palgrave MacMillan, 2013), 13. Her proposal is an expansion of W. E. B. Du Bois's work on "the white gaze" and "double consciousness" that she finds has actually reinforced patriarchal structures in the Black church.

[59] These terms are hotly debated and of great import in and of themselves.

These three aspects of the person are practiced through the act of remembering itself. Memory here is an act of resistance and agency for life, not a mythologized heroism in survival or suffering. Critically, memory work, like all work for justice, is an activity. It is ongoing. As Monica Coleman puts it, "It is a verb, a gerund. Health and wholeness come through teach*ing,* heal*ing,* remember*ing,* honor*ing,* possess*ing,* adopt*ing,* conform*ing,* and creatively transform*ing.*"[60] The lived examples of these "verbs of work" on the micro level are as multiple as the individuals who enact them. Coleman herself uses a multitude of pathways to healing, including Western psychotherapy, pharmaceutical treatment, West African dance and spiritual ritual, Christian fellowship and "traditional" church, theological scholarship, group therapy, artmaking, public speaking/advocacy, and more. All of these actions affirm and work toward the empowerment of her individual agency and integrity as self, in and through relationship.

Without attending to the individual's embodied strengths, needs, and desires, the work for justice within an enfleshed counter-memory cannot be realized in the concrete. If not oriented by real persons, memorative justice, at best, defaults

---

I am using them as shorthand here to gesture toward the necessary attention to the multifaceted person at the center of enfleshed counter-memory as a social ethic—weaving together insights from womanist thought and Metz that have to balance each other, the personal and the mystical-political, to be a proper and robust response to trauma. It is also not to premise a fullness of the capacity (holding to Haslam's critique of disability/capacities above) but to say we must engage these aspects of the person.

[60] Monica Coleman, *Bipolar Faith: A Black Woman's Journey with Depression and Faith* (Minneapolis: Fortress Press, 2016), 169. There is also a very necessary conversation to be had about the "right to forget" explored by Miroslav Volf that is of particular importance in contexts of communal, political trauma, *The End of Memory: Remembering Rightly in a Violent World* (Grand Rapids: William B. Eerdmans, 2006).

into reinforcing limiting social norms via benevolent paternalism, and, at worst, it inflicts further harm.[61] As theologian Melanie May reflected on her own experiences of sickness and near-death trauma, the body is not just material or passive, nor is it just a symbol or sign. Rather, it is an active and real disclosure of the nature of God in human existence. For May, her

> body's theological knowledge is neither symbolic nor is it a proposal for the production of a form of fixity. What I know from my flesh and blood fixes me on trespass ... for the sake of the transfiguration of my mind as well as the resurrection of my body.... This blessing is the clarity and courage to participate—my body a textured verb—in the ongoing process of naming and renaming, of making and remaking, of binding and loosing, trusting the end to God.[62]

As she suggests, individual trauma healing is not static, but is necessarily dynamic, rooted in the concepts of transfiguration and resurrection that guide Christian belief. Recognition of these categories as central to the self allows for expanded notions of healing and justice, and specifically that these aims are not always practiced in an upward trajectory with a clear and achievable goal. Seeing the incarnate a priori in the context of the resurrection finally promises a healing of self that belongs ultimately to God, but also fuels our continued "work in the dark" to empower individual agency, integrity, and empowerment in light of God's promises of liberation.

---

[61] A moving example of this risk can be found in Susanna Snyder, "'La Mano Zurda with a Heart in Its Palm': Mystical Activism as a Response to the Trauma of Immigration Detention," in *Post-traumatic Public Theology*, ed. Shelly Rambo and Stephanie N. Arel (London: Palgrave Macmillan, 2016), 217–240.

[62] May, *A Body Knows*, 104.

Community Support and Participation in Re/integration of Persons (Mezzo)

> There are so many of us now, we could hardly be called strange fish anymore. We have made a place in this sea. All the fluttering, building, loving, hunting, embracing, mating, we hear it all, our presence unmistakable. A whole chorus of the deep. *Wajinru.* We are not zoti aleyu. We are more vast and more beauteous than that name implies. We are a song, and we are together.
>
> We remember.
>
> —Rivers Solomon[63]

In Rivers Solomon's novella, we learn about an underwater society built by the water-breathing descendants of pregnant enslaved African women thrown overboard from trans-Atlantic ships. In the resulting Wajinru culture, a certain member is tasked with keeping history, with holding the memories of their entire population, so that others can live without this burden. When Yetu is chosen, the memories begin to kill her, driving a story of self and communal responsibility for memory, no matter how painful. It is only through the sharing of memory, the cooperation toward healing, and the recognition of traumatic pasts that Yetu is saved, the Wajinru survive, and together they begin to create a new world.

A critical element that is often missing from proposals regarding traumatic memory is the role of the larger community. What I mean by "community" is admittedly undertheorized and requires the individual evaluation of a person, group, or both to determine aspects of best fit and responsible activity. Here it suffices to say that I am using the sociological paradigm of "mezzo" actors that

---

[63] Rivers Solomon, *The Deep* (New York: Saga Press, 2019), 64.

are often described as local institutions with direct relationship to the individual, such as families, churches, community centers, schools, towns, and so on. Importantly, communities are not singular but multiple. Often it is the "cloud of witnesses"—from family to friends to parish to small group to geographical location to ethno-racial identity—that constitutes the definition of one's community and that would be present in mezzo-level support. It is within these communities, and particularly those defined by the Christian faith, where we have the potential and responsibility to cultivate enfleshed counter-memory: naming suffering and related problems, seeking justice for and beyond the individual, and providing grounded hope.[64]

Beyond a more robust vision of the human person offered through the theological anthropology presented in this project and the need for individual healing justice, Christian communities have, since their inception, confronted and reinterpreted traumatic events and related suffering. Arguably such confrontation and reinterpretation are the ethical foundations of the faith. It is not only the role of the community to work for justice in the face of suffering as an external moral obligation, but we must do so also to resist our own internal complicity in the creation or continuation of pain. Beyond taking an abstract social stand, the mezzo form of justice calls us toward this internal work through the cultivation of intimate relationships. Within enfleshed counter-memory, this is based on the relationality of the Trinitarian God, as well as the model of accompaniment in the Gospels. As Jesus shared intimate "being-with" with those whom society deemed most abhorrent, so Christians are called to do the same.

---

[64] Drawn from Townes, *Breaking the Fine Rain*, 25, as well as Shelly Rambo, *Spirit and Trauma: A Theology of Remaining* (Louisville, KY: Westminster John Knox Press, 2010). Also, strategies for healing such as community-based healthcare have shown themselves to be more effective in resource use than top-down models. Townes, *Breaking the Fine Rain*, 158.

In the hyperindividualized United States, this can be a difficult proposal. However, trauma healing best practices clarify that we require some form of truth telling, for a "community in conversation," because "if [survivors] lay our bodies bare in our world so inhospitable to truth and to vulnerability we need to be in the company of others—a communion of saints, indeed—who choose to live with thin skins."[65] Choosing to live with "thin skin" is an uncomfortable proposition, but one that communities seeking memorative justice must embody. It allows for strength to be founded in shared vulnerability, asking those of us who witness to hold and carry the weight of trauma *with* survivors, and, at times, *for* them. Importantly, this is in no way about stripping away one's agency, but instead a call toward communal responsibility and love in action. This is Christian agapic *and* erotic love: first it is agapic in that it is "unselfish and seeks the good for all of us—not just the common good . . . [and] the erotic dimension of this care is our individual and collective creative energy that makes us feel what we are doing passionately and fully."[66] Through practices of community support, love, and participation, we cultivate the paths to feel, act, and remember rightly. We also allow for possibilities of future growth, of "how to remember the loss and still go on—not only as survivors in defiance or desperation, but with a measure of commitment to life and its goodness."[67] Here, like the Wajinru, we learn to honor past pain together while we build environments of hope and possibility.

Yet appropriate formation of community support and participation must be in response to the survivor or survivor group's self-defined needs (recall CHRYSALIS above). Too often, well-

---

[65] May, *A Body Knows*, 86. She also tempers this with the need for balance and space (91).

[66] Townes, *Breaking the Fine Rain*, 175.

[67] Keshgegian, *Redeeming Memories*, 87.

intentioned actions are rushed, and such rushing not only quickly expends limited resources (of energy and material goods), but actually does a disservice to traumatized persons and the social nature of their experience. This is often well-meaning action, but supportive communities too often claim to speak for a person or group, misrepresent the desires of a person or group, and/or occupy physical or rhetorical space to which the impacted person or group has the primary right. Heeding disability advocates' cry of "nothing about us without us," public actions must be survivor-led, even if it means delay. With Swinton, we must remember that God's time is "slow," that our work is a way of being that exceeds its perceived productivity or success.[68] This orientation encourages communities to first, and perhaps exclusively, sit *with* in accompaniment rather than act *for* the survivors who ask for support. Recalling brown's *emergent strategy*, she encourages cultivating such communities of depth rather than breadth, emphasizing the need for enduring commitment that only thrives within intimate groups.[69]

A corporate body with preexisting roots in Christian communities can develop a central role in traumatic memory through communal ritual practices such as lament. While lament is practiced with some regularity in communities that observe Lent, the Longest Night, or other annual liturgical moments, lament is still an underutilized aspect of the US Christian tradition. We may not share the same pain, but all suffering is interconnected, and "lament enables us and even requires of us to acknowledge and to experience the fullness of our suffering."[70] Lament also forms a

---

[68] John Swinton, *Becoming Friends of Time: Disability, Timefullness, and Gentle Discipleship* (Waco, TX: Baylor University Press, 2018), 74. Delaying might also be a good, as large-scale movements often only function to make communities feel they are "helping" or "fixing" rather than being led by attention to the harmed person/group.

[69] brown, *Emergent Strategy*, 10.

[70] Townes, *Breaking the Fine Rain*, 24.

responsible faith with a "hefty hope," as Townes puts it, that has the capacity to hold the memory of trauma in resistance to both personal despair and death-dealing hegemonic forces. It makes space for genuine covenantal interaction with God that holds grief as well as praise, that is full in its expression of life.

> When we grieve, when we lament, we acknowledge and live the experience, rather than try to hold it away from us out of some misguided notion of being objective or strong. We hurt; something is fractured, if not broken. A foul spirit lives in and among us. We are living in structures of evil and wickedness that make us ill. We must name them as such and seek to repent—not out of form but from the heart. It is only then that we can begin to heal.[71]

Naming pain in lament, a community surfaces trauma so that the group can hear its expression and hold the story together. In this holding, lament pushes us toward action in repentance, for both the current situation of pain and its historical roots.[72]

After Hurricane Katrina hit Mississippi, one congregation returned to find their church completely destroyed: "All that remained of their house of worship was a concrete slab. During the week, the pastor spread the word that they would still meet for worship like they did every week. Because that bare concrete foundation was all that remained, the church ... referred to that

---

[71] Townes, *Breaking the Fine Rain*, 24.

[72] For example, "As a white person by denouncing slavery I affirm a linguistic anti-racist position. However, by defining chattel slavery as only in the past, I am insulating myself from my/our individual and 'collective role(s) in the perpetuation of racism.'" Cassidy quoting Alice McIntyre; Laurie Cassidy, "Learning to Enflesh Freedom: Returning to the Clearing," in *Enfleshing Theology: Embodiment, Discipleship, and Politics in the Work of M. Shawn Copeland*, ed. Robert J. Rivera and Michele Saracino (Lanham, MD: Lexington Books / Fortress Academic, 2018), 56.

moment as 'Slab Sunday.'"[73] Singing songs with all they had left, their voices, the people cried out to God. The pastor provided time for members to name—specifically or abstractly—what had been lost, and members wept, leaned on one another, and prayed. Lament naturally resists the triumphalism often encouraged or even mandated by survival. Rather, it forces us to sit in our discomfort with our or others' loss and express pain in whatever means we have available. Enacting such ritual as community also contextualizes pain in a larger narrative, allows people to interact with memory through a "third" space outside of any direct victim-offender scenario, and resists victimization rhetoric that can dominate traumatic memory.[74] As Soong-Chan Rah reflects on his time with a relief agency responding to events like Katrina, "Lament does not simply explain away suffering. Instead lament allows for the suffering to speak and contribute to the larger story. The narrative is not merely an expression of the privileged and the powerful but of the humble. Lament is not a passive act but a subversive act of protest against the status quo."[75] Holding painful memory within the liminal space of community lament (neither a solely internal nor solely external practice) offers fertile ground for cultivating enfleshed counter-memory and fostering creative healing rituals focused on memory for life.

---

[73] Jamie D. Aten, "The Radical Power of Lament," *Sojourners,* April 12, 2019, https://sojo.net/articles/radical-power-lament.

[74] Keshgegian, *Redeeming Memories,* 87, and Townes, *Breaking the Fine Rain,* 183. Whether calculated for gain or out of mindless reliance on easy answers, victimization rhetoric is sinful in nature but often clung to in opposition to socially mandated triumphalism. The rhetoric of victimization tells a story that does not include redemption or acknowledge the chaotic nature of suffering. It positions suffering as central to the identity of a person/group, and pain is therefore necessary, deserved, and to be expected.

[75] Soong-Chan Rah, "Lament Is a Necessary Step toward Healing," *Sojourners,* June 15, 2017, https://sojo.net/articles/faith-action/lament-necessary-step-toward-healing.

While lament is only one example of potential community-level action, it is an example of how groups rooted in the Christian story have unique tools to assist in trauma healing and holding traumatic memory rightly. Others may include social or political activism based on the teachings of the gospel, public rituals such as communal penance or prayer that surface communal accountability for trauma as well as healing, small group spiritual support (such as the Christian Life Community model popular on many college campuses), and trauma-sensitive liturgies that speak to and hold the reality of ongoing trauma healing. While these practices are in no way exhaustive, nor can they attend to every need in the wake of trauma, the use of similar activities in communal spaces can empower survivors, resist the isolation too often experienced by those in the throes of debilitating trauma, and help us all learn to remember suffering rightly.

Solidarity and the Preferential Option for the Poor (Macro)

> The struggle against power is the struggle of memory against forgetting.
>
> —Milan Kundera[76]

The final level of action for justice in response to trauma is necessarily global. As revealed by the work of Metz and womanist thought, suffering is not just personal but structural and systemic, and memory is a site of resistance to its grip. Forgetting itself can be a manipulation of power, as Kundera reflects. For the Christian, Townes argues, forgetting is particularly dubious, as the "ability

---

[76] Milan Kundera, *The Book of Laughter and Forgetting* (1978; New York: Harper Perennial Modern Classics, 1999), 3; also cited by Susan Brison, *Aftermath: Violence and the Remaking of a Self* (Princeton, NJ: Princeton University Press, 2002), 58.

of the fantastic hegemonic imagination to forget is both a serious medical condition and an astute strategy of domination. It is not healthy—not even for the dominant elite—to fail to remember the textures of our common humanity.... It is strategic in that to 'forget' is to be able to feign ignorance and lack of agency."[77] Losing our agency in this way compromises our covenantal connection with God, becoming overwhelmed by earthly dominance at the cost of salvific memory.[78] Ignoring the "textures"—particularly those that do not fit neatly into our shared woven garment, those that trouble us and demand attention and action like a loose thread—is a specific tool for the continuation of oppressive structures that create and uphold trauma. Whether because oppression supports one's social location, or because it is simply "too hard" to act, most individuals will look for simple solutions or ways to extricate themselves from responsibility. The Christian faith asks more of its followers. Instead of turning away, Christ asks us to turn *toward* those most in need, no matter their location.

Without the central grounding of solidarity and preferential option for the poor, the hard work of community participation and individual empowerment remains isolating and dislocating. Trauma exists and functions in a global environment and within sociohistorical locations. The Christian mandate of solidarity, of standing with those most in need, is to resist *all* machinations that attempt to circumscribe full human flourishing. We are asked to

---

[77] Townes, *Womanist Ethics*, 27. See also Monica Coleman, *Making a Way out of No Way* (Minneapolis: Fortress Press, 2008), 33. On a sociocultural level, focusing on fallen moral exemplars, Karen V. Guth explores how we can do this work in *The Ethics of Tainted Legacies: Human Flourishing after Traumatic Pasts* (Cambridge: Cambridge University Press, 2022).

[78] "If the cries of the victims are the voice of God, then the faces of the victims are the face of God, the bodies of the victims are the body of God. The anguish of the victims of history and the demand of authentic solidarity plead for the presence of the supernatural in the concrete." Copeland, *Enfleshing Freedom*, 101–102.

resist a world that tries to force us "to accept the is-ness of our lives as the ought," and instead remember how to weave with God: binding the threads of our lives together to create masterpieces.[79] Within our weaving, the greater work of God in humanity and within all creation emerges—a deep incarnation—where humans are endowed with a greater sense of purpose, and a greater hope. It is out of this hope that Christianity, modeled on the life of Jesus, asks us to stand with those most broken by the world. As such, solidarity and the preferential option for the poor are not only ethical but anthropological and even soteriological. Our deepest selves and ultimate telos are not simply choosing for the good but are rooted in a way of being that transcends moral "rules" and instead are enlivened by our whole selves grounded in Love.[80]

Even on a global scale, we can begin the work of healing justice by listening to impacted persons, and then "accepting individual and communal accountability and complicity in how we have and have not responded" that is not overly burdensome to one individual, but appropriate to the sinful structures in which we exist.[81] This is the necessary position of theology in response to theodicy, as Metz puts it, positioning "discourse about God as the cry for the salvation of others, of those who suffer unjustly, of the victims and the vanquished in our history."[82] If we are to take seriously the task of trauma healing, it must be located within such a global view, as "it is in society that people acquire their memories. It is also in society that they recall, recognize, and localize their

---

[79] Townes, *Breaking the Fine Rain*, 179.

[80] Roberto Goizueta, "'A Body of Broken Bones': Shawn Copeland and the New Anthropological Subject," in *Enfleshing Theology: Embodiment, Discipleship, and Politics in the Work of M. Shawn Copeland*, ed. Robert J. Rivera and Michele Saracino (Lanham, MD: Lexington Books / Fortress Academic, 2018), 7, 11.

[81] Townes, *Breaking the Fine Rain*, 183.

[82] Johann Baptist Metz, *A Passion for God: The Mystical-Political Dimension of Christianity* (New York: Paulist Press, 1998), 55.

memories."[83] Without the overarching orientation of solidarity and preferential option for the poor framing how we confront and interpret trauma, the memories of individuals remain limited to potentially damaging social scripts and available cultural metaphors that tend to trap victims within interpretations of their experiences that at best are reductive and that at worst reinscribe harm. Orienting trauma healing within God's promises to humanity can perhaps respond to philosopher and rape survivor Susan Brison: "As irrational as it is, I want to believe that, just as there is such a thing as irreparable damage, there might be such a thing as irreversible repair."[84]

Although these three levels of justice, from the singular individual to the global context, are necessarily generalized, they indicate how all-encompassing change must be to truly address trauma and its impacts. In micro-level interactions, enacting a Christian enfleshed counter-memory demands accompaniment, empowering individual agency, and fostering integrity of self, rather than abandoning complex and often difficult individuals. For mezzo-level communities, a Christian enfleshed counter-memory supports the work of survivor-led rituals and public actions that encourage narrative integration and participation, whether within religious institutions themselves, or in the broader public sphere. Finally, the concepts of solidarity and preferential option for the poor continually challenge any assumption of privilege, or the belief that oneself or one's community can stand completely "outside" of the trauma experience.[85] Christian enfleshed

---

[83] Brison quoting Halbwachs, *Aftermath*, 31.
[84] Brison, *Aftermath*, 116.
[85] Cassidy, "Learning to Enflesh Freedom," 62. Here Cassidy is reflecting on Sarah Lucia Hogland's engagement with white-Black feminisms, where "We who are white can decide to see white privilege as part of our theological trajectory or not. The self that makes this decision is essentially autonomous in relationship to women of color.... 'We are positioned to act for the other, to represent the other, but never to recognize ourselves as dependent upon her'" (59).

counter-memory resists an epistemology of ignorance; instead, it insists that we recognize how to "rage with compassion"[86] in the face of ongoing radical evil while at the same time holding strong to the hope for radical change offered through Christian faith.

Conclusion

"I love the thing that I most wish had not happened."[87]

Christian enfleshed counter-memory takes Colbert's assertion seriously and provides a tool that helps us construct such a language of life for all. Fostering enfleshed counter-memory as a Christian ethical task does not valorize pain. It seeks healing through and within memory, rooted in hope. This is by no means a pat response to the hard work of encountering trauma. Rather, we are each and together called into further collaboration, engagement, and struggle within our own lives and communities.[88] Enfleshed counter-memory follows in the lineage of Martín-Baró, who framed his efforts in liberation psychology as "writings for," where the phrase is intentional, capturing "the open-ended and unfinished nature of [the] work as well as its explicit directionality."[89] Enfleshed counter-memory is, by its very nature, the central work of the Christian ethical life in response to trauma: covenantal, committed, ongoing, and primarily focused on work with and for the oppressed. It is an ethic that reaches beyond traditional

---

[86] See John Swinton, *Raging with Compassion: Pastoral Responses to the Problem of Evil* (Grand Rapids: William B. Eerdmans, 2007).

[87] Lovell, "The Late, Great Stephen Colbert."

[88] "*Gaudium et Spes* teaches us that we are mistaken when we think that we may overlook or push aside our social responsibilities. As followers of Jesus, 'The joys and hopes, griefs and anguish of the people of our time, especially those who are poor or afflicted' are our joys and hopes, our griefs and anguish. There should [be] no dichotomy between the faith we profess and our daily lives (nos. 1, 43)." Saracino and Rivera, "An Interview," xxxviii.

[89] Mishler, "Foreword," xii, reflecting on Martín-Baró's title.

ethical categories, holding together the nuanced justice practices that are required to prevent trauma healing and memory from disintegrating into nothing but the "business of planning."[90] We must and we can experience survivors' truth with compassionate respect that is premised on concrete action. We must and we can root our actions in an incarnational theological anthropology and a mystical-political reality that contribute to our flourishing, not just our survival. We must and we can heal—together.

---

[90] Johann Baptist Metz, *Faith in History and Society: Toward a Practical Fundamental Theology* (New York: Crossroad, 2011), 101. Also a critique of Robert J. Schreiter regarding reconciliation work, see, *Reconciliation: Mission and Ministry in a Changing Social Order*, Boston Theological Institute Series (Maryknoll, NY: Orbis Books, 1992), 70.

EPILOGUE

et lux in tenebris lucet

There is no simplicity in this task.[1] And there is little proof that the field needs another white, Catholic, middle-class woman writing this book. Yet I take this as a challenge, a demonstration of the very task at hand, rather than a negation of its validity. Since my coming into consciousness, the Catholic Church has been rife with controversy, rather than a beacon of God's love. In fact, taking seriously the pain, trauma, and sinfulness that the church has wrought is another inspiration for my undertaking this writing. The rape, molestation, and mistreatment of children and adults, alongside the criminal cover-ups of those actions and others is not, and never will be, made "right." And yet I cling to hope in the siblings in Christ with whom I have walked—victim/survivor, witness, and otherwise—who steadfastly demand that this church is *theirs,* maybe even more so than those who sit in its offices or hold power in its halls.

While I write mostly using the term "Christian" (as my work is squarely rooted in the teachings of Jesus), I am inextricably Catholic. I want to hold myself and my church specifically accountable to its own grounding in the gospel as well as the best of its theological thinking. As a Catholic ethicist, I am so tired of "scandal" being a primary concern for my church rather than honesty, humility, and

---

[1] The epigraph is John 1:15: "et lux in tenebris lucet et tenebrae eam non comprehenderunt" [the Light shines in the darkness, and the darkness did not overcome it].

responsibility. We are not perfect—myself very much included—and yet we, as a magisterial body, are so wedded to a vision of perfection and purity that we would rather commit further crimes and stay within a system of injustice than admit publicly and without reservation that we were wrong—intentionally or not—and co-create systems of service for and with those most harmed.[2]

The knowledge of our sinfulness is present, but true accountability is not. *Learning* how we are all embedded in systems we did not choose, let alone create, is not the end of the task—the *doing* is. Looking to ethical action, however, is not an urge to rush to total, perfect resolution. As Laurie Cassidy reminds us,

> The desire to alleviate suffering is not the problem, the problem is that, as white people [her writing here is focused on race], we have an urgency to act so as to overcome our discomfort, we need to be in control, we need to have an action plan. History is littered with the plans (and human bodies) of the powerful who have created plans to bring about a better world.[3]

While this book is, in a way, my own urge to "plan" taken to the extreme, I take Cassidy's words to heart: trauma asks first and foremost that we sit with complexity, that we recognize tension and discordance, that we do the hard work of what F. Scott Fitzgerald

---

[2] Not to mention the myriad other historical and present injustices permeating the life of the church. For further discussion on this topic in particular, see John Sheveland, ed., *Theology in a Post-traumatic Church* (Maryknoll, NY: Orbis Books, 2023). I have also written on the intergenerational harms of clergy-perpetrated sexual abuse with Kimberley Humphrey: "Haunted Salvation: The Generational Consequences of Ecclesial Sex Abuse and the Conditions for Conversion," *Journal of Moral Theology* 9, no. 1 (2020): 51–74.

[3] Laurie Cassidy, "Grotesque Un/Knowing of Suffering: A White Christian Response," in *Christology and Whiteness: What Would Jesus Do?*, ed. George Yancy (New York: Routledge, 2012), 47.

called a first-rate intelligence: "the ability to hold two opposed ideas in mind at the same time, and still retain the ability to function. One should, for example, be able to see that things are hopeless yet be determined to make them otherwise."[4] Seeking a Christian social ethic of trauma is not about "fixing," or handing down a technocratic plan that will have little impact and less heart.[5] Instead, building an enfleshed counter-memory is finding a way of *being* and *becoming* that can hold all our suffering and our hope in light of the gospel. It is trying to build a way of mending ourselves together to do the hardest work of our lives.

---

[4] F. Scott Fitzgerald, *The Crack-Up* (New York: New Directions Publishing, 1945), 69.

[5] Inspired here by Robert Schreiter, C.PP.S., and his work on reconciliation. I have no desire and feel no need to write apologetics; instead I respond to a similar call that Hans Zollner defines in light of the clergy sex-abuse crisis: I "cannot help but speak," confronting the reality of sin and yet in faith. Zollner, "Foreword," in Sheveland, ed., *Theology in a Post-traumatic Church*, x.

Permissions

Excerpt from *I'm Still Here: Black Dignity in a World Made for Whiteness* by Austin Channing Brown. Copyright © 2018 by Austin Channing Brown. Used by permission of Crown Books, an imprint of the Crown Publishing Group, a division of Penguin Random House LLC. All rights reserved.

Excerpt from *On Earth We're Briefly Gorgeous: A Novel* by Ocean Vuong. Copyright © 2019 by Ocean Vuong. Used by permission of Penguin Press, an imprint of Penguin Publishing Group, a division of Penguin Random House LLC. All rights reserved.

Excerpt from *The Deep* by Rivers Solomon with Daveed Diggs, William Hutson, and Jonathan Snipes. Copyright © 2019 by Daveed Diggs, William Hutson, and Jonathan Snipes. Reprinted with the permission of Saga Press, an imprint of Simon & Schuster, LLC. All rights reserved.

Excerpt from *The Deep* by Rivers Solomon with Daveed Diggs, William Hutson, and Jonathan Snipes. Copyright © 2019 by Daveed Diggs, William Hutson, and Jonathan Snipes. Reproduced with permission of Hodder and Stoughton Limited through PLSclear.

Excerpt from *The Deep* by Rivers Solomon with Daveed Diggs, William Hutson, and Jonathan Snipes. Copyright © 2019 by Rivers Solomon, Daveed Diggs, William Hutson, and Jonathan Snipes. Reprinted with permission of Clipping Touring LLC. All rights reserved.

Excerpt from *The Katrina Papers: A Journal of Trauma and Recovery*, by Jerry W. Ward Jr. Copyright © 2008 by The University of New Orleans. Used by permission. All rights reserved.

Index

Abraham, Susan, 98, 99–100
Ahmed, Sara, 41
Anzaldúa, Gloria, 110, 115–16
apophaticism, 28
Ashley, James Matthew, 129, 134, 150, 155

Beste, Jennifer, 25–26, 28–30, 105
Bipolar Faith (Coleman), 62
The Body Keeps the Score (van der Kolk), 15, 107
border thinking, 115–16
bourgeois man, framework of, 131, 148
Brison, Susan, 211
brown, adrienne maree, 173–74, 205
Brown, Austin Channing, 185, 189

Cadwallader, Jessica R., 41–42
Calvin, John, 27
Caputo, John, 101, 110, 119, 121–22, 124
Carnal Hermeneutics (ed. Kearney/Treanor), 113
Caruth, Cathy, 21–23, 25, 103
Cassidy, Laurie, 2, 52, 216–17
Christian Justapaz groups, 191
Christian Life Community model, 208
Christian memory, 148, 177
 divine sense of time, as positioned in, 147
 enfleshed counter-memory, as ethical expression of, 184–95
 existential contours of trauma, examining, 45
 language of life for all, providing, 212
 metanarrative of, 129
 in micro-level interactions, 211
 proposals for building, 160–61, 167
 secular memory, as radically different from, 46, 47, 53
 social ethic of Christian memory, 4, 173
 in womanist theological anthropology, 36, 48, 62
CHRYSALIS program, 194–95, 204
Coddington, Kate S., 18
cognitive praxis, 88–89
Colbert, Stephen, 169–70, 212
Coleman, Monica, 48, 77
depression, identifying, 84
faith communities, on healing with the aid of, 82, 157
health, relating to Jesus Christ, 66, 83
old self, allowing to die, 81
on recovery as ongoing, 66, 200
religious institutions, on accountability of, 62–63
rituals, on healing through the practice of, 80
combative epistemology, 120, 189
Copeland, M. Shawn, 48, 78
 on Black embodiment, 68
 on cognitive praxis, 88–89
 on the inseparability of the body from ourselves, 187
 on memory, 47, 53, 76
 on the Mystical Body of Christ, 73–74
 structural historical amnesia and, 46
 on suffering, 53, 71, 76, 94
 theological anthropology of, 69–70, 75

cosmetic neurology/cosmetic
  psychopharmacology, 39–40
Council of Chalcedon, 72
counterdiscourse and noncompetition,
  145–46
COVID-19 pandemic, 6–8, 17, 93–94
Creamer, Deborah Beth, 175, 176
cultural production of health, 48,
  58–61, 62

dangerous memory, 127, 157
  as disruptive, 150
  of humanity, as a liberating
    response, 142–43
  as life-transforming, 166
  narrative, cultivating through, 136,
    138, 161
  redemptive action of, liturgy
    exemplifying, 134
  trauma as, 128, 132, 143–49, 159,
    162–63
  truth over fact in, 135
  wounds of Christ, reading
    through, 151–54
Danielson Institute, 188, 194
Derrida, Jacques, 24, 119
disability theology, 172–73, 175–79,
  186
Douglas, Kelly Brown, 86–87
Du Bois, W. E. B., 145–47

Eckhart, Meister, 119
Edkins, Jenny, 34–35
Ellacuría, Ignacio, 183
emergent strategies, 173–74, 205
Empire of Trauma (Fassin/Rechtman),
  31
enfleshed counter-memory, 148,
  170
  autonomy, surpassing, 187–89
  Christian liberation psychology
    and, 180–84
  disability theology, grounding in,
    172–73, 177
  distributive justice, as beyond,
    192–95
  epistemology of ignorance,
    resisting, 211–12

ethical expansion of, 151, 184–86,
    212–13
  as an intentional term, 171
  justice, as the work of, 173,
    195–98, 199, 200
  Keshgegian proposals for building,
    160–61
  non-maleficence and beneficence,
    more than, 189–92
  social ethic of, 49, 124, 168, 172,
    173, 186
  on suffering as holding in being
    and becoming, 217
  trauma memory and, 174, 179
  in womanist theological
    anthropology, 36, 45, 48, 49, 62,
    88–90
epigenetics, 10–12
ethic of care, 193

Fanon, Frantz, 97–98, 117–18
Farley, Margaret, 192
Fassin, Didier, 31–32, 35
Faulkner, William, 109
Felman, Shoshana, 21, 25, 137–38
Fitzgerald, F. Scott, 216–17
flight response, 9, 38
Floyd-Thomas, Stacey M., 85–86
Ford, David, 95
Frances, Allen, 105
Freud, Sigmund, 14, 22, 99

Gadamer, Hans-Georg, 93, 95
Godzeiba, Anthony, 95, 101–2
Goizueta, Roberto, 76
grace, 114
  choice for grace as open to all, 28
  enfleshed counter-memory and, 191
  Lange on grace, 111, 112
  mystery of grace, 162
  in trauma theory, 27, 106
Green, Garrett, 96
Gudorf, Christine, 193

Halbwachs, Maurice, 85
hegemonic imagination, 60, 80, 209
Heidegger, Martin, 95, 119
Herman, Judith, 25, 27

Index

community, emphasis on, 119
 on enfleshed counter-memory, 195–96
 feminist lens, applying to trauma framework, 19–21
 hegemonic and violent power, on the proper response to, 107–8
 hermeneutics, 3, 150
 complexity, trauma hermeneutic revealing, 105
 culture and, 12–14
 describing and defining, 92–93
 face of the other in trauma hermeneutics, 119
 liberation hermeneutics, 96–98, 106
 life, hermeneutics for, 100–102
 negative hermeneutic of impaired thinking, 177
 postcolonial hermeneutics, 97–98, 107–8, 120–21
 public truth-telling, as including, 19–20
 radical hermeneutic, 121–22
 theological hermeneutic of trauma, 30, 93, 108–9, 124, 127
 trauma and encountering hermeneutics, 102–3, 118
 traumatic imagination and, 94–95, 100, 106
 womanist hermeneutics, 99, 104
Hinze, Bradford E., 95, 101–2
Hurley, Elisa A., 41
Hurricane Katrina, 206–7

imago Dei, 53
 community affirmation of, 65
 lament of the sufferer as a part of, 80
 memory and, 36, 133
 in womanist thought, 77–78, 83, 167, 187

Jennings, Willie James, 94
Job, 139
Jones, Serene, 25–26, 27, 111, 114
Jones, Tamsin, 119–20

Kamieński, Łukasz, 40–41
Kearney, Richard, 113
the kenotic person, 101
Keshgegian, Flora, 168
 complex narratives, on practicing, 161–63, 167
 the cross, decentering, 161, 163–65, 167
 on cultivating memories for life, 161, 170, 183
 Metz and, 127, 128, 151, 160, 165
 multiple memorative practices, calling for, 161, 165–67, 192
 survivors, on memory as a resource for, 122–23
Kolber, Adam, 43
Kundera, Milan, 208

lament, 85
 as a community-level action, 208
 hefty hope, as forming, 205–6
 in liminal space, 115, 207
 as public prophecy, 49, 77, 78–81, 89
Lange, Dirk G., 25–26, 27, 111–12
Laub, Dori, 21, 25, 137–38
Laws, Terri, 84
Leiden an Gott, 139, 143–45, 147–48, 164
Levinas, Emmanuel, 119
Levine, Rebecca Leah, 178
liberation psychology, 173, 180–84, 186, 212
liberation theology, 96, 100, 182
liminal space, 26–27, 113, 115–16, 118, 207
Loughry, Maryanne, 32–33, 35
Luther, Martin, 112

Marshall Turman, Eboni, 48, 66–67, 69, 71–73, 199
Martín-Baró, Ignacio, 173, 181–83, 191, 199, 212
Massingale, Bryan, 97
May, Melanie, 114–15, 184, 201
mental health, 17, 84
 Black women and, 48, 62–67
 enfleshed counter-memory and, 181
 global mental health and PTSD diagnosis, 5–12

mental health *(continued)*
  lack of access to mental health care, 15, 192
  situational mental health, 103, 105–6
  theology not a mental healthcare provision, 118
  trauma and, 31, 32–33, 58, 59, 60, 195
  virtue, conflating with, 55–57
Merleau-Ponty, Maurice, 117
Metz, Johann Baptist, 165, 208
  the crucifixion, importance in thought, 133, 151–54, 163
  dangerous memories and, 127–28, 132, 134–36, 143, 149, 157, 158–60, 161, 168, 183
  enfleshed counter memory concept and, 171
  forward memories, cultivating, 128, 151, 156–60, 168, 190–91
  as a German soldier, 126–27, 135
  Leiden an Gott theology, 139, 143–44, 145, 147, 164
  on memory, 127–28, 132–36, 139, 142, 149, 166, 167
  mystical-political framework, 127, 128, 148, 150–51, 186
  on narrative, 127–28, 132, 139–40, 141, 142, 149, 161, 166, 167
  open eyes, on the mysticism of, 130, 145, 146, 149
  the person, centralizing in theology, 128, 131, 132–33, 135–36, 139, 142, 167–68
  on solidarity, 127–28, 132, 139, 141–43, 148, 149, 158, 159, 166, 167
  suffering, on the interruption of, 128, 151, 156, 168
  theodicy, responding to, 129, 143, 210
  traumatic imagination, reading Metz with, 93, 127, 143–49
mezzo, sociological paradigm of, 30–31, 202–8, 211
Miller, Chanel, 91, 92, 94
mirroring, 64–65

moral memory, 87
Morrison, Toni, 52

narrative
  Christian memory, metanarrative of, 129
  dangerous memory, cultivating through narrative, 136, 138, 161
  Keshgegian on practicing complex narratives, 161–63, 167
  Metz on narrative, 127–28, 132, 139–40, 141, 142, 149, 161, 166, 167
  suffering, narrative as dangerous stories of, 136–37
"The Negro and the Warsaw Ghetto" (Du Bois), 145
nepantla as in-between space, 116

Oakes, Matthew Bretton, 7
ontological instability, 7
the Other, 51–52, 64–65

Pestana, Michael, 55–59
political theology, 147, 149
Porter, Stanley E., 100–101, 121
posttraumatic stress disorder (PTSD), 3, 32
  cultural production of health and, 59
  diagnosis, not presupposing, 15
  ethics of tampering with memory and, 43
  flashbacks, 9, 38, 109
  global mental health and PTSD diagnoses, 5–12
  memory in patients with PTSD, 37–39
  in US combat troops, 40
preferential option for the poor, 76, 134
  authority of those who suffer and, 156
  enfleshed counter-memory and, 173
  solidarity and the preferential option, 197, 208–12
  in womanist theological anthropology, 67–68

Index

Rah, Soong-Chan, 207
Rahner, Karl, 28, 30, 126, 143
Rambo, Shelly, 25–26, 115, 120, 151–53
Rechtman, Richard, 31–32, 35
Requiem for a Nun (Faulkner), 109
resilience, 160, 163
   in Catholic healthcare guidelines, 190
   CHRYSALIS, as part of, 194
   in combative epistemology, 189
   good for all, as an act seeking, 191
   integration and healthy resilience, 103
   the margins, resilience of people in, 51
   in post-trauma contexts, 104
Resurrecting Wounds (Rambo), 151
Ricoeur, Paul, 95, 99
Rivera, Mayra, 116–17
Robinson, Jason C., 100–101, 121
Romero, Oscar, 185
Rose, Marika, 92
Rosenberg, Leah B., 42–43
Rosner, Elizabeth, 1, 2
Rothberg, Michael, 145–47, 173

Sales, Ruby, 172, 199
salvation, 28, 86
   crucified peoples participating in, 165
   external salvation, 97, 121
   forward memories and the promise of, 157
   incarnate enfleshment and, 189
   Metz on, 135, 149, 159, 210
   wounds not stumbling blocks to, 152
Sandage, Steven J., 188
Scarry, Elaine, 22–23, 80
Schreiter, Robert, 106
sexual abuse
   of children, 26, 28, 161
   clergy-perpetrated abuse, 105–6, 171, 215–16
   sexual assault, 13, 26, 104
Sheppard, Phillis I., 66, 69, 77
   on black women and mental health, 48, 64
   community, emphasizing centrality of, 82
   on grief and lament, 78–79, 81
   negative societal mirroring, on overcoming, 65
the Shoah, 21, 34, 126–27, 137, 161
sin, 153, 164
   accountability for sins, 79, 216
   as blocking transformation, 77
   the church, sinfulness of, 215
   enfleshed counter-memory and, 171
   sinful powers, turning prophetic fury toward, 196
   sin of the fall, Tolkien on, 169
   social sin and those who suffer, 188
   structural sin, 59, 148, 210
Slaubaugh, Samantha, 131
sociomas as social problems, 60
Soelle, Dorothee, 135, 140
solidarity, 2, 104
   anamnesis, solidarity beginning in, 76
   divine solidarity, 114
   Du Bois, in the work of, 145, 146
   enfleshed counter-memory and lived solidarity, 174
   healing solidarity in *nepantla* space, 116
   Metz on, 127–28, 132, 139, 141–43, 148, 149, 158, 159, 166, 167
   preferential option for the poor and, 173, 197, 208–12
   in womanist theological anthropology, 67, 74–75, 82, 89
Solomon, Rivers, 202
Spivak, Gayatri, 100
Sri Lankan tsunami victims, 15–16
structural historical amnesia, 46
suffering, 17, 21, 34, 61, 91, 113, 123, 157
   agential capacities of the sufferer, 81
   alleviation of, 168, 170, 178, 216
   authority of the sufferer, 130, 136, 156

suffering *(continued)*
  of Black women, 66–67
  bonds of suffering, cultivating, 145
  in Christian theology, 3, 48, 94, 112
  chronic suffering, 44
  community response to, 33
  complete healing, the sufferer as seeking, 172
  enfleshed counter-memory and, 191, 198, 203, 217
  the face of the sufferer, 119, 120, 122
  instrumentalization and the suffering of others, 161
  in intergenerational storytelling, 86–88
  interruption of suffering, 128, 150, 151, 156, 168
  of Jesus, 70, 115, 131
  lament as a response to, 79, 80, 205, 207
  in *Leiden an Gott* concept, 139, 143–45, 147–48, 164
  medical methods of confronting suffering, 175
  memory of suffering, 3, 130, 133, 145, 147, 149
  Metz on suffering, 136, 141, 143, 149, 153, 156, 159, 160, 162, 165
  narrative as dangerous stories of suffering, 136–37
  neutrality as willful ignorance of suffering, 154
  noncompetitive connection rooted in, 146
  outsiders' knowledge of suffering, 2, 25
  pain of the sufferer, awareness of, 22, 138, 193
  personal suffering as never isolated, 107
  preferential option for the sufferer, 134
  resisting suffering, 104, 127
  romanticization of, Keshgegian on, 166–67
  similarities across suffering, detecting, 155
  social responses to, 30, 32, 53, 59, 60, 85, 135, 188, 190
  spiritual responses to, 47, 129
  as structural, 59, 148, 183, 208
  traumatic experience and, 42, 71, 166, 194
  victims, blaming for their suffering, 55
  Western response to suffering, 16, 35
  womanism on, 67–68, 70–71, 74–75, 76, 77, 83, 154
  the world, suffering of, 2, 129, 140, 173
  See also trauma and suffering
Summerfield, Derek, 31
Swinton, John, 177–78, 181, 205

Testimony (Laub), 21
theodicy, 26, 87, 129, 143, 210
third naïveté, 102
Thomas, Saint, 151–52
Townes, Emilie, 63, 66
  on healing as shaped by how we are, 176
  health, on the cultural production of, 48, 61
  on hegemonic imagination, 59–60, 208–9
  on lament, 79, 205–6
  postmodern discourse, on the Other in, 51–52
  on the social fabric and its impact on memory, 85
trauma, general, 7, 17, 140, 165, 202, 209
  agency and trauma healing, 81–84, 187
  biological trauma, 10–12, 161
  Christ, reading through a trauma lens, 151–54
  Christian communities and traumatic events, 26–27, 157, 203, 205
  Christian memory and, 45, 47
  church-caused trauma, 71, 215

Index

as communal, 80, 128
contagious trauma, 18
the cross and, 163, 165
cure *vs.* healing of, 175, 177, 179
defining trauma, 3, 4, 5, 12, 19, 20, 32, 35
ethical response to, 48–49, 50, 68, 78, 154–56, 164, 189
feminist lens, applying to trauma framework, 19–21
first-rate intelligence, meeting trauma with, 216–17
forgetting and, 38, 42, 67, 85, 116, 155, 208–9
grace in trauma theory, 27, 106
growth of trauma diagnoses, 14–15
hermeneutics and, 93, 94–95, 100, 102–3, 106, 108–9, 118, 124, 127
as a hidden disability, 176
intergenerational storytelling and, 84–88
interruption of trauma, 156
lament as a response to, 78, 80–81
mental health and, 8, 31, 32–33, 58, 59, 60, 103, 105–6, 195
mystery as a response to, 28, 92
as particular and universal, 37, 63–64, 197–98
positionality, considering, 113–18, 123, 124
psychiatric nosology, framing trauma through, 16
in seminary students, 194
social experiences of trauma, 59–61, 64, 66–67
as structural violence, 107–8
theological engagement with, 3, 25–30, 118–23, 124, 165
time, taking into account, 109–13, 123, 124, 132
trauma as uneven and unstable, 146, 166
trauma discourse, 3–4, 19, 31, 32, 105
trauma in enfleshed counter-memory, 170–74, 177, 183–86, 188, 191, 192, 195–96, 212
trauma survivors, 23, 62–63, 135
womanist lens, viewing trauma through, 50–51, 53, 54, 66–67, 70, 73, 84, 89, 128, 208
Trauma and Recovery (Herman), 19–20
trauma and suffering, 4, 104
forgetting the trauma of suffering, 42
historical suffering, trauma related to, 166
in intergenerational storytelling, 86
overwhelming suffering, initial traumatic response to, 8
particular suffering in modern trauma discourse, 31
post-traumatic stress and suffering, 10, 43
suffering of trauma survivors, 63–64
suffering unto God response, 144
theological reframing of, 47
the world, trauma in the suffering of, 2
trauma healing, 117, 213
beneficence in trauma treatment, 190
best practices, 103, 204
Christian approach to, 26, 208
dynamic nature of, 201
in a global view, 210–11
individual agency in, 81
moral memory, cultivating for, 87
remembering for in trauma healing, 161
storytelling, beginning with, 88
in theological anthropology of Metz, 139
womanist thought and, 167–68
trauma memory
as dangerous memory, 128, 132, 143–49, 159, 162–63
enfleshed counter-memory and, 174, 179

trauma memory *(continued)*
  incarnational createdness approach to, 89
  lament as a Christian reaction to, 205–8
  larger community, taking into account, 202–3
  manipulation of, 47–48
  in mystical-political framework, 150–60
  remembering *for* concept, 161, 164, 166, 168, 170
  traumatic memories, 9, 31, 33, 36–43, 44
  virtue, taking into consideration, 55, 58
  womanist construction of, 53, 54, 67–77
trauma studies, 23, 137
  Herman as sparking a renaissance in, 20–21
  liminal space in, 115
  publications dedicated to, 25–26
  trauma critique, 13, 30–35
  unknowing asserted by, 27
  as victim-centered, 1–2, 140
  womanist thought in, 50, 72
traumatic imagination, 93, 101
  on gaps as incarnational solidarity, 104
  hermeneutical basis for, 94–100, 108, 124
  Metz, reading with, 127, 128, 143–49, 151, 160, 190–91
  position as featured in, 113–18
  praxis as an aspect of, 118–23
  radical humility, calling for, 106
  time as a feature of, 109–13
Treanor, Brian, 113
trigger warnings, 13
Truth and Repair (Herman), 107
truth testimony, 34–35

Tubman, Harriet, 66
Tuskegee syphilis experiments, 84

Unclaimed Experience (Caruth), 21

van der Kolk, Bessel, 15, 107
virtue, conflating with mental health, 55–58
Volf, Miroslav, 3, 44
Vuong, Ocean, 198, 199

Ward, Jerry W., Jr., 180
Williams, Delores, 164
withness, practice of, 124, 162, 164
womanism, 52, 184
  community response, focus on, 64–65
  cultural production of health, recognizing, 59, 62
  enfleshed counter-memory and, 36, 45, 48, 49, 62, 88–90, 171
  healing, womanist practices of, 77–88
  hermeneutics of, 93, 96, 99, 100, 104
  imago Dei, viewing persons through lens of, 187
  incarnate personhood in, 163, 167, 186
  lament as public prophecy in, 89
  on suffering, 67–68, 70–71, 74–75, 76, 77, 83, 154
  trauma in womanist theological anthropology, 51, 70, 73, 77, 89, 168
  womanist lens on trauma, 50, 53, 54, 66–67, 84, 128, 208
World Health Organization (WHO), 5, 7

Yehuda, Rachel, 12